1991

The Darker World Within

The Darker World Within

Evil in the Tragedies
of Shakespeare and His Successors

Molly Smith

DELAWARE

Newark: University of Delaware Press
London and Toronto: Associated University Presses

Associated University Presses
440 Forsgate Drive
Cranbury, NJ 08512

Associated University Presses
25 Sicilian Avenue
London WC1A 2QH, England

Associated University Presses
P.O. Box 39, Clarkson Pstl. Stn.
Mississauga, Ontario,
L5J 3X9 Canada

The paper used in this publication meets the requirements
of the American National Standard for Permanence of Paper
for Printed Library Materials Z39.48-1984.

Library of Congress Cataloging-in-Publication Data

Smith, Molly, 1958–
    The darker world within : evil in the tragedies of Shakespeare and his successor / Molly Smith.
        p.   cm.
    Includes bibliographical references (p.) and index.
    ISBN 0-87413-400-5 (alk. paper).
    1. Shakespeare. William, 1564-1616—Tragedies.   2. English drama (Tragedy)—History and criticism.   3. Evil in literature
4. Tragedy.   I. Title.
PR2983.S57 1991
822.3′3—dc20   89-40763
                                                                              CIP

PRINTED IN THE UNITED STATES OF AMERICA

Contents

Acknowledgments

Research for this book was conducted while I was on a doctoral fellowship at Auburn University. I wish to thank the many librarians at Ralph Brown Draughon library for their assistance in helping me with interlibrary loans and for providing me with access to the latest books as they were acquired by the library.

I would also like to thank all those who read this study while in manuscript, in particular Miller Solomon, Margaret Kouidis, and Pat Morrow, but especially Drew Clark without whose patience and insightful criticism I would never have completed this project. To the work of Stephen Greenblatt, whom I met only after the bulk of this book was completed, I owe an inspirational debt that is readily apparent in the following pages.

1

Dramatic Fascination with Evil: Its Sociopolitical and Philosophical Implications

Theories of Evil

Intense fascination with evil clearly demarcates early seventeenth-century literature from that of the Elizabethan and Restoration eras. This is not to suggest that evil is absent in the earlier and later periods, but concern with this theme appears to have been particularly intense in the literature composed during the early Stuart periods. Thus, although Kyd inaugurated the tragedy of concentrated violence on the Elizabethan stage, the Jacobean and Caroline dramatists show a particular preoccupation with the darker side of the human psyche, with the themes of madness, violence, revenge, adultery, incest, and with the psychological state of melancholia. Using psychological criteria, we might even separate seventeenth-century drama into two periods; drama before 1660 concentrates on the inner man, while Restoration drama concentrates on the outer. If linguistic patterns can be treated as a sympton of psychological states, then it may be relevant that seventeenth-century literature is "particularly replete with words beginning with 'mal'" (Mora 1984, 49).

That Jacobean and Caroline drama presents a darker vision of humanity than the Elizabethan and that a marked transition occurs in the texture of literary productions in the seventeenth century, have, of course, long been recognized, but no really substantial efforts have been made to study the phenomenon of evil in these plays, particularly as a phenomenon directly related to the sociopolitical and philosophical atmosphere of Jacobean and Caroline England. Dramatic fascination with evil closely corresponds to the sociopolitical atmosphere of the early seventeenth century, and was perhaps partly responsible for the social, political, and intellectual temper of the subsequent ages, the periods of the Interregnum and the Restoration.

In other words, Stuart dramatic concern with evil had *creative* effects; it did not merely indicate moral or social decadence. Unlike Rowland Wymer, therefore, I do not believe that dramatists of this age, "like most writers, found it easier to convey the reality of evil than to show virtue" (1986, 102). The marked decrease in depictions of virtue, in comparison with those of the previous age, stems from a great deal more than mere representational facility. Repeatedly, Jacobean and Caroline dramatists, even while they seem to support the hierarchical system, locate villainy among those who exercise power and thus, the plays posit a stark criticism of social morality. Even an early play such as *The Shoemaker's Holiday*, written in 1599, proffers such a criticism, although its tone as a whole appears less harsh than the Jacobean and Caroline dramas.

A deliberate contrast between Rowland Lacy and Ralph, the nobleman and the journeyman, is suggested in this play through the ease with which Lacy escapes fighting in the war in order to woo Rose Oteley, the Lord Mayor's daughter, while Ralph, although recently married, is forced to go to battle, loses his leg, and almost loses his wife because of it. When Ralph appears at the shoemaker's after the wars, Lacy disguised as the journeyman, Hans, is present through the entire scene, and on stage we are confronted with a disturbing visual representation of social inequality. The audience is forced to consider the unfairness of the situation when Ralph returns lamed to discover that he has lost his wife and his place among the shoemakers, especially because the agent of some of that loss is present on stage, and has himself escaped a similar situation by usurping Ralph's role. A deliberate irony may also be intended in that Lacy has to usurp the role of the lower classes, the shoemakers, to rise to a new moral awareness by the end of the play. The play, therefore, is not so pure a comedy of mirth as it has traditionally been regarded.[1]

The plays of the Jacobean and Caroline theater seem to go a step farther in their exposition of social ills; they dispense even with the facade of theatrical idealization and their criticism is overt and blatant. The darker aspect of these plays and of the period in general has always received considerable attention from both critics and historians. Lynne White, for example, describes the period between 1300 and 1650 as "the most psychically disturbed era" in history, and argues that this psychic disturbance became more pronounced as the age came to its close (1974, 26). Causes of the drastic change that occurs after 1650 have also been a matter of inquiry and dispute; "why about 1650 did social manifestations of aggression and personal disorientation so markedly diminish" (44)? Lately, since critics have become conscious of the allusive significance of Stuart plays, dramatic fascination with the darker aspects of the psyche has come to be regarded as symptomatic of other things, of social and political factors. These later plays do more than argue with conventional notions of hierarchy; they trace evil through metaphor, allusion, and suggestion to the very roots of the hierarchical system, to kingship itself. The potency of the dramatic argument arises, therefore, from its united force as a criticism of monarchy as it then existed. The drama of the period destroys metaphorically those conventional hierarchies and systems that had provided the basis for the arguments of such Renaissance theorists as Richard Hooker and Sir Thomas Elyot. This dramatic destruction symbolically prefigures the actual violence against monarchy and hierarchy that took place in the 1640s. "The historical task effectively accomplished by the form," Stephen Greenblatt argues, referring to Stuart tragedy, "was precisely the destruction of the fundamental paradigm of the dominant culture," and an anticipation of the new one that was to emerge (1982, 7). In fact, dramatic fascination with the darker world within precipitates this cultural transformation, although the final message of the Stuart plays remains ambivalent and complex. My study will focus on the ambivalent, paradoxical, and multifaceted nature of early Stuart drama.

This ambivalence may relate directly to the upheavals that took place in the 1640s. In the summer of 1642, when King Charles and his opponents prepared for war against each other, few suspected that these preparations would climax in the dramatic public spectacle of 30 January 1649. For the first time in European history, a monarch was publicly tried and beheaded. Charles's trial took place before a partial Parliament consisting of a depleted lower house, the peers having conveniently disappeared to the country sometime earlier. His execution, performed in the open street outside his own Banqueting house of Whitehall, clearly attacked the institution of monarchy itself. And yet, ironically, as Maurice Ashley argues, by his death Charles might have saved rather than destroyed the monarchy in England (1987, 216). Contemporaries viewed these events of the mid-century according to their own political allegiances, either as a theatrical example for the world to emulate or as a world-upside-down that would ultimately be reversed and set aright. The ambivalence that characterizes seventeenth-century attitudes toward these political upheavals evolves also in the literature of the period.

Increasingly, however, historians have acknowledged that despite the seeming abruptness with which these political events developed, they might have been in the making throughout the early half of the seventeenth century. Indeed, concentrated dramatic interest in evil, which intensified in conjunction with the political turmoils of the era, might be studied as an index to the sociocultural upheavals that occurred in the mid-century.

Perhaps a definition of the term *evil* as used in this study is necessary. The *OED* describes *evil* as in some senses an obsolete word, no longer used in its strong sense to indicate intense villainy. Anthropologists give varying reasons for the gradual elimination of the term from our casual vocabulary, but most agree that the term went into obscurity sometime in the seventeenth century. Some believe that this resulted naturally from the advent of rationalism and an increasing disbelief in supernatural forces as controlling man's destiny, changes which occurred in the late seventeenth century, and others that the very elimination of the term from our casual vocabulary indicates the potency of the phenomenon of evil in post-seventeenth century society.[2] Whatever the reasons for its weakening after the seventeenth century, in that period, the term still retained its strongest sense; seventeenth-century writers more than any others concerned themselves overtly and almost exclusively with exploring the phenomenon of evil among men.

The category of evil as an other-worldly force resulting from the superhuman powers of ghosts, demons, or witches has received considerable critical attention, and recently, several excellent studies has explored this aspect of Elizabethan and Stuart culture.[3] My study will draw on this literature as it becomes necessary, but evil as a supernatural phenomenon, as demonology or witchcraft, is not my central concern.

The most compelling reason for the omission of this category of evil is the diminishing interest in witchcraft and demonology in the period itself. Although records indicate a rather large number of witchcraft trials during the period, these were considerably fewer than in the preceding age and steadily diminished in number as the period reached its close.[4] Of course, King James himself showed great interest in witchcraft and actively participated in several witchcraft trials. His *Demonologie* became an influential and important tract on the matter simply because it was a product of his pen, even if it offered very little new information on witches and demons. But James's active interest in witchcraft was limited to Scotland and to the last decade of the sixteenth century.[5]

James's ascension to the English throne was followed by a diminishing interest in the subject, and in some cases, by active participation in the exposure of false witches (S. Clark 1977, 160).

Although this may be the result of the social temper in England at the time, we must assume that kings being public personalities, James was probably as responsible for England's diminishing interest in supernatural phenomena as England was for his. Thomas Fuller provides us with an account of the King's change in attitude during the latter part of his reign, a change we might regard as taking place in the entire nation as well.

> The frequency of such forged Possessions wrought such an alteration upon the judgement of King JAMES, that he receding from what he had written in his *Demonologie*, grew first diffident and then flatly to deny the workings of Witches and Devils, as but Falsehoods and Delusions. (Cited by S. Clark, 162)

Several other influential figures in England both before and during James's reign, in particular Reginald Scot, George Gifford, John Cotta, and William Perkins, expressed skepticism about witches and demons. Evidence suggests that seventeenth-century England was little involved in searching out and convicting witches; the witch craze died during the last years of Elizabeth's reign.

Major differences between representations of evil in sixteenth- and in seventeenth-century drama also suggest a decreasing interest in the supernatural in Stuart England. Despite Marlowe's interest in hell as a state of mind rather than as a fixed location, *Doctor Faustus* (ca. 1594) ultimately asserts the origin of evil in a primordial figure of villainy, Lucifer. In a later play such as Shakespeare's *Macbeth* (1606–7), however, supernatural power exerts an important influence, but the play emphatically asserts the presence of evil within the individual; villainous action, although accentuated and provoked by the promptings of the witches, originates in the desires of Macbeth and Lady Macbeth; little in the play suggests a primordial source of evil. Still later plays such as *The Revenger's Tragedy* (1607), *The Maid's Tragedy* (ca. 1610), *The Duches of Malfi* (1614), or The *Changeling* (1622), dispose of the supernatural even more emphatically; evil arises either as a result of the social environment or from within the characters themselves; villains such as Vindice in *The Revenger's Tragedy*, the Cardinal and Ferdinand in *The Duchess of Malfi*, the king in *The Maid's Tragedy*, and De Flores in *The Changeling* are prompted to initial action by the situations in which they are placed, but the intensity of their actions as the plays progress emphasizes the origin of evil within their own natures.[6] A similar transition occurs even in the formula of the revenge play in the seventeenth century; revenge springs from within protagonists such as Vindice, and the murdered individual's ghost, the strong motivating force in *The Spanish Tragedy* and *Hamlet*, disappears quite completely. In fact, it may be argued that Stuart drama, which dispenses quite completely with supernatural evil and which repeatedly depicts evil as intrinsic to human nature, represents "the dawn of modern conscience and the first step towards modern psychiatry" (Mora 1984, 56).

Neither is the concept of evil that I pursue the "pure" evil that Georges Bataille designates as basic to the work of Emily Brontë, the Marquis de Sade, John Ford, and William Blake, among others. He defines "pure evil" as evil without a purpose, evil in which harm is caused for the sheer pleasure of witnessing hurt and destruction (1973, 5). On the contrary, evil in Stuart drama emerges as a creative and transformatives force. Bataille himself indicates some interest in this aspect of evil (1973, 61). Indeed, in the sense in which I deal with it, evil emerges as a version of what Bataille describes as the "hypermorality" of evil, which he defines as the factor in representations of evil that becomes the "basis of intense communication" between reader and text (8); the creation of a new sociopolitical and philosophical environment may be regarded as part of the "intense communication" between drama and seventeenth-century (and post-seventeenth-century) society.[7] Depictions of evil on the early Stuart stage function as one element in the cultural transformation that takes place during this period.

In a purely theoretical sense, my treatment of evil draws on three philosophical definitions that seem especially relevant to the Jacobean and Caroline periods: Saint Augustine's, Paul Ricoeur's, and Emile Durkheim's. Chapter 2 will concentrate on the Augustinian concept of evil as incompleteness. The primordial image of Satan as less that whole in contrast to the whole, that is, God, derives from this view of evil.[8] Although seventeenth-century drama is little concerned with depicting evil as emanating from a superhuman and primordial villain, it nevertheless portrays its villainous protagonists as essentially incomplete human beings. Drama thus reasserts the notion of evil as inherently a result of spiritual and psychological incompleteness; Stuart depictions of physical and mental fragmentation fall under this category. The theme of violence, central to depictions of physical fragmentation, and the themes of madness and melancholia, central to depictions of mental fragmentation, may be treated as instances of incompleteness, and therefore, as evil in the Augustinian sense. Indeed, violence, madness, and melancholia acquire new connotations in Jacobean and Caroline drama.

Related to the Augustinian notion of evil as incompleteness, Ricoeur's idea of evil as a defilement of that which was pure or clean, offers a definition sanctioned also by Christian and Jewish theology.[9] Chapter 3 will address this category of evil by concentrating on Stuart depictions of patriarchy. Many plays represent the patriarchal system in a state of decline or corruption; in some cases, they even represent parricide as a natural and inevitable, although unfortunate result of this decline. Stuart theatrical depictions of parricide may have had much to do with the sociopolitical violence against patriarchy and monarchy in the mid-century. But the relationship between these theatrical depictions and the social drama of the mid-century cannot arbitrarily be reduced to a cause-and effect scheme, for many plays seem ultimately to reassert rather than destroy the declining patriarchal system. The ambiguous and multi-faceted nature of Stuart tragedy emerges especially in its treatment of patriarchal authority.

Thus, drama both criticizes and harks back to Elizabethan sociopolitical norms asserted by writers such as Richard Hooker and Sir Thomas Elyot. And while at first it may seem that literature turns "radical" in its opposition to king and social system (as Jonathan Dollimore has recently argued), it is actually the deviation by society as a whole from desirable norms that prompts criticism from the dramatists. Emile Durkheim's definition of evil becomes especially relevant to Stuart depictions of things gone awry. Intrinsic to the entire body of Durkheim's influential sociological studies is the belief that human society functions as an essentially moral system in which social conformity constitutes "goodness" and nonconformity "evil."[10] Many Stuart dramatists seek through depictions of evil and things gone awry to transform a society that has failed to conform to desirable moral norms. Images of the world-upside-down and the woman-on-top drawn from such plebian activities as the carnival and the charivari recur in the drama. Chaper 4 will concentrate on Durkheimian evil and on Stuart tragedies that draw on these images from plebian culture.

The concluding chapter will discuss the intellectual effects and implications of Stuart dramatic fascination with evil by focusing on the issue of transformation. Finally, despite our awareness of Milton's Satan as primordial evil, many of the aspects outlined in the drama apply also to Milton's creation. Despite inherent ideological differences, Milton's potent and influential depiction of evil which culminates the period, owes more to contemporary stage representations than has generally been acknowledged.

Critical Methodology

My work, therefore, owes much to recent studies that have emphasized the sociopolitical contexts within which literature was produced. New Historicists, feminists, Marxists, and most post-structuralist theorists have contributed to this recent interest in contexts.[11] My study is partially rooted in the New Historicist trends of the past decade, and I am especially indebted to the radical re-evaluation of the sixteenth and seventeenth centuries by Stephen Greenblatt, Jonathan Goldberg, and Jonathan Dollimore, but I will strive to combine rather than eschew other methodologies.

New Historicist methodology has been particularly popular among students of Elizabethan literature. That Renaissance scholars have been the first to embrace this theory is perhaps not a surprise, for students of the sixteenth and seventeenth centuries generally have been more reticent about applying psychoanalytical and deconstructionist theories to the works of the period.[12] So perhaps the glimmer of a new critical theory has been on the horizon for a long while; it was certainly in the making long before the term "New Historicism" itself came into being.

The English Institute volume, *Literature and Society*, edited by Edward Said in 1980, for example, contains various essays that are New Historicist in temper, although no specific terminology is used to classify the whole as belonging to a single trend.[13] Said, in his important preface, voiced a general discontent with the state of criticism then, and perhaps captured the frustration of many scholars at what seemed to be an increased distancing of criticism from reading rather than a merging of the two. "To read an 'advanced' critic today," Said notes, "is often to read writing that is essentially a highly rarified jargon . . . the issues debated are about 'texts,' . . . they deal in complex abstractions whose main reference is to other complex abstractions" (ix). Since 1980 a great deal has changed, yet if Said's volume and the proceedings of the English Institute did not inaugurate the reinstatement of literature as "writing in history and human society," they were certainly at the very heart of that development. Marjorie Garber's preface to the volume, *Cannibals, Witches, and Divorces: Estranging the Renaissance* (1987), for example, firmly establishes the link between the English Institute meetings and the success of the New Historicism.[14]

Recent Marxist theories have also done much to re-emphasize social and political contexts, but New Historicists have widened the very concept of contexts. The New Historicism, as Edward Pechter points out (in a useful although somewhat unsympathetic evaluation of New Historicist practice), is "interpretation judged as an expression of the political interests of the audience—sometimes the contemporary audience, sometimes the modern one, sometimes both" (1987, 292). In other words, New Historicists have expanded the term *context* to include not only the context of creation of a text, but *every context that preceded and therefore influenced the creation of the text and every subsequent context within which the text was a factor*. In New Historicist criticism, context also includes political, social, and other activity, besides the phiolsophical and literary ones that old historicists emphasized.

Peter Erickson, although he has criticized new historical practice for its failure to expand the term *context* to include the present, has defined new historical theory and intentions accurately:

> Historicism, when fully historicized, implies historical consciousness of our immediate context as well as of the Renaissance; the latter does not reduce the former, but the two are incxtricable. This means that the present cannot be treated as a nuisance or irrelevance ... but must be accorded the same intellectual sophistication and emotional investment as our assertions about the past. (1987, 336)

Thus, while it was customary under old historical practice to study the influence of previous and contemporary periods on a work of art, New Historicists tend to emphasize periods that followed the written text, insisting that texts mold and modify sociocultural environments.[15]

What exactly makes the New Historicism so new, and why is it particularly relevant to the study of the seventeenth century? The New Historicism's departure from conventional historical studies, which regard literature as a reflection of the philosophical temperament of an age, lies in the equal significance it attaches to literature and to philosophical/social/political events. All these areas are seen as equally interrelated and as yielding only a complex and often conflicting (rather than coherent and unified) image of society. "The Elizabethan World Picture," in other words, becomes to the New Historicist an inadequate representation of matters. At best, it is only a partially valid theory, and, at worst, an artificial and ex post facto construct, a reduction for the sake of convenience made by the literary historian.

Works are no longer regarded as self-sufficient entities conveying an entire meaning on their own, "as a fixed set of texts that are set apart from all other forms of expression," as the New Critics seemed to regard them; nor are they simply chronicles of their time, that is, a "stable set of reflections of historical facts that lie beyond them," as traditional historical critics have regarded them (Greenblatt 1980, 6). As Greenblatt has said, the New Historicist is interested not only in the "social presence of the world in the literary text," but in the social presence to the world of the literary text" (6). The importance of the literary artifact lies, then, in its power to provoke the creation of new social, political, and philosophical situations.[16]

Many New Historicists, therefore, are involved in indicating the subversive functions of texts that had hitherto been regarded as upholding and maintaining the status quo. In their readings, Shakespeare no longer emerges as a spokesman for the "Elizabethan world picture," but rather, as one who repeatedly depicts the tensions inherent in that worldview; his works represent the dichotomy between Elizabethan theory and practice. In their concern with authority and subversion in the age, many of these critics tend, however, to stress the latter.[17] But is the drama a vehicle of social control or of subversion? Both, I would say, as do most New Historicists in theory. As Richard Burt in a recent essay on Ben Jonson argues, "any attempt to interpret the politics of the early Stuart theater in terms of a strict global antithesis between authority on the one hand, and subversion on the other" proves inadequate (1987, 552). He cites the example of the "anti-theatricalism" of Jonson, who turned away from theater and often criticized it, to argue for the "cultural contradictions" in which the Stuart court, the Puritans, the playwrights, and the theatrical companies were involved.[18] "Socio-cultural systems," as Victor Turner insists, "are never harmonious *gestalten*, but are fraught with structural contradictions and conflicts" (1982, 76), and in his reading of Stuart culture, Burt exemplifies the foremost desire of exponents of the New Historicism to provoke an awareness of the dialectical interplay between theater and court and between literature and society.

The particular relevance of such a theory to so turbulent and productive a period as the seventeenth century is readily apparent, as Jonathan Dollimore has pointed out (1984, 5). The age inaugurated later radical changes in politics, religion, and society. Although the beginnings of modern thought can be located squarely in the rationalism of the eighteenth century, the factors that permitted those changes already existed in the preceding age. And to locate the source of this shift toward rationalism, one might turn to some of the voices of the seventeenth century (the voices most available to subsequent audiences through their transmission via the written word) to the drama and the poetry, in short, to the literature of the period.[19]

My own study of Jacobean and Caroline drama will be related to New Historical studies such as Greenblatt's, Dollimore's and Goldberg's, although I would like ultimately to modify certain of their claims. Unlike Greenblatt, I do not believe, for instance, that despite the creative significance of this literature, "there is little in English tragedy that anticipates the new age, opened up, as it were, by the stroke of an axe" (1982, 7). On the contrary, not only was Jacobean and Caroline literature partly responsible for English civil war, it actually inaugurated the intellectual environment of the Restoration and the eighteenth century; the roots of both Lockeian and Hobbesian theories may be traced to Stuart fictions and anatomies of the self. Again, whereas Dollimore and other English New Historicists—*Cultural Materialists* is the term that they prefer—stress the political meaning of the text and the creation of new political events by the text, I would like to suggest that these Jacobean and Caroline texts make possible not only a new political situation, but a new social and intellectual environment. In other words, while my exploration roots itself in the New Historicism's concern with the power of the text, I am least interested in characterizing that power in terminology that is wholly Marxist (and political/economic) in implication.

Instead, I propose to rely on a variety of other fields, on related concepts in psychology, anthropology, and sociology, and especially on the theories of Carl G. Jung, Erich Neumann, Antonin Artaud, Victor Turner, Rene Girard, Mikhail Bakhtin, and Tzvetan Todorov. At least part of my purpose in this study is to re-emphasize the need for interdisciplinarity, to counter those voices that have recently been raised against it.[20]

Jungian theory provides a means of understanding the creative and transformative power of Stuart fascination with evil. Read in Jungian terms, Stuart interest in the darker world within may be regarded as the first step in the movement toward rationalism. Although Jung's theories about the collective psyche have received much attention, his belief in the distinguishing aspects of social character have generally been ignored. But belief in social character, that is, character as molded by a particular social environment, is central to Jungian psychology. In fact, Jung's concept of the function of the artist is intimately linked to a perception of the artist's relationship to his particular age. According to Jung, "the work of the poet comes to meet the spiritual need of the society in which he lives" (1933, 171); "an epoch is like an individual; it has its own limitations of conscious outlook, and therefore requires a compensatory adjustment" (166). Jung sees this adjustment as being made by the "visionary" poet who draws on archetypal patterns.

Jung's comparison of the individual psyche and social character proves particularly relevant to seventeenth-century dramatic concern with evil. According to Jung, a similar dynamics motivates both the individual and society; underlying Jung's insistence on the existence of a social character is a belief in what Erich Fromm has described as the "social unconscious" (1962, 88). The striving toward psychic wholeness is a goal shared by entire communities, and may be categorized as a process germane to historical and social change. According to Jung, the conscious mind in its progress toward psychic wholeness must confront and come to terms with its darker aspect, the "shadow" within its psyche. This confrontation has dual possibilities; the mind can either confront and overcome its darker self, that is, progress toward psychic wholeness, or succumb to its power, that is, regress into psychosis. Jacobean and Caroline dramatic fascination with madness, melancholia, violence, and death may be regarded from this standpoint as representing a confrontation of the collective psyche of the age with its darker inner self, its "shadow." This confrontation with the darker world within made possible society's progress toward rationalism and enlightenment in the subsequent age. A Jungian, then, would find it no accident that the age of rationalism, a cultural change which may be regarded as a movement toward psychic wholeness, should have been preceded by an age intensely concerned with representations of evil and violence. Even the violence of the 1640s may be seen in sociopsychological terms from society's standpoint as the "temporary retrogression into chaos" that precedes every movement towards wholeness (Eliade 1969, xii).[21]

Thus, Stuart protagonists who exist in the liminal stage between powerful and extreme mental states (Malevole in *The Malcontent* [1604] and Vindice in *The Revenger's Tragedy* [1607], for instance) dramatize the liminal psychological state of the entire society; their schizophrenia and their multiple inclinations represent the impending psychological and political catastrophe which was to close the age.[22] But it is precisely this delving into the psyche by the collective mind of the age, by its creative artists, that made the creation of a new social environment possible. As George Mora point out, "something creative is involved in becoming conscious of one's own evil" (1984, 55).

Stuart fascination with evil, therefore, provides an instance of what Victor Turner characterizes as "plural reflexivity," in which groups "strive to see their own reality in new ways" (1982, 12). Durkheim also argues that social harmony must be renewed periodically using the ritual intensification of the collective cultural experience. Depictions of madness, violence, and melancholia in seventeen-century drama may be treated as part of this process of "ritual intensification" in society. In this sense, dramatic fascination with the darker world within represents metaphorically, a collective journey by society into the underworld, into the realm of the chthonic, a realm "frequently associated with the principle of evil." But as in all myths and legends which represent such journeys, the act is itself a productive one, for the underworld also symbolizes fertility and the womb (Russell 1977, 62). Dramatic fascination with these themes represents an "activation of the power of the symbolic," and constitutes a recognition by elements in society (dramatists and their audiences) of society's "instinctual, irrational, primitive, violent side"; thus fascination with evil constitutes, to borrow an expression used by Halverson in an entirely different context, a "critical phase in the process of transformation," in seventeenth-century society (1970, 334). Ultimately, Jacobean and Caroline fascination with evil may be related to the temporary disruption and subsequent re-establishment of monarchy in England. Thus, one might categorize Stuart fascination with evil as transformative and creative. The theme of transformation is, in fact, a central aspect of the plays of this period, an aspect that distinguishes these works from those of subsequent periods. Figures who usher in processes of transformation—Proteus, the trickster, and the masque magician—become important archetypes in this literature. Kenneth Burke once noted that "Critical and imaginative works are answers to questions posed by the situation in which they arose. They are not merely answers, they are *strategic* answers, *stylized* answers" (1973, 1). Through its preoccupation with evil, Stuart drama perhaps poses an answer to the cultural crisis of the seventeenth century. In these terms, psychological and New Historicist readings of Renaissance texts may not be incompatible, as Greenblatt has recently made them out to be.[23]

To a degree, therefore, Jacobean and Caroline drama presents true tragedy as Antonin Artaud describes it. Artaud, pleading for the resurrection of authentic drama in the twentieth century, calls for the establishment of what he describes as the "theatre of cruelty." To Artaud this "theatre of cruelty" is intensely concerned with evil:

"The terrifying aspect of Evil produced in unalloyed form at the Eleusinian Mysteries being truly revealed, corresponded to the darker moments in certain ancient tragedies which all theatre must rediscover" (1970, 20). To Artaud, theater also has a therapeutic purpose, a claim which recalls the Aristotelian notion of "catharsis" (and which is not incompatible either with the above Jungian reading or with recent New Historicist claims); according to Artaud, "like the plague, theatre is collectively made to drain abscesses" (22). This "theatre of cruelty," as one example of which he cites John Ford's *'Tis Pity She's a Whore* (c. 1633), is concerned with violence and death; "it destroys, but it is a revenging scourge, a redeeming epidemic" (22).[24] Early Stuart tragedy both symbolizes the destructive desires within the psyche of seventeenth-century society and ultimately permits, through an intellectual transformation, the creation of a new society.[25]

One might even say that Stuart drama functions as a transformation ritual. Theories about ritual activities, in fact, throw considerable light on the transformative effects of this drama.[26] In general, as Frank Wadsworth argues, although "Historians of the English drama have charted its artistic development in impressive detail ... they have made less sense of its folk origins"; "Elizabethan playwrights," he insists, "were absorbed by and in social ritual" (1984, 72).[27] If this is true, and there can be little doubt that it is, recent anthropological speculations about folk culture and ritual performances have much to offer to students of the Elizabethan and Stuart drama.

This approach proves especially valid because texts had an essentially pre-literary status at this time; the theater was a part of the sociocultural environment and catered to a large and heterogenous group of people. Thus, theatrical representations of patriarchy in decline, for example, which drew their impetus from patrician theories, may have activated the scapegoat mechanism in society and thus made possible the scapegoating of Charles I in 1649. Erich Neumann's and Rene Girard's recent theories about the scapegoat in culture and society may prove especially relevant to Stuart depictions of parricide. Bakhtin's and Todorov's theories about plebian activities such as the carnival also illumine the ritual inversions which increased and intensified in seventeenth-century drama and which ultimately functioned as agents of social liberation. The plays of the period thus functioned as formalized social rituals.[28]

Barbara Myerhoff's definition of ritual, which emphasizes its social importance, is especially relevant within seventeenth-century contexts: she argues that "ritual is prominent in all areas of uncertainty, anxiety, impotence, and disorder" and that "in requiring enactments involving symbols, it bids us to participate in its messages." Ritual dramas "are elaborately staged and use presentational more than discursive symbols" and "by high stylization and extraordinary uses—of objects, language, dress, gestures, and like—ritual calls attention to itself" (1984, 151–52). She further insists that "ritual appears in dangerous circumstances and at the same time is itself a dangerous enterprise," because its failure, a potential that exists with its every performance, calls everything, including the very basis of culture into question and thus posits that culture itself may be an entirely artifical and man-made construct. Something similar to what Myerhoff claims results from the cultural performances of the Stuart reigns; drama calls into question the systems on which English society was based, and after the Restoration, in the theories of writers such as Hobbes, society and monarchy emerge as entirely artificial constructs.

Tragedy and Social Turbulence

The ritualistic links between art and society are especially vivid in Stuart tragedy, a form which encapsulates the philosophical essence of the age. Greenblatt makes a similar point when he notes, "Only tragedy looks the new prince straight in the face, taking his absolutist claims at their word and systematically elaborating them. Alone in the Elizabethan period, tragedy is truly modern, truly rigorous" (1982, 14).

My choice of tragedy over other forms of drama perhaps requires some explanation, especially because generally, more comedies were composed in the period than tragedies. Significantly, however, the number of tragi-comedies, plays which verge on the tragic despite their ultimately comic resolution, increased drastically. Moreover, the comedies of the period, with few exceptions, are darker in conception than those of the preceding era, as has generally been recognized with Shakespeare's later comedies, for instance. However, few critics have acknowledged the darker elements that exist even in the most festive of the Jacobean and Caroline comedies. Beneath their jollity, even these plays posit a stark criticism of social inequality and proclaim their festivity as an illusion possible only within the artificial confines of the theater. This change in tone does not, of course, manifest itself suddenly in 1603. On the contrary, the emergence of this darker vision is gradual, and the transition apparent most clearly in the comedies written close to the turn of the century, in such plays, that is, as *The Shoemaker's Holiday* (1599) and *The Merchant of Venice* (1597).

But the cynical tone appears more marked in later plays. Chapman's *The Widow's Tears* (ca. 1605), for example, hovers between comedy and tragedy. Indeed, many critics have been reluctant to classify it as a comedy, because of its trenchant and bitter denunciation of women.[29] Marston's *The Malcontent* (1604) with its Machiavellian protagonist, Malevole; Shakespeare's *Measure for Measure* (1604); Jonson's *Volpone* (1607); Middleton's *More Dissemblers Besides Women* (ca. 1615); Massinger's *The Bondam* 1624); and Shirley's *The Grateful Servant* (ca. 1629) are a few examples from a vast number of plays that validate what has now become a commonplace of literary criticism; namely, the increasing cynicism or bitterness of early seventeenth-century drama, even the comedies. This bitterness emerges most vividly, however, in Stuart tragedies.

The most potent "renaissance public symbolism" (Diehl 1980, 28) lies in the tragedies, where the pervasiveness of the public symbols unites these plays into extended metaphors in which the theatrical world becomes the equivalent of the social and political world of the seventeenth century. In the later seventeenth and early eighteenth centuries, the allusive mode is very different; the new social environment was accompanied by different images. As Girard argues, the tragic spirit "never widespread even in periods of crisis, vanishes without a trace during periods of cultural stability" (1972, 66–67). The popularity of tragedy in seventeenth-century England points to the sociocultural instability of the period, and the form may be studied as an index to that instability.

Recent histories of the later Tudor and early Stuart reigns have established the ironies and turbulence that lay beneath the achievements in art and culture during these periods. Jonathan Dollimore describes the later Elizabethan and early Stuart periods as a time of great social change, when social mobility "was more extensive than at any other time before the nineteenth and twentieth centuries" (1984, 84). Christopher Hill describes in detail the increasing class antagonism that accompanied this change and insists that "Not far below the surface of Tudor society . . . discontent was rife," a statement equally applicable to Jacobean England (1972, 20). James's ascension to the throne increased social change; his (and Charles's) extravagance in conferring titles on favorites accelerated class mobility and provoked the antagonism of those opposed to such extravagance. Statistics indicate a dramatic difference between

Elizabeth's and James's treatment of favorites; 878 knights were created during the whole of Elizabeth's reign, while the first four months alone of James's reign saw the creation of 906 knights (Ashton, 1969, 105). The dramatic growth in population in major cities also was important; "by the beginning of the seventeenth century, wages had fallen to their lowest level in three centuries, while geographic mobility had surged to what was perhaps its highest point" (Agnew 1986, 52). Social disruption, however, was only one factor among many kinds of tensions. Hill posits that "in addition to these class tensions ... there was a tradition of plebian anti-clericalism and irreligion" (1972, 25). Historians emphasize the increasing political turbulence in the age, growing doubts within the culture about the systems as they existed. In politics, in society, and in religion, therefore, the seventeenth century was in a state of flux.

A great part of this turbulence manifests itself in Stuart theatrical productions. Victor Turner insists on the importance of drama as a gauge of social disharmony:

Social life ... even at its apparently quietest moments, is characteristi-cally "pregnant" with social dramas. ... By means of such genres as theatre ... performances are presented which probe a community's weaknesses, call its political leaders to account, desacralize its most cherished values and beliefs, portray its characteristic conflicts and suggest remedies for them. (1982, 11)

Of course, the public theaters of the seventeenth century probably recorded this turbulence to a greater degree than the private. But most of the plays staged at the public theaters such as the Fortune and the Globe are now lost to us. Besides, the demarcation between public and private dramatists does not seem to have been quite as marked as we once thought it was, and in general, I will draw no distinctions between private and public theater plays. Webster, for example, was primarily a writer for the private theaters, but *The Duchess of Malfi* was a public play; Massinger, "the most popular and fashionable dramatist for the Blackfriars," wrote at least one play for the Globe (Heinemann 1980, 136); Middleton seems to have moved from an early career in the public theaters to the private theaters during his later years. The plays cannot be divided distinctly according to these two categories either. As Margot Heinemann points out, *A Game at Chesse*, for example, seems to cater to an audience both "public" and "select" (165). Nor was criticism of the social structure restricted to the public theaters and the plebian world; "the best courtly plays were vehicles of criticism rather than compliment" (Butler 1984, 3). The line between Puritans and theater-goers seems to have been similarly fragile (Heinemann 1980, 19–22). Middleton, for example, had Parliamentarian and Puritan patrons, and after his death, was hailed by William Henninge as the Puritans's favorite dramatist (Heinemann 1980, 126, 171). Thus, we do not have to look within plebian settings for records of the cultural upheavals taking place throughout seventeenth-century England. Despite patronal obligations, all theater in varying degress records this general discontent and through its awareness of social change, engages in a productive discourse with court and society.

Mimesis, Rivalry, and Theatrical Subversion

In the broadest sense, this mutual discourse between court and theater and between society and theater involves both an imitation and a modification of each other. Theater in society, theater as society, society in theater and society as theater—all the variations seem to apply to seventeenth-century England. In the seventeenth century, society is theater, theater is society. Facetious though this equation may sound, this factor most clearly demarcates seventeenth-century attitudes toward the theater from our own and most clearly aligns the age with all ages and societies in which theater functioned as an integral aspect of society, in which drama, spectacle, ritual, and symbol have coalesced into a single spectrum of socially relevant meaning.

Recently, critics have studied the extent to which the monarchs, Elizabeth and James, viewed themselves as theatrical performers. Their performances, of course, differed, perhaps consciously, but basic to their function as monarchs was a realization of their roles as performers *within* the spectacle of the court, as theatrical players being scrutinized and evaluatd constantly by the entire populace. Elizabeth, it seems, was particularly adept at exploiting the dramatic analogy to its fullest advantage, but James was equally conscious of his function as central player within the royal spectacle. References to his role as a theatrical player are made twice overtly in the *Basilikon Doron*, written as advice to young prince Henry in 1599, and the idea is implicit throughout the text. In his introduction to the work he notes,

Kings, being publike persons, by reason of their office and authority, are as it were set (as it was said of old) upon a publike stage, in the sight of all the people; where all the beholders eyes are attentively bent to looke and pry in the least circumstances of their secretest drifts. (1981, 5)

He reiterates the idea later in the third book, emphasizing the public scrutiny which the king undergoes and the symbolic possibilities of his every action and gesture:

It is a trew old saying, That a King is as one set on a stage, whose smallest actions and gestures, all the people gazingly doe behold: and therefore although a King be neuer so praecise in the discharging of his Office, the people, who seeth but the outward part, will euer iudge of the substance by the circumstances; and according to the outward appearance. ... (1981, 43)

James's sons, Henry and Charles, were introduced at an early age to their father's ideas of monarchy, and Charles was probably just as conscious as James had been of the theatrical nature of the life of public figures, especially the king. He was, moreover, particularly interested in the theater. But unlike James, who always remained a spectator rather than a participant in royal entertainments and masques, Charles insisted on being a part of court productions. Thus, while James had sought the static image of the patriarchal and benevolent monarch as his public face (his figure as it is represented on the front page of his *Collected Works* published in 1616 is probably the image that comes most easily to mind), Charles actively participated in a variety of roles and the image of the patient sufferer (the picture on the front page of the *Eikon Basilike* [1649] with its Christ-like pose, for instance) was an association consciously cultivated during his later years and popularized by sympathetic historians after his execution.

Of course, to a degree, every public personality's life, especially the monarch's, may be regarded as a performance. As Erving Goffman defines it, performance is "all activity of an individual which occurs during a period marked by his continuous presence before a particular set of observers and which has some effect on the observers" (1959, 22). But in the seventeenth century, the typical equation between King and player and between society and theater worked both ways. Elizabeth, James, and Charles may have seen themselves as players in constant performance, but this did not reduce their relationship to society to one between actors and spectators. Theater in the age had not yet erected a wall between performers and spectators, and the analogy between the two, suggested by such well-known expressions as Shakespears's "All the world's a stage," was not simply a metaphor of theatrical convenience. The world was quite literally regarded as analogous to the theater even as theater functioned as a little world. This is most

clearly apparent, of course, in the royal masques that often began
casually and into which royal personages could stroll, as Elizabeth
did frequently. But the analogy was equally valid to theatrical
performances in general. The image of the mirror, therefore, which
was so popular in the age, indicated a double movement; theater
reflected society and society reflected the theater.[30]

Analogous to the image of the mirror is the Aristotelian notion of
mimesis, sanctioned and championed in the sixteenth century by
writers like Sir Philip Sidney. Recently, the concept of mimesis has
been brought back into the spectrum of critical discourse; this revival
of interest has, of course, been accompanied by an enlargement of
its meaning, by an awareness of the complexity of the term, and by
a recognition of the need to understand its relevance as more than
simply imitation.[31] Awareness of the degree of mimetic interaction
between court and theater and between society and theater is crucial
for an understanding of the transformative power of Stuart drama.
To a great degree, the power of Stuart theater as a maker of history
lies within its mimetic impulses.

Rene Girard traces mimesis to the desire to rival and surpass the
model and argues that intrinsic to the notion of mimesis is conflict
or rivalry; if I understand him correctly, one imitates another
through the desire to surpass and perhaps even to negate the other's
achievement. In this sense, Shakespeare's depiction of Shylock in
The Merchant of Venice, for example, may be regarded as an
attempt both to surpass and suppress all previous depictions of the
Jewish character, especially successful ones such as Marlowe's
Barrabas in the *Jew of Malta*.[32] This important dimension to the
concept of mimesis has been, as Girard emphasizes, virtually ignored
in most treatments of the subject. "Not only in philosophy, but also
in psychology, sociology, and literature," he argues, "a mutilated
version of imitation has prevailed"(1978, vii). While Girard stresses
only the *conflict* between emulator and emulated, I would like to
suggest that mimesis springs from the simultaneous though
dialectically opposed desires to emulate and negate. The imitator
both compliments the initiator and attempts by the imitation to
render null or negligible the achievement of his predecessor.[33]

The importance of mimesis in the sixteenth and seventeenth
centuries, in both social and literary activity, can hardly be
underestimated. As historians have shown, the court of James, even
from its inception, competed with images of Elizabeth's court in the
popular mind. James's arrival in London in 1604 (a delay caused by
the presence of the plague in London 1603) replayed Elizabeth's

similar march in the previous age in every detail, but the whole event was deliberately planned to surpass the Queen's in grandeur and extravagance (Goldberg 1983, 30). The event provided, at least in conception if not in execution, theater in its purest sense. Similarly, although Elizabeth had been cast frequently in the role of the virgin goddess, Diana, an apt metaphor for James seemed to be the sensual and wise figure of Solomon, an association consciously cultivated by the King himself. If restraint characterized the Elizabethan court, extravagance typified the Jacobean. The competition with the Elizabethan court seems to have increased in intensity during the later years of James's reign, when idealized visions of the past were constantly evoked in deliberate contrast to the less than ideal present.[34]

Charles, like James, cultivated the aura of lavish splendor particularly through his acquisitions in art and the artists he managed to bring from Europe into England, but having succeeded to a depleted Exchequer, his extravagance was confined to the privileged few. The vast majority of the people, excluded from participation in courtly extravagance even if only as spectators, naturally grew increasingly dissatisfied with the court and courtiers.[35] But the Caroline court, like the Jacobean, still competed with exaggerated images of opulence and peace in Elizabethan England, visions kept alive in the public mind by those dissatisfied with the Stuart monarchy. Distance in time seems only to have increased the mimetic impulses of the court and the public.

Similarly, many Stuart plays clearly invoke earlier ones. As Tzvetan Todorov argues, voicing a belief that has received much support among recent critical theorists, "There is no utterance without relation to other utterance. . . . No utterance is devoid of the intertextual dimension" (1984, 60, 62). The tendency to see all Jacobean and Caroline drama in relation to the drama of the Elizabethan age, to see the ghosts of Shakespearean plays beneath the structures of the later plays is, therefore, not a pointless exercise or an unfair comparison. It is perhaps the most valid methodology that might be adopted. Even as mimetic impulses increased with distance in time, later dramatists such as Ford and Shirley incorporated more ghost structures within their plays than any of the Jacobean dramatists. In plot, theme, and language, the plays of the seventeenth century often invert and parody earlier drama; they function, thus, as "discourses" in the truest sense of that word, though their vision of humanity is decidedly darker than in earlier plays.

The Changeling, for example, consciously parodies the plot of *Othello*.[36] Othello's testing of Desdemona's fidelity with the "magical" handkerchief undergoes a cynical variation in *The Changeling*, when Alsemero tests Beatrice-Joanna's virginity through the use of magical potions. What appears to be a trifle gains magical (and grim) relevance in the earlier play, whereas what are presented as real magical potions provide an occasion for tomfoolery and laughter in the later one. The role of the villainous accomplice, likewise, also reverses: De Flores functions as the manipulating heroine's trusted accomplice while the unsuspecting husband is duped. Even the underplot of the play in which Lollio spies on Alibius's wife, echoes Iago's similar function as Othello's spy, but Isabella's fidelity carries comic overtones. The later play thus concerns itself with the same themes as the earlier, the chastity of women and the duping of indivuduals by villains like Iago and De Flores whose malignancy transcends comprehension. Even Beatrice-Joanna's reaction in act 5 when called a "whore" by her husband echoes Desdemona's horror regarding adultery. She cannot even conceive of such an action, and expresses her dismay thus to Emilia:

> I have heard it so. O, these men, these men!
> Dost thou in conscience think—tell me Emilia—
> That there be women do abuse their husbands
> In such gross kind?

> (4.5. 63–66)

She reacts with equal horror when called a strumpet by Othello shortly before he kills her. Beatrice-Joanna in Middleton's tragedy reacts in similar fashion, but the audience, now privy to her guilt even as they had been to Desdemona's innocence, perceives the intense irony of her statements:

> What a horrid sound it hath.
> It blasts a beauty to deformity;
> Upon what face soever that breath falls,
> It strikes it ugly.

> (5.3. 31–34)

The lines are parodic, for Beatrice-Joanna emerges as the type of woman Desdemona does not even regard as a possibility in the world. Middleton's play thus modifies and reworks Shakespeare's central concerns.

But if the earlier play makes a point about the relationship between appearance and reality, that they do not necessarily coincide, the latter deliberately complicates the issue. In *Othello*, the point emerges clearly: the black moor is not a villain but a victim of villainy cunningly imposed by the seemingly honest Iago. In *The Changeling*, these distinctions collapse. The play suggests that De Flores's appearance is disquieting even as Othello's had been to some in the earlier play, but like Iago, De Flores is trusted and referred to frequently as loyal and honest. In other words, the play conveys a complicated message; it deliberately muddles the dichotomy that the earlier play had erected so carefully. The play thus, like many others in the period, varies patterns begun earlier.[37] This intertextuality between Stuart plays and their earlier models is, however, frequently accompanied by a darker vision of human relationships, a vision (or fascination with evil) that may provide a key to the sociopolitical temper of early Stuart England and the subversive-creative power of theater in particular.

An understanding of the extent to which imitation dictated seventeenth-century behavior (not only literary activity) certainly modifies our perception of the function of theater itself in the age. On some level at least, the dramatists sought by imitation to negate and surpass the ideology of the court that sanctioned their activities, even as they sought to modify the ideologies of the previous century in order to create new (and what it saw as more viable) ones. In its function, therefore, drama both reflected and worked counter to the desire of James himself; like James, it sought to surpass the models of the previous age, but at the same time, it sought to counter the ideology of his court. These dual and dialectically opposed functions make the drama of the period particularly complex; mimesis as it was practiced seems to have been more complex than any vocabulary we have yet devised to describe it.

The *creative power* of Stuart drama rested on these dual inclinations of court and theater. The term *power* has almost always carried connotations of repression and restraint. But, as Michel Foucault insists, "it needs to be considered as a productive network which runs through the whole social body much more than as a negative instance whose function is repression" (1980, 119). Seventeenth-century drama provides a vivid example of this positive power that creates rather than represses. Foucault claims that Western preference for seeing power as a repressive force is closely allied to the institution of monarchy. He goes on to argue that an intellectual destruction of monarchy is necessary to install a belief in the positive function of power: "We need to cut off the king's head," he notes, for "in political theory that has still to be done" (121). The creative function of power in seventeenth-century drama relates explicitly to the intellectual destruction of monarchy in the psyche of the age. Thus, Stuart theater did not function simply as rebellion but as a creative force; as Greenblatt points out, theatricality in the seventeenth century "is not set over against power but is one of power's essential modes"; the "English form of absolutist theatricality" permitted the plays to be "relentlessly subversive" in an environment subjected to the strictest state censorship (1981, 56). But the subversive power of these plays did not preclude their ability to act as court propagnanda; dramatists simultaneously spoke for and against the court.

The coexistence of intellectual destruction in the drama with the social phenomenon of patronage perhaps requires some explanation. Dramatists came to be increasingly under the control of public figures, and were recognized by their allegiance to particular royal households. Chapman and Dekker, for example, belonged to the household of Prince Henry, who even at a very young age had his own establishment and was an avid patron of the arts; Ben Jonson's stature in court increased dramatically with the ascension of the James, although in Charles's court he lost ground after 1632 to his arch rival at court in the creation of masques, Inigo Jones. Several recent books have explored the issue of patronage in the age, and we are only now beginning to understand the complexity and intricacy of social allegiances between writers and the court.[38]

But patronage in the Stuart court does not seem to have been incompatible with dramatic criticism; writers took their cues from the ambiguities at court and "found authority in the royal prerogative of double speech "Goldberg 1983, 147). Patronage was, moreover, in a state of comparative decline as the period progressed; as Leo Salingar has shown, "the portrayal of wealth and patronage by Marston, Tourneur, and Webster indicates the decay of the Tudor aristocracy" and a decreasing respect for it (1986, 438). But radical criticism could coexist with censorship. As Christopher Hill points out, "popular revolt was for many centuries an essential feature of the English tradition," and it seems to have increased in intensity during the early Stuart reigns (1972, 13). Jonathan Barry, in his discussion of the simultaneous existence of conformity and subversion in the popular culture, cites the incident of the apprentice riots of 1660 which incorporated Shrove Tuesday games of football and throwing stones at hens and bitches, thus both obeying and ridiculing the Council's proclamation against the abuse of cocks and dogs, a traditional Shrove Tuesday pastime (1985, 70). Something similar happens in early Stuart drama.

Radical criticism was especially possible because of the nature of drama which, while it could draw the audience into participation by suggesting similarities, could also distance itself from them by invoking the concept of spectacle, as many plays do through blatant and stylized exaggerations. Playwrights simultaneously insist on the alienness of their characters and actions by setting their plays in Italy, and yet proclaim the hollowness of their public lie by making these characters and actions recognizably English. The concern with censorship also explains the allusiveness of these plays; "under censorship men restrained themselves from telling the whole truth as they saw it, proceeding by analogy, implication, and innuendo" (Hill 1984, 21). Dramatists criticize existing structures not overtly, but, as Dollimore argues, by "the inscribing of a subversive discourse within an orthodox one," by providing "a vindication of the letter of orthodoxy while subverting its spirit" (119). Thus, even the most subversive and revolutionary statements are conveyed through the modes of allegory, metaphor, and symbol, and concealed beneath a facade of social and political conformity.

When we speak about the revolutionary nature of the drama in the Stuart periods, however, we refer to a rebellion that was still "orthodox." Parliament (edpecially during the early years) still worked within the established English system, and, in essence, despite the violent action of 1649, the English rebellion differed greatly from later, more radical revolutions such as the French Revolution in 1789. Dollimore argues that the play *Selimus* (1594), for example, "might well have persuaded the audience that religion was indispensible for maintaining the social order while at the same time casting serious doubts as to its veracity" (1984, 86). The same might be said about the revolutionary tone of Stuart drama in general as it raises questions about the monarchical system.

Of course, the subversive power of this drama may even have been a product of the patronage system. The acquiring of gentlemen's privileges by the King's Men was an important event; social status determined power and guaranteed a voice that would be taken seriously. It may be true, as Stephen Orgel argues, that the actual running of the theaters was probably no different than during the Elizabethan age (Lytle and Orgel 1981, 267), but the acquisition of a social "voice" by the theatrical companies permitted the drama to be both official and subversive at once. Strategies of power are intimately linked to language potential; "society shapes and is shaped by the possibilities in its language and discursive practices" (Goldberg 1983, xi). Official sanction both ensured security and guaranteed authority; it made the relationship between the stage and the Crown, as Orgel describes it, "a complex mixture of intimacy and danger" (Greenblatt, 1982, 47).

But the voice in theater involves more than words; in the theater, "verbal means of expression is only one element, with scenery, lighting, music, acting, etc. as other, equally important components in a conglomerate and highly complex structure" (Limon 1986, 16). The language of theater is the sum of its gestures, both verbal, physical and metaphoric; as Owen Feltham noted in 1628, "The Stage feeds both the eare and the eye" (quoted by Diehl 1980, 33). And the reliance on gesture and symbol becomes even more pronounced when theater is forced to conform in verbal and formal matters to outside authority. Thus, the greatest possibilities for subversion exist not in the literal text, which through transmutation into the written word can be subject to the strictest scrutiny, but in physical and metaphoric gestures which are capable of infinite variations. In discussing subversion in Stuart drama, therefore, one is forced to deal especially with meta-theater, the modes of symbol, metaphor and allegory, with what Artaud describes as the "active metaphysics" of theater (1970,33). We deal not only with ideas, but with the function that these ideas serve; we indulge in what J. B. Russell characterizes as "functionalism" (41 n.7).

If I were to reduce the argument of this study to a single statement, it would be that seventeenth-century stage drama in its concern with evil contributed much to the social drama (sociopolitical events) of the period. Victor Turner defines social dramas as "units of disharmonic process arising in conflict situations" (1982, 106). The "conflict situations" of the seventeenth century that resulted in the social drama of the Interregnum may be viewed within the precincts of the Stuart theatrical enterprise; the plays have what Greenblatt recently characterized as "social energy" (1988, 6). Thus, ultimately my study will be as much a cultural analysis as a literary one, for the two realms are inextricably related and may not be viewed except in mutual terms. But even as all "cultural analysis is intrinsically incomplete," as Clifford Geertz insists (1973, 29), so the following is only introductory and essentially incomplete.

2

Evil as Nonbeing: Physical and Mental Fragmentation

The Human Body in Stuart Monarchical Theory

The Augustinian concept of evil as lack of essence is dramatized in Stuart tragedies through depictions of mental and physical fragmentation invariably represented through violence done to the human body. I will concentrate in the following pages on stage violence and on the image of the body in the rhetoric of the court and in the drama.

Violence acquires new connotations in the drama of this period. In earlier plays, such as *The Spanish Tragedy* (1585), *Edward II* (1590), or *Titus Andronicus* (ca. 1590), violence had been primarily a matter of thematic and structural resolution. When it carried symbolic implications, the symbolism had extended only to the context of the play. Hieronimo bites his tongue off in the final scene of the *The Spanish Tragedy* mocking the inadequacy of words, and thus aptly denounces the course of events in the play. The final scene in *Edward II*, in which the murderer thrusts a red hot iron into Edward's anus, provides a grotesque parody of the homosexual act and thus functions as a condemnation of the king's actions throughout the play. In *Titus Andronicus*, Titus murders Chiron and Demetrius and feeds them in a pie to their mother, the Empress Tamora; Titus thus literalizes Tamora's voracious and consuming appetite for power.

In Jacobean and Caroline drama, on the other hand, violence both reveals the sexual and moral depravity of the characters who practice it and symbolically offers a commentary on the dramatist's social context. We should not regard the grim humor that accompanies violence in many of these plays as simply "laughter that celebrates anarchy" (Brooke 1979, 2); stage violence in this period is not a matter of mere sensationalism but of signification, as Huston Diehl has pointed out (1980, 29). The plays explore with greater tenacity the relationship between body and psyche, and violence done to the body almost always symbolizes violence committed on the social and political body by those in power. As Vera Foster asserts, "early seventeenth-century tragedy is characterized by its emphasis on a whole social group rather than on the tragic individual as in the Elizabethan era" (181).

By rooting violence in images of the body, dramatists necessarily imitated the court and the church; this interaction makes the image one of the most consistently important images in Stuart drama. The image of the body also relates expressly to the theme of evil; violence done to the body, resulting in physical fragmentation, often becomes a metaphor for psychological and sociopolitical fragmentation. Because identity in the Renaissance related closely to theories about the body, dramatists could, by destroying, disguising, and multiplying the body, raise questions about being itself. Thus, Stuart theatrical depictions of mental and physical fragmentation ultimately reiterate the Augustinian notion of evil as lack of essence.

The villainies of many Jacobean and Caroline protagonists may, in fact, be traced to the state of mental fragmentation, often symbolically reiterated on the stage through depictions of dismemberment and disguise of the body. As Robert R. Reed argues, the treatment of madfolk in the seventeenth century was "similar to the treatment of devils in medieval drama" (1952, 6). Depictions of madness increase in number and variety in this period. Michel Foucault has argued in his remarkable study of European attitudes toward madness that while "in both Shakespeare of Cervantes, madness still occupies an extreme place in that it is beyond appeal," "the world of the seventeenth century is strangely hospitable to madness. Madness is here at the heart of things and men" (1965, 31, 37). Interest in madness became a general cultural phenomenon that the literature of the age reflects through its increased theatrical concern with the theme.[1]

The age's interest in the theme of mental fragmentation may be seen also in the number of plays that represent the state of melancholia, in the interest which Robert Burton's *Anatomy of Melancholy* (1621) provoked, and in playwrights such as Ford whose work shows the direct influence of the *Anatomy*. As is commonly known, the term *melancholy* signified more than simply depression or listlessness; it described a variety of psychological states. Many tragedies (especially the revenge plays) of the period appropriated the melancholy protagonist and denote violence and madness as proceeding from the psychological state of melancholia.

From one perspective, the image of the human body, central to Stuart depictions of violence, madness, and melancholia, may be classified as a natural symbol, for, as Leonard Barkan notes in his study of the image in early England, "In the life of primitive man, the self, and hence the body, is the only wholeness that can be grasped" (1975, 8). "Significance is inherent in the human body" as Julia Kristeva argues (Suleiman 1985, 193), and "most symbolic behavior must work through the body" as Mary Douglas demonstrates in her influential study of natural symbols (1970, xix). But, as Douglas goes on to qualify, universal though the general relevance of a natural symbol might be "systems of symbols . . . get their meaning from social experience. They are coded by a community with a shared history." The image of the human body in Stuart drama provides a vivid example of what she characterizes as a "social symbol" (xx).

By the time of the late Tudor and early Stuart reigns, the image of the human body, through repeated political and ecclesiastical use, had become a charged metaphor signifying a variety of things. That the dramatists turned to this, the most common image in the Church's and James's vocabulary, provides an instance of mimesis as I described it earlier. Its use placed theatrical productions well within the parameters of orthodox representation, even as it provided dramatists with a potent weapon of political, social, and religious subversion. The image of the fragmented body thus provided dramatists with a metaphor through which they could represent social disintegration and the breakdown of conventional beliefs.

Its frequent use by the monarchs, especially James, increased the potency of the body as a public symbol. In medieval theory the king had two bodies, one divine, the *corpus mysticum*, and the other human, the *corpus naturalis*.[2] The theory ensured the perpetual acceptance of monarchy itself no matter how tyrannical a particular monarch might be. In his human body, the king was necessarily prone to error and deviation from moral norms, but as monarch, in the governing of his kingdom, he was a divine instrument and therefore above reproach. A tyrant monarch was a plague sent by God to torture a wicked people and thus still beyond the people's judgment.

While the fiction of the king's two bodies thus had earlier precedents, it was, as Ernst Kantorowicz points out, a "distinctive feature of English political thought in the age of Elizabeth and the early Stuarts" (1957, 42.).[3] James's *Basilikon Doron* is probably the most useful source book of monarchical use of the theory. Written when he was king of Scotland only, its aim was to provide the people for the first time with an inside theory of monarchy. As such, it became a reference book for succeeding Stuart monarchs who wished to reassert the divine right of the king. *Basilikon Doron* was hurriedly republished in England in 1604 shortly before James's coronation, and to some degree, it was the only introduction the literate English populace could have had to their new monarch. It was, at any rate, a text with which most learned Englishmen were acquainted.

James had first made similar claims for the divinity inherent in the monarch earlier in "The True Lawe of Free Monarchies," published anonymously in 1598. Written in the voice of a concerned citizen, the work exhorts against harming the monarch, however evil he might be. In the *Basilikon Doron*, written in his "divine" voice as monarch, James articulates the notion of kingship even more vividly by using images central to Renaissance hierarchical and patriarchal theory. Here he makes substantial use of the human body as an image to reaffirm hierarchy; the king was to be regarded as analogous to the head, and as the head rules the body, so the king had to be in absolute control over his kingdom, his social body (1918, 272). The idea became an essential aspect of James's public rhetoric and behavior. Commenting on the formation of the "commonwealth" of England and Scotland under his kingship, he noted in his first speech to Parliament:

> I am the Head and it [the commonwealth] is my Body; I am the Sheperd, and it is my flocke: I hope therefore no man will be so vnreasonable as to thinke that I that am a Christian King vnder the Gospel, should be a Polygamist and husband to two wiues; that I being the Head, should haue a diuided and monstrous Body .... could euer the Body bee counted without the Head, which was euer vnseparably ioined therunto? So that as Honour and Priuiledges of any of the Kingdomes could bot be diuided from their Soueraigne; So are they now confounded and ioined in my Person, who am equall and alike kindly Head to you both. (1918, 272)

To sanction the divinity of the monarch and his role as head of the kingdom, James selected frequently from the Bible, especially the Old Testament, passages which described how Saul, David, and Solomon were appointed kings; the anointing of their mortal bodies transformed them into divine instruments. The image of the dual bodies of the monarch was itself a theological one, traditionally used to characterize Christ as both man and Son of God. The image thus linked the king overtly with Christ and guaranteed his acceptance; the king was a *typus Christi*. The Christ anaolgy was used frequently during the Stuart reigns, for Christ as the ideal monarch emphasized both the divinity and the humanity of kings. Francis Bacon's introduction to the second edition of the *Advancement of Learning*, for example, calculated to gain James's support for his plans, draws the anaolgy (1954, 263), and Bishop Williams in his funeral oration for James explicitly makes the connection after drawing on the Solomon analogy, for "Salomon was a type of Christ himself, and by consequence a Patterne for any Christian" (Ashton 1969, 43). The name of Christ could be derived anagrammatically from Charles Stuart's name; the image became particularly popular during Charles's last years and is evoked quite explicitly in the picture on the front page of the *Eikon Basilike* (1649). The Church also made much of the image; it represented the body of Christ and thus functioned as an extension of divinity. The Church's theory made possible the analogous notion of the kingdom as the extended body of the monarch; it was his social and public body. Royalty was thus expounded during the early Stuart reignes in specifically christological terminology.[4]

But the notion of the dual bodies and of hierarchy within the body, while intended to indicate unity among seemingly discrete parts, could also indicate the very opposite. Duality itself created the possibility of schisms, of fragmentation, as James himself seems to have been aware. And fragmentation in the king would result in fragmentation in the social body and vice versa. Thus, Lear's act of dividing his social body, his kingdom, into three parts, symbolically prefigures his own psychological fragmentation later and the sociopolitical crisis that the rest of the play enacts. And viewed within the context of seventeenth-century monarchical theory, the Puritan cry of "We fight the king to defend the king," was still a very "orthodox" revolutionary program, questioning the king in his *corpus naturalis*, while still accepting the fiction of the *corpus mysticum*. This uniquely English concept of the dual bodies of the monarch permitted Parliament in the name of King Charles I (his body politic) to wage war against the same Charles I (in his natural and hence corrupt body). And Parliament could declare about its own actions sentencing Charles to death that "what they do herein hath the stamp of Royal Authority, although his Majesty ... do in his own Person oppose or interrupt the same" (McIlwain 1910, 389f). The fiction of the dual bodies implied that death could affect the king only in his physical body and that his mystical body was immortal. Thus, Charles's execution in 1649 dispensed of his mortal body, which alone was perishable. The irony is that logically interpreted, the notion of the king's two bodies, so tacitly embraced by the Stuart monarchs, actually permitted the events between 1642 and 1649.

Dramatic reliance on the image of the human body shows how an idea drawn from patristic culture could become a vehicle of subversion and criticism even within a literary form subjected to the strictest censorship and royal scrutiny. The image functioned as a natural and charged metaphor for voicing discontent, for representing the domino-like effects that any displacement within the scale could cause. By subjecting the body to the evils of dismemberment and melancholia, dramatists could indicate political, social, and moral degeneration both in particular individuals and in society as a whole.

Physical Fragmentation: The Body Divided

The intensity of Stuart fascination with the fragmented body becomes most apparent when we compare Jacobean treatments of the subject with earlier depictions that emphasize the unity rather than fragmentation between the dual bodies of the monarch. In an early Jacobean play such as Shakespeare's *Measure for Measure* (1604), the notion of the dual bodies of the king figures without the intense criticism and sense of irremediable fragmentation that accompanies its depiction in later plays. In this play, Angelo and the Duke may be treated as mirror images of each other. The idea of the mirror, so popular in the age, points to more than simple reflection; in a mirror, things appear in reverse. Thus, Angelo, the stickler for rules, turns out to be corruptible; but the Duke, a lax and careless ruler, emerges as moral and just. Angelo, deputized to govern by the Duke, may represent the corruptible body of the ruler, the *corpus naturalis*, while the Duke embodies the *corpus mysticum*, the body divine. The sense of identification between them is suggested by the Duke himself in the opening scene, when he entrusts the welfare of his kingdom to Angelo:

> But I do bend my speech
> To one that can my part in him advertise.
> Hold therefore, Angelo:
> In our remove be thou at full ourself.
>
> (1.1 41–44)

The lines are echoed later by Isabella, who, however, stresses the differences between the divine and the corrupt ruler when she compares the absent Duke to the "stern" Angelo:

> If he had been as you and you as he,
> You would have slip'd like him; but he like you,
> Would not have been so stern.
>
> (2.2. 68–70)

Escalus similarly asserts the divine presence of the Duke among his deputies when he says, "The Duke's in us" (5.1. 330).

Critics and audiences of *Measure for Measure* have been troubled by how the Duke sets about correcting the villainies in his kingdom. He deliberately obscures facts and holds back information so that his final plan can be properly executed. The conclusion of the play, where he makes convenient marriage arrangements among unwilling characters, is likewise problematic. Angelo's crimes go unpunished, and marriage to Mariana, the woman he had rejected and abused earlier, is foisted on him; Lucio is wed to the "woman wrong'd by this lewd fellow" despite his plea that he should not be married to a whore. The Duke's proposal of marriage to Isabella also jars with her previous determination to join a nunnery. In fact, her silence through the last few pages of the play (which contrasts sharply with her vocal intensity earlier) may suggest her discomfort with the new arrangements for her future made by the Duke arbitrarily and in public. Critics have argued that the Duke behaves as if he were a divine agent as he moves through the play manipulating events and characters. Although modern audiences are troubled by this, it may, in fact, be the way we are expected to see him. In *Measure for Measure*, written so early in the Jacobean period, we may have a script on the dual bodies of the monarch, an enactment of this uniquely English theory of kingship.

In fact, the figure of James may be invoked in the Duke. This becomes especially relevant when we remember that the play was staged for the new monarch in 1604. Historians have pointed out that James disliked crowds and that he openly revealed his impatience of public shows. During James's procession through London, his dislike of public contact became most apparent; the new king may have furnished Shakespeare with some of the characteristics he gives to the Duke. Thus, in the opening scene, the Duke declares:

> I love the people,
> But do not like to stage me to their eyes;

> Though it do well, I do not relish well
> Their loud applause and eyes vehement
>
> (1.1. 68–71)

And yet, ironically, only by mingling with his people can he gain true knowledge about his kingdom and its citizens. The play perhaps written as advice to the new monarch, calls for a perfect balance between tyranny and kindness, for a true merging of the natural and divine bodies of the monarch. The play ultimately suggests the integration of power and mercy in the ruler who should be "terror" as well as "love," mortality" and "mercy" to his people (1.1. 20, 45).

Hamlet also may be read allegorically as a script on the dual aspects of the monarch. Through Hamlet, the play repeatedly stresses the radical differences between the virtuous Hamlet senior and the corrupt Claudius. And the play emphasizes the irrevocable gulf between these bodies: one transmutes into the supernatural form, but still commands respect and awe; the other, despite the paraphernalia of sovereignity with which it surrounds itself, is stabbed, mutilated, and desanctified by the end of the play. In this rendering, the rift between the divine and corrupt bodies of the monarch has decidedly disastrous effects on the kingdom, which passes into the hands of an old enemy, Fortinbras of Norway.

Later representations of the dual bodies of the ruler are not quite as indulgent of the theory as *Measure for Measure* had been.[5] In effect, the later drama demystifies the language of the monarchs about the body (Goldberg 1983, 85). In Stuart plays, therefore, we encounter the image in its demystified and fragmented form, or "in the process of its effective dismemberment" (Barker 1984, 24). And, as Francis Barker insists, these images of the dismembered body are "systematic rather than personal," and spread across the whole of Jacobean and Caroline writing. Physically present on the stage in their fragmented forms, these images ultimately question humanist claims about the essential divinity of man and royal claims about the divinity of the king's body. They raise doubts both about the welfare of the body politic and ultimately about entrusting that welfare to the physical (and therefore potentially at least corruptible) body of the monarch. Most importantly, by raising doubts about the very basis of these systems, the plays fomented intellectual revolutions making possible the actual social revolution of 1642; as Franco Moretti remarks about tragedy, "having deconsecratd the king, it made it possible to decapitate him" (1983, 8).

Fragmentation in these plays may be devided into two distinct groups: fragmentation by division, in which grotesque parts of the disjointed body are brought on stage, and fragmentation by multiplication, in which characters seem simply to be caricatured variations on each other or where individual figures multiply into a variety of persons. In both cases, characters emerge as psychologically and emotionally fragmented.

The fragmented human body has been the focus of several recent studies of the Jacobean theater, and I will deal only briefly with the image of the body fragmented by division in these plays.[6] The vividly sexual nature of these depictions, what J. L. Simmons characterizes as "Jacobean fascination with phallic evil," also has received considerable attention. Simmons argues that "Had King James not existed, dramatists would have had to invent such a monarch to preside over the Jacobean fascination with phallic evil" (1980, 160). It seems more likely that dramatic fascination with phallic evil took its cue from the court and might not have existed in different circumstances. Precisely because of the intense interaction between court and theater, concern with sexual and phallic evil often manifests itself in images of the human body, images central to James's monarchical and patriarchal theory. These depictions probably resulted from sexual ambiguities in James's behavior and vocabulary.

The conventional image of the human body itself provided for an easy association between the sexual and political halves of the monarch. But James's public rhetoric and behavior made the association even more potent. The sexual implications of James's entry into London have been noted by Goldberg; it was expressly described in terms of the groom's arrival to take his bride (1983, 142). James was himself fond of the biblical/sexual/patriarchal image, and declared about his monarchy, "I am the Husband and all the isle is my Wife" (272). His series of ambiguous relationships with male favorites, the last of whom was Buckingham, was no secret. Thus, as Goldberg argues, encouraged by conventional analogies between the body and the state and by James's ambiguous public behavior, dramatists could, for example, "glance at the marriage of James to his kingdom" in terms of "the homosexuality of Tiberius" (142). "Jacobean fascination with phallic evil" thus took its cue from James's ambiguous language and public behavior. Depictions of the fragmented body in plays such as *The Changeling* may be regared as vividly grotesque manifestations of Jacobean fascination with phallic evil.

In *The Changeling*, act 3, scene 4, we have one of the most vividly sexual instances of stage violence in Jacobean tragedy. Having murdered Alonso Piracquo at the request of Beatrice-Joanna, Alonso's fiancée, De Flores brings her the finger of the murdered man with the engagement ring she had once given him still on it. Formerly a token of her love for Alonso, now the ring is a token of De Flores's deed, and soon it will be a token of her liaison with De Flores during the rest of the play. De Flores brings the finger, too, because, as he says, he "could not get the ring without the finger" (1.30). Of course, having sliced off the finger for the ring, De Flores should have had access to the ring. The reason De Flores gives, therefore, explains why he had to slice off Alonso's finger, but it does not explain the presence of the finger on stage with the ring still on it. In other words, De Flores intends to convey a message through his "token," and his desecration of Alonso's body is not gratuitous violence. Middleton conveys a vivid sense of the impending action in the rest of the play through the manner in which the characters handle this token in this scene.

The finger projects an obvious phallic symbol and conveys De Flores's triumphant emasculation of Piracquo. The fact that he leaves the ring still on the finger as he offers it to Beatrice-Joanna makes his intentions clear to the audience, although Beatrice-Joanna remains (either intentionally or as a mater of convenience) oblivious to his hints. The ring was a common feminine symbol on the Renaissance stage; we encounter it in many of Shakespeare's plays. *The Merchant of Venice*, for example, closes with a bawdy joke that explicitly treats it as a sexual image. Here, in Middleton's play, more than De Flores, it is finally Beatrice-Joanna who loads the image with explicit sexual meaning. Offered the ring and finger, she asks De Flores to keep the very token she had given earlier to Alonso. Thus, even before she does, the audience perceives her inclinations. She has permitted the transference of the ring from Piracquo to De Flores; and the emasculation of Piracquo has endowed the once ugly De Flores with sexual appeal. Beatrice-Joanna transfers both her "love" and Piracquo's masculinity in this scene. Their guilty alliance through the rest of the play has already been anticipated metaphorically through this dramatic transference of a bloody token.

The iconographic significance of this transference adds to the dramatic intensity of the scene. Huston Diehl, discussing violence in Renaissance drama, points out the iconographic traditions on which dramatists invariably drew; "to see stage violence as iconographic," she points out, "is to see it in terms of Renaissance aesthetics" (1980,

33). Christ's injunction, "If thy right hand offend thee, cut it off," produces in a Renaissance emblem book the image of a knife slicing off a finger (Diehl 1980, 36). In this scene in *The Changeling* in which a sliced off finger is presented on stage by De Flores in full sight of the audience, we have, I believe, a corruption and subversion of that emblematic depiction. Beatrice-Joanna has tried to do precisely what the biblical text warns against; she has tried to close her eyes to the enormity of her own actions, to the villainy she herself has initiated. She gas tried to commit murder by proxy. The finger disgusts her, and De Flores's just reply, "Why, is that killing more than the whole man?" is a comment on her hypocrisy. The finger thus both recalls and parodies the biblical text and its conventional emblematic interpretation.

Stuart tragedy provides numerous other examples of such theatrical fascination with the body fragmented by division. The body devoid of flesh and artificially refashioned to resemble a country lass, the bloody head brought on stage by the executioner moments after the execution, and the disjointed tongue in *The Revenger's Tragedy*, the hand given to the Duchess shortly before she is killed in *The Duchess of Malfi*, the limbs of Tymetheus hanging on stage during the concluding scenes of *The Bloody Banquet*, and the heart on a dagger brought into the middle of a feast in *'Tis Pity She's a Whore* provide examples of the body fragmented by division. What John Hunt has said about *Hamlet* holds true for many plays of the period: "the play looks like a dissecting room, stocked with all of man's limbs, organs, tissues, and fluids" (1988, 29). The plays repeatedly present partial and grotesque images of the body fragmented during processes of sexual and political corruption by madmen and melancholics.

Gilles Deleuze and Felix Guattari in their extraordinary book, *Anti-Oedipus*, note:

> The body without organs is the model of death. . . . Zero intensity. The death model appears when the body without organs repels the organs and lays them aside; no mouth, no tongue, no teeth—to the point of self-mutilation, to the point of suicide. (1972, 329)

In Jacobean and Caroline tragedy we encounter two kinds of "zero intensity," the body without organs and organs without the body. Both cases constitute deconsecration; the images provide dramatic commentary on the inadequacy of the body, on the inadequacy of organs. Ultimately, these depictions of the fragmented body raise questions also about the fragmented self; they constitute both a deconstruction of the body, as Hunt argues about *Hamlet*, and, as I hope to show, a deconstruction of being or selfhood itself (1988, 30).

Mental Fragmentation: The Body Multiplied

Fragmentation by multiplication, equally common in the plays, often allies with the popular device of the disguise. Disguise serves a very different function in Jacobean plays than in Elizabethan. The adoption of masks becomes a preliminary action that lures men into corruption; disguise often functions as a metaphor for the multiplication of the body, for mental fragmentation and for the phenomenon we now describe as schizophrenia. The idea of the dual bodies, so intrinsic to the notion of the divinity of kings, thus receives an ironic twist. In many plays the disgusied body ultimately succumbs to melancholy obsessions and villainy, which can in most cases be traced directly to the initial action of disguising the natural body. The mental and physical fragmentation in the protagonists as they take on a variety of personalities ultimately points (as do the images of the divided body) to schisms in the social (and political) structure.

Interestingly, this concept of the multiple and fragmented self becomes a crucial argument later in John Milton's denunciation of Charles I: "Which of him shall we believe? For he seems not one, but double" (1953, 3: 371). Milton's charge, offered as justification for regicide, posits that lack of an identifiable self in Charles made him evil. The same claim might be made about a large number of Jacobean and Caroline heroes and antiheroes. Two things need to be stressed here, however: first, not merely depicting dissembling and disguise, many Stuart plays even suggest that character may be artificial construct; second, they do not always restrict this suggestion to villainous characters, but often extend the claim to ambiguous and even positive figures. Iago provides an instance of the multifaceted nature of evil, as does De Flores in *The Changeling*, or Bosola in *The Duchess of Malfi*. Malevole in *The Malcontent*, however, remains an ambiguous figure, for his disguises and manipulations ultimately bring about social and moral order. The same might be said about the Duke in *Measure for Measure*. Vindice's villainy in *The Revenger's Tragedy*, however, begins with his departure from a definite self. In Shakespeare's *Hamlet*, on the other hand, we encounter a decentered self in the figure of Hamlet, and yet, in this instance, the decentering can hardly be attributed to evil as in Tourneur's play.

The Renaissance equivalent term for schizophrenia (among other ailments), and for the state of mental fragmentation in general, seems to have been *melancholy*, the term discussed in what was the most important psychological/philosophical treatise of the age, Robert Burton's *Anatomy of Melancholy*. Melancholy described mental imbalance between bodily and emotional desires caused by fragmentation. The term *melancholy* as it was used in the sixteenth and seventeenth centuries included more than mere alienation from and discontent with the world, although both of these were necessary adjuncts to the melancholic disposition. It was an all-encompassing term inherently contradictory, as Lawrence Babb points out (1951, 59–60). Extreme sorrow often caused melancholy (Burton 1927, 225); intemperance of the body could also extend to intemperance of the mind and result in the malady (Babb, 20); immoderate passion, such as the desire for revenge could also be attributed to melancholy (Burton 1927, 231–35); and the appearance of the melancholy man often indicated the malignancy of his heart (Babb 58, 75). The melancholy condition was not, however, a wholly negative one; its emotional intensity could lead one to both intellectual creativity and satanic viciousness. Melancholy could thus generate extraordinary intellectual and imaginative powers; the melancholy man was indefatigable in the exercise of his wits, a power which he could choose to use creatively or destructively (Babb 58–59).

Revenge and melancholy emerge as closely allied in Burton's *Anatomy of Melancholy* (1927, 232–35). A similar theory can be seen earlier in Sir Francis Bacon, who condemns revenge as a "wild justice," a necessary result of mental unhealthiness: "A man who studies revenge keeps his own wounds green, which otherwise would heal and do well" ("On Revenge," 1927, 15–16). Even earlier Thomas Elyot likewise had seen the effects of revenge as a progessive deterioration of the mind (Prosser 1967, 8). That the revenger was thought to be not merely diseased but also allied mentally and spiritually with supernatural forces of evil is abundantly clear in Bacon, who sees such figures as living the "life of witches" (1927, 16). Timothy Bright also defended the theory that Satan forever hankers after melancholy men (Reed 1952, 105), an analogy which allows the merging of the revenger with the Vice figures of the medieval morality tradition.

The revenge plays in particular, therefore, appropriated the melancholy protagonist. Concern with melancholia is not, of course, restricted to the revenge plays, and one encounters it in almost all the literary forms of the period (Reed 1952, 71–72), but the revenge tradition seems to have adopted the melancholy man as a necessary and particularly suitable protagonist. To a degree, the history of the revenge tradition in England coincides with the development of ideas about the melancholy man. Gradually the negative connotations of melancholia seem to have been subsumed, and in dramatists such as Ford, the melancholy condition, although still resulting in unnatural violence, becomes infinitely more fascinating. The extent to which the revenge tradition and public fascination with melancholia coincided has not, I believe, been explored adequately. In conjunction, the terms *revenge* and *melancholy* provided for the kind of tension so basic to the dramatic productions of the period, for revenge, like melancholy, was a complex term. It was at once a condemnable violation of social codes and an act evoking sympathy and emotional support.

Early plays such as *The Spanish Tragedy* and *Titus Andronicus* had been concerned with melancholy, but as the revenge tradition developed, many plays became anatomical studies of the disease. In fact, *The Revenger's Tragedy*, written as early as 1607, and Ford's *'Tis Pity She's a Whore* (1632–33), seem to be less revenge plays than dramatically realized satires on the revenge tradition and on earlier melancholy heroes. Melancholy even overrides the movive of revenge in later plays of the genre. Although the early tragedies represent the revenger's increasing propensity toward melancholy, they rarely include fragmentation and multiplication of the body beyond all recognition, as the later plays do. Increasingly, by multiplying and duplicating the body, these later plays also suggest a lack of essence at the core of being and thus deconstruct being itself.

And in keeping with the general temper of the seventeenth century, these later plays are little concerned with supernatural phenomena; the alliance between the ghost of the deceased and the avenging hero, a central factor in earlier plays, no longer figures, and the protagonist's desire for revenge springs from within himself. The revenge ghost, it should be remembered, came from "hell" under the stage in the earlier plays; by rooting the desire for revenge within individuals, later dramatists emphasize the psychological origins of evil. Later dramatists also show greater interest in exploring the psychology of revenge than in depciting its successful accomplishment. Ford's tragedy, *'Tis Pity* offers the freest, boldest, and most ironic treatment of these subjects. To understand fully this freedom of conception in Ford, we have to deal first, however with the conjunctive treatment of revenge and melancholy in early plays such as *The Spanish Tragedy*, which presents a similar juxtaposition with perhaps greater intensity, and in later plays such as *Hamlet* and *The Revenger's Tragedy*, which first anatomized melancholy and revenge. In Tourneur's tragedy especially, melancholy coexists with irremediable mental fragmentation and multiplication of the body.

In *the Spanish Tragedy* (1594), Hieronimo, the Marshall of Spain, is the most important melancholy figure. After the inhuman murder of his son, Horatio, his desire for justice prompts him at first to take his case through the proper channels:

> I will go plain me to my lord the King,
> And cry aloud for justice through the Court,
> Wearing the flints with these my withered feet,
> And either purchase justice by entreats,
> Or tire them all with my revenging threats
>
> (3.7. 69–73)

Grief has not yet overthrown his reason, but when his griefs increase over the suicide of his wife, and when justice seems an impossibility, Hieronimo's degeneration into melancholy begins. Fron here on, his psychological conflict between reason and passion, a conflict he himself recognizes, becomes the central focus of the play: "As I am never better than when I am mad; then me thinks I am a brave fellow; then I do wonders; but reason abuseth me, and there's the torment, there's the hell" (4.6, 163–64). He becomes more and more like a melancholic obsessed by a single passion (Babb 1951, 43). Because of his position as a judge, Hieronimo constantly faces the task of providing justice to otehrs similarly wronged; thus reminded of his own inability to act, he becomes more and more obsessed with the idea of revenge.

Fredson Bowers seems to be ignoring psychological degeneration when he sees as inexplicable Hieronimo's desire to delay his revenge in order to work it cunningly and under cover (1940, 70). Hieronimo's decision to work cunningly indicates a development towards Machiavellianism, which Renaissance theorists saw as the inevitable result of the melancholic's constant mental activity (Babb 1951, 58). The pride of the Machiavellian intriguer surfaces in Hieronimo's statements later as he vows to revenge his son's murder:

> I will revenge his death.
> But how? not as the vulgar wits of men,

> with open, but inevitable ills,
> As by a secret, yet a certain meane,
> Which under kindship will be cloaked best.
>
> (4.6. 188–92)

Ture, Hieronimo's reasons for delay at this point are not valid, as Bowers points out, but Kyd here depicts the psychological degeneration that later dramatists such as Tourneur and Ford develop into the central focus of their plays. As the play progresses, Hieronimo's mental activity increases, culminating in a macabre grand finale of multiple deaths ironically accomplished before an entirely unsuspecting audience.

The scene between Hieronimo and the painter (3.12) shows early the malancholic's intellectual and creative inclinations. Hieronimo desires to create, and requests the painter, who pleads justice for his own murdered son, to paint a picture that will capture in minute detail Horatio's murder and Hieronimo subsequent discovery of the body. Hieronimo transfers some of his hatred of the murderers by requesting that they be painted in a manner that will immediately suggest their villainy: "stretch thine art, and let their beards be of Judas his own color; and let their eyebrows jutty over" (3.12, 134–36). But painting, a static art, proves unsatisfactory, as Hieronimo quickly realizes. He can ask the painter to paint Horatio's murder and his subsequent discovery of the body, but can go no further to present the murderers brought to justice. The painter's query when Hieronimo closes with a description of himself in a trance after discovering the body, "And is this the end?," pointedly comments on the inadequacy of the painting if it will not also incorporate justice. Hieronimo, realizing that he cannot describe a scene that is so far from being realized in action, reacts by beating the painter. The scene, although purposeless in accomplishing revenge, banishes Hieronimo's final vestige of rationality and leads him to creative madness.

Later, in a parallel scene (4.2), his wife, Isabella, attempts to destroy the garden, the scene of their son's murder.. Disappointed that the murderers have not been brought to justice, she speaks of her desecration of the arbor as a substitute revenge:

> Oh monstrous homicides!
> Since neither piety nor pity moves
> The King to justice or compassion,
> I will revenge myself upon this place,
> Where thus they murdered my beloved son.
>
> (4.2, 1–5)

But her act remains unsatisfying like the art of painting, because it establishes only an illusory spectacle of destruction without affecting the outside world which is the source of her sorrow and which continues to exercise the same powers that had resulted in the initial tragedy. Her realization of the inadequacy of her efforts leads her to suicide at the end of this scene. Her violence, although different from Hieronimo's in the earlier scene because it is misdirected against herself, remains pointless, like her husband's.

Hieronimo's and Isabella's failed attempts at revenge provide interesting contrasts to each other. Hieronimo seeks revenge in static artistic representation that will capture in vivid detail the unnatural and horrifying murder; he wants an exact replica of the original scene. Isabella wishes to erase all memory of the murder by destroying the arbor where it occurred: she wishes to efface rather than recreate. Ultimately, dramatic reenactment, which simultaneously recreates the original murder and destroys those who committed it, thus uniting Hieronimo's and Isabella's desires, provides the most satisfying form of revenge.

The play within the play planned by Hieronimo and enacted before the entire court near the end of the tragedy (4.4) thus accomplishes what the scene with the painter and the scene in the garden failed to achieve, because it succeeds in removing the "roots from whence the rest is sprung" (5.2. 9). The original murders are reenacted and the murderers killed. The King and the Duke, whose sons participated in the play, are left without heirs, and Hieronimo thus ensures that their social power will transfer to outsiders. The killing of the Duke of Castile, which Bowers categorizes as unsatisfying (1940, 70–71), is thus both dramatically necessary if the revenge is to be complete and evidence of the extreme power of malancholy to convert its victims to primordial evil. Ironically, Hieronimo's public tragedy manifests a highly creative power used wholly for destructive purposes. Thus, Kyd's play foreshadows later dramatic depictions of revenge as a destroyer of the moral barriers that initially separate the avenger from the villains who have wronged him.

The dramatic grand finale that concludes Kyd's tragedy has its parallel in the concluding act of *Titus Andronicus*. But Shakespeare's early experiment in the revenge tradition obsessively insists from the very beginning on its relevance as a dramatic reenactment of earlier revenge tales. The story centers on Titus's revenge enacted on the family of Saturnius, the emperor of Rome. At the beginning of the tragedy, Titus returns to Rome with Tamora, queen of the Goths, and her sons after victorious wars against them.

He delivers Alarbus, Tamora's oldest son to be ritually sacrificed by the Romans in honor of their victory. The incensed Tamora vows revenge, and perceives her opportunity when she becomes Empress of Rome shortly after through marriage with Saturnius. Tamora thus emerges as the initial avenger, although the motives for her actions against Lavinia, Titus's daughter, and his sons, Quintus and Martius, appear to be motivated by jealousy, fear of their popularity, and sheer pleasure in inflicting curelty rather than vengeance. Depicted throughout as a vicious and ambitious outsider, Tamora never evokes sympathy despite the initial wrongs done to her.

The primary revenger and melancholic in the play is Titus himself who faces a series of losses and debasements. Tamora permits her sons, Demetrius and Chiron, to murder Bassanius, Lavinia's husband, so that they might rape her; afterwards, to prevent detection, they chop off her tongue and her arms. With the help of Aaron, Tamora's secret lover and a Moor, they succeed in accusing Titus's sons, Quintus and Martius, of Bassanius's murder. Both are beheaded by Saturnius's orders immediately.

The parallel between the Ovidian tale of Philomel and Chiron's and Demetrius's outrage on Lavinia is overt, but by their actions, Tamora's sons do not merely reenact the original story; they seek to render it anew with variations that will prevent discovery such as had occurred in the original. In the process, they also make their rendering more viciously brutal, because they at once double the dismemberment and jointly enact the villainous actions. But the tale on which they model their behavior also becomes their means of discovery and their eventual ruin. Marcus Andronicus, Lavinia's uncle and brother to Titus, devises another variation on the original by having his niece use his staff, guiding it with her mouth and feet, to reveal the names of the brothers. Lavinia's revelation produces a ritualistic and joint avowal by the Andronici to revenge her rape and dismemberment at all costs.

Thereafter, we perceive Titus's increasing melancholia; in keeping with traditional conceptions of the malancholy mind, he reveals his greatest intellectual abilities when fully committed to revenge. In a grotesque grand finale that surpasses Kyd's in dramatic effect, he returns to the Ovidian story invoked earlier by Tamora's sons in their actions, and by Lavinia. His successful final act of vengeance is preceded, however, by other re-renderings of earlier texts, which reveal the intellectual intensity of his mind in its melancholy state. In an earlier scene, shortly after Lavinia's revelation, he sends the young Lucius, his grandson, to Demetrius and Chiron with weapons wrapped in Latin literary verses. The young messenger presents the weapons with the following explanation:

> May it please you,
> My grandsire, well advis'd, hath sent by me
> The goodliest weapons of his armory
> To gratify your honourable youth,
> The hope of Rome; for so he bid me say.
> And so I do, and with his gifts present
> Your lordships, that, whenever you have need,
> You may be armed and appointed well.
>
> (4.1. 9–16)

Chiron and Demetrius appear puzzled by Titus's actions, although they recognize the verse on the wrapping: "*Integer vitae, scelerisque purus, / Non eget Mauri iaculis, nec arcu.*" Translated, the passage reads "He who is spotless in life and free of crime needs not the Moorish bow and arrow." Maurice Hunt argues that Titus's message constitutes an attempt to avoid performing revenge:

> Reading the verses, whose message argues for a breaking of relationship between the man and the Moor, Chiron and Demetrius might, flattered by the hope of a pure life ensuing, turn upon Aaron and kill him. Conversely, Aaron, aware of Titus's knowledge and the poetry's relevance, might decide to kill the boys before they slay him. (1988, 203)

Intriguing possibility though this might be, it is, I think, hardly likely. Already aware of the callous brutality of these men, Titus would surely not trust to a possible change of heart on their part to accomplish revenge. Besides, even if they did turn against Aaron, Titus would surely have accomplished little, for it is Demetrius and Chiron who have violated his daughter and it is on them that Titus intends to wreak vengeance. To rely on Aaron's recognition of the relevance of the verses would also be taking a chance. In fact, Aaron does realize that Titus has discovered their villainy, but if Titus expected him to murder the brothers as a result, we must regard Titus's action in this scene as a complete failure. Most importantly, Titus has gone to considerable lengths to circulate the notion that he is mad; to openly vaunt his knowledge of their villainy before his enemies would undo this masquerade and jeopardize his own safety. The relevance of Titus's gifts and the poetry that accompanies them, therefore, lies elsewhere.

In light of the above reasons, we must presume that Titus intends Demetrius and Chiron to miss the point of his message; indeed, that is precisely what happens. Aaron alone recognizes Titus's intent and applauds his skill:

> Here's no sound jest! The old man hath found their guilt,
> And sends them weapons wrapp'd about with lines
> That wound, beyond their feeling, to the quick.
> But were our witty empress well afoot,
> She would applaud Andronicus' conceit.
>
> (4.2. 26–30)

Remarkably, even Marcus Andronicus earlier had presumed that Titus, refusing to indulge in bloody vengeance, intended his gifts as a gesture of conciliation:

> Marcus, attend him in his ecstasy,
> That hath more scars of sorrow in his heart
> Than foeman's marks upon his batt'red shield,
> But yet so just that he will not revenge.
>
> (4.1. 127–30)

Thus, despite the earlier ritual avowal of familial conspiracy, Titus intends to act alone; indeed, the tongueless Lavinia is the only individual privy to his plans.

Thus, the Horatian verse, which Hunt suggests refers to the brothers, must, on the contrary, refer to Titus himself, the great general and warrior, "spotless in life and free of crime," who single-handedly will bring about divine justice. Unlike the villainous brothers, he will not need "the Moorish weapons" or aid from others. Ironically, Titus also suggests through his gift (and the message conveyed by the young Lucius) that Demetrius and Chiron, although they might be well armed, have no defense against him. Titus's gift of the weapons and the verses present a Machiavellian show of superiority, intended to beat the sons at their own game, namely, the reenactment of original tales of violence and evil. His actions constitute a veiled warning of his own power and the impending disaster. By couching his warning as a well-known Horatian verse, Titus both reveals and conceals his hand; he reveals his method of vengeance without revealing his knowledge, although neither Chiron nor Demetrius perceive the threat. Aaron guesses rightly that Tamora might have applauded such a design, for she had shown similar Machiavellian industry and creativity earlier when she provoked her sons to murder Bassanius.

Shortly after this, in a similar scene, Titus sends the Clown to the Emperor with two pigeons and a knife wrapped in a written supplication. Presumably, Titus does not sign this supplication, although Saturnius immediately recognizes his hand in it: "I know from whence this same device proceeds" (4.4. 52). Already vexed by the arrows carrying supplications to the gods, which Titus and his friends have been shooting at the Emperor's palace, Saturnius shows his impatience with this new interference by callously having the Clown beheaded. The scene has puzzled most critics who dismiss it as a filler primarily intended to convey Titus's melancholy distraction and frustration at being unable to accomplish revenge. But perhaps the scene parallels his earlier action of sending gifts to Chiron and Demetrius; it at once reenacts and extends the earlier action.

Earlier, as Titus solicits the gods to help him in his vengeance, he had insisted that the arrows being shot at the palace were not directed at Saturnius:

> *Ad Jovem*, that's for you: here, *Ad Apollinem*
> *Ad Martem*, that's for myself:
> Here, boy, to Pallas: here, to Mercury:
> To Saturn, Caius, not to Saturnine;
> You were as good to shoot against the wind.
>
> (4.3. 53–57)

Although it would appear at first to the reader or viewer that these pleas remain unanswered, the Clown's arrival immediately after is hailed by the shooters as a divine response. Indeed, they question the Clown about Jupiter's answer to their requests: "News, news from Heaven! Marcus, the post is come. / Sirrah, what tidings? Have you any letters? / Shall I have justice? What says Jupiter?" (4.3. 76–78). When asked by Titus if he is not Jupiter's carrier, the Clown replies, "Ay, of my pigeons, sir; nothing else" (l.86). The two pigeons, therefore, become to Titus symbols of divine sanction for the vengeance soon to be enacted on the Emperor's family. Having received such sanction, Titus takes an even bolder step than he had earlier with Chiron and Demetrius; he sends a more overtly contentious letter and a dagger whose message is unmistakeable, this time to the Emperor himself. The scene presents his moment of resolution, but also reveals his pleasure at taunting his enemies; these overt warnings can only increase our (and his family's) perception of the horrible ingenuity of his final plans.

The Clown with his message from Jupiter also functions as an exact contrast to the later messenger, Tamora, sent by Saturnius to bargain with Titus. The correspondence between the scenes is striking. Even as the clown had descended from above, Tamora, pretending to be Revenge, claims to have arisen from the Underworld. And like the Clown, she brings twin gifts, Chiron and Demetrius, whom Titus characterizes as Rape and Murder, respectively. Tamora believes that her melodramatic performance has deceived the lunatic Titus and actually suggests an outline for the forthcoming events:

> But would it please thee, good Andronicus,
> To send for Lucius, thy thrice-valiant son,
> Who leads towards Rome a band of warlike Goths,
> And bid him come and banquet at thy house,
> When he is here, even at thy solemn feast,
> I will bring in the Empress and her sons,
> The Emperor himself, and all thy foes,
> And at thy mercy shall they stoop and kneel,
> And on them shalt thou ease thy angry heart.
>
> (5.2. 111–19)

Confident of her dramatic success, Tamora leaves Chiron and Demetrius at Titus's house to continue the "determin'd jest" that they had concocted. But again, Titus seizes on the initial plot outline suggested by his enemy and converts it into a more dramatic and horrifying drama of successful vengeance. With Lavinia's help, he murders Chiron and Demetrius and serves them in a pie to his royal guests. Before he kills Tamora's sons, he insists on his actions as an extended reenactment of the Philomel story on which Chiron and Demetrius had originally patterned their behavior: "For worse than Philomel you us'd my daughter, / And worse than Progne I will be reveng'd" (5.2. 194–95). Titus's dramatic concoction, like Hieronimo's at the end of Kyd's play, reveals highly imaginative and creative talents used for wholly destructive purposes.

At the close of the tragedy, Marcus tries to understand the preceding events by evoking another literary parallel:

> Speak, Rome's dear friend, as erst our ancestor,
> When with his solemn tongue he did discourse
> To lov-sick Dido's sad attending ear
> The story of that baleful burning night
> When subtle Greeks surpris'd King Priam's Troy.
> Tell us what Sinon hath bewitch'd our ears,
> Or who hath brought the fatal engine in
> That gives our Troy, our Rome, the civil wound.
>
> (5.3. 80–87)

Shakespeare's tragedy of evil presents itself as a reenactment and variation on earlier tales of woe. Thus, while an exact dramatic reenactment accomplished revenge in *The Spanish Tragedy*, modified and expanded reenactments succeed in Shakespeare's early revenge play. The later play, *Hamlet* continues the discourse by suggesting that even such reenactment might be inadequate.

While in *The Spanish Tragedy* and *Titus Andronicus*, we actually witness the protagonists' transition from rationality to obsessive melancholy, *Hamlet* opens after the death of Hamlet's father, with the hero already on the precipice of melancholia. By his training as a scholar, Hamlet would have seemed to the Renaissance mind particularly prone to melancholy. Indeed, his initial complaints about human nature and the conditions in Denmark establish his melancholy inclinations, as do his habit and demeanor. We learn, though, that these remarks have valid causes. When the play opens, therefore, he presents himself as not yet a fully melancholy figure, although certainly on the verge of becoming so. As it progresses, the play, like Kyd's *The Spanish Tragedy*, shows an increasing dramatic concern with liminality, with depicting the protagonist's precarious psychological position between sanity and excessive melancholia. Like Hieronimo Hamlet is essentially a passive figure called upon to take an active role in the accomplishment of revenge. Because the motive of revenge is established early in the play, we are catapulted immediately into the central psychological conflict between reason and passion.

Hamlet's initial reaction to the ghost's revelation of murder is passionate—"Haste me to know't, that I, with wings as swift / As meditation or the thoughts of love, / May sweep to my revenge" (1.5 30–32). But as the play progresses, he shows, like Hieronimo, an awareness of the tension within him between emotion that wishes to efface memory and reason that wishes to dwell on it:

> Now whether it be
> Bestial oblivion, or some craven scruple
> Of thinking too precisely on the event—
> A thought which, quartered, hath but one part wisdom
> And ever three parts coward—I do not know
> Why yet I live to say, 'This thing's to do.'
>
> (4.4. 39–44)

Three times Hamlet tries to resolve this conflict by means of creativity. His early attempts look back, as Titus had done repeatedly, to similar tales of revenge from the past. The earliest instance occurs in the scene with the players where he calls on them to recite the lines about Pyrrhus's slaughter of Priam, an act of revenge for his father's murder. Like Hieronimo's similar attempt to achieve satisfaction in art by evoking a parallel situation, the reenactment proves unsatisfactory, because it also emphasizes the serious repercussions of revenge. All of Illium suffers from Pyrrhus's slaughter, and Hamlet's revenge will similarly affect Denmark. Dissatisfied with the implications of the reenactment, Hamlet has himself to create the speech "of some dozen or sixteen lines" to find an adequate dramatic equivalent for his emotional state. True, the play within the play provides a partly successful attempt at creativity, for it has its desired effect of catching the conscience of the King, but, like Hieronimo, Hamlet is caught in the web of his own creation, and by arousing the suspicion of the King, he prompts Claudius to have him banished and killed. In both these intances of creativity, Hamlet gets similarly interrupted—in the scene with the players, by Polonius who considers the speech too long and boring, in the scene of the play within the play by Claudius's passionate exit. Hamlet's most successful act of creativity is probably the letter he composes to lead Rosencrantz and Guildenstern to the fate that had been intended for him. Hamlet's bragging narration of the event to Horatio recalls Hieronimo's attitude immediately after the success of his intrigues, and significantly, Hamlet claims to have thwarted Claudius's creativity by rewriting events:

> Being thus benetted round with villainies,
> Or I could make a prologue to my brains,
> They had begun the play. I sat me down,
> Devis'd a new commission, wrote it fair.

> (5.2. 29–32)

In *Hamlet*, Shakespeare explores more fully than Kyd the creative power of the melancholy mind by providing three important melancholy figures: Hamlet, Claudius, and Laertes. All are constantly creative, although each is only partially successful in his attempts in every instance. In fact, the latter half of the play is as much a play about Laertes's and Claudius's revenge as about Hamlet's. Moved to melancholy passion by grief like Hamlet, Laertes conspires creatively with the King to fix the duel. But he has a weak mind easily manipulated by Claudius's clever machinations. Both Claudius and Laertes reveal a melancholy disposition, but their melancholy differs significantly from Hamlet's. Laertes's initial desire for revenge springs, like Hamlet's, from grief. Claudius, like Hamlet and Hieronimo, emerges indefatigable in the exercise of his wits, as his repeated plans to be rid of Hamlet reveal, but he functions as a purely Machiavellian melancholic, seeking not to avenge a wrong done against him but to preserve his state and reputation. Both Laertes and Claudius, in accordance with the formulaic revenge pattern, become entangled in their own plot of treachery and are destroyed.

But Shakespeare makes a significant alteration to the revenge pattern in this later play. *Hamlet* questions the very notion of revenge itself. Neither Hieronimo nor Titus seriously questioned what had to be done; they both delayed only because they could not find the appropriate moment at which to work their revenge. Hamlet, on the other hand, raises the question of the endless circularity of the act of revenge; as Rene Girard argues,

> The trouble with the hero is that he does not believe in his play half as much as the critics do. He understands revenge and the theater too well to assume willingly a role chosen for him by others. His sentiments are those, in other words, which we have surmised in Shakespeare himself. What the hero feels in regard to the act of revenge, the creator feels in regard to revenge as theater. (1986a, 284)

This is nowhere more apparent than in Shakespeare's modification of the dramatic metaphor first used by Kyd to declare its effectiveness. In Kyd's tragedy, reenactment of events in dramatic form provided the most appropriate means of revenge. *Titus Andronicus* also sanctioned modified reenactment. Shakespeare's later play suggests that even reenactment may prove only partially successful: the player's rendering of Aeneas's tale duplicates emotion, but cannot hold the attention of its audience; the play within the play duplicates action and thus arouses the King's conscience, but postpones revenge; but Hamlet's rewriting of Claudius's play, however, at least produces his first successful attempt at remedying matters by permitting his return to England. Shakespeare's revenge tragedy, itself a rewriting of Kyd's earlier version, thus extends the discourse about revenge and creativity begun in the earlier play by raising questions even about theatricality itself.

Indeed, even as *Titus Andronicus* had repeatedly evoked earlier literary parallels, *Hamlet* reminds us throughout of its theatricality; "the actor who plays Hamlet, plays one who is an actor" (Wilshire 1982, 64). *Hamlet* is a play written by a playwright and actor; it is a play written by an actor for an actor who plays an actor and who also in the course of the play creates a play for actors who also play actors. In short, "Shakespeare turns a typical revenge topic, *Hamlet*, into a meditation'' not only ''on his predicament as a playwright'' (Girard 1986a, 284) but also on his predicament as an actor. We might keep in mind that Kyd's similar meditation had concluded with an emphatic assertion rather than questioning of the dramatic medium. Shakespeare's tragedy provides a calculated response to that emphatic assertion of theater.

The Spanish Tragedy, Titus Andronicus, and Hamlet focus on the protagonists's dilemma in accomplishing revenge and on the actual act of revenge itself. The hero's ambiguous madness in these plays, his destructive melancholia, becomes the central focus in Tourneur's The Revenger's Tragedy and Ford's 'Tis Pity She's a Whore, anatomies of revenge and melancholia. The later plays deconstruct all morality as they raise rather than answer questions. Tourneur's tragedy provides an intense study of melancholia and depicts fragmentation both by division and by multiplications. While Shakespeare had extended the theme of melancholia by presenting three melancholy although somewhat different figures, in Tourneur's tragedy, we encounter characters again and again who prove to be mere duplications of ones we had met earlier. The multiplication of bodies through disguise and duplication is extensive.

Renaissance and Jacobean theorists believed that man's central psychological dilemma arose from the moral necessity to control his passions, which could, if left to go berserk, lead him to destruction. The passions most to be feared were anger and lust (Burton 1927, 233). Because man's greatest enemies lay within himself, his greatest moral problem involved self-mastery, which had to be preceded by self-knowledge or ''understanding,'' what Hooker called the ''director of man's will by discovering in action what was good'' (1954, 187). Vindice's primary psychological problem may be described as lack of self-understanding. Hamlet shows an awareness of his lack of self-mastery in the speech before his confrontation with Laertes:

> Was't Hamlet wronged Laertes? Never Hamlet.
> If Hamlet from himself be taken away,
> And when not himself does wrong Laertes,
> Who does it then? His madness. If't be so,
> Hamlet is of the faction that is wronged;
> His madness is poor Hamlet's enemy.
>
> (5.2. 222–28)

But Vindice's problem figures early in Tourneur's play and therefore appears to be more accute.

Both Bacon and Elyot saw the passion for vengeance as self-destructive, an extension of the Senecan axiom that "anger, like ruin, breaks itself on that it falls" (Bacon 1876, 142). This suicidal inclination in those consumed by the passion for vengeance dramatically resolves in the revenge plays through the inevitable death of the protagonist at the close of the play. In *The Spanish Tragedy*, Hieronimo, caught in the web of his own creation, is forced to kill himself; Titus is stabbed by Saturnius as he avenges Tamora's death; Hamlet, though sole heir to the throne of Denmark, must necessarily die for his justifiable although nevertheless criminal regicide. In *The Revenger's Tragedy*, we may see the extension of this idea to include not only Vindice's death, but the earlier deterioration of his mind through an increasing loss of identity in the course of the play. The destruction and fragmentation here is both physical and mental, dramatic and psychological. *The Spanish Tragedy*, *Titus Andronicus*, and *Hamlet* had both hinted at such a motif, but in none of these plays is madness an established characteristic of the protagonist. In *Hamlet*, at least part of the audience's interest springs from the dramatic tension created by the protagonist's precarious position between madness and sanity. Although particularly prone to melancholy because of his position as a scholar, Hamlet consciously cultivates his melancholy desposition through the course of the play; his melancholia, especially at first, is a matter of cultivated and dramatized show.

Tourneur's play, however, concerns itself less with exploring the dramatic possibilities of liminality. Vindice's melancholy carries no traces of show, and he is immediately recognizable as an emblematic representation of melancholia when he first appears on the stage. As Bridget Lyons points out, the representation of melancholy traditionally took the pattern of a man or woman brooding over a skull (1971, 121). The opening image of Vindice with the skull of his beloved in his hand recalls the image of Hamlet in the graveyard scene holding the skull of Yorick, even as it evokes the general Renaissance iconographic tradition in depictions of the melancholy man. But the scene in *Hamlet occurs late in the play*. The opening scene in *The Revenger's Tragedy* indicates early that Vindice personifies more than revenge, which his name implies; he also represents the mental condition of melancholia. In fact, the play takes off quite deliberately from the point at which *Hamlet* had ended; Tourneur's tragedy thus adds to the discourse on revenge and melancholia initiated by *The Spanish Tragedy* and furthered by *Hamlet*.

The melancholic's characteristic state of mind was "discontent," a term used repeatedly by Burton, and used in the play surprisingly of both Vindice and Antonio, an indication that the latter is potentially as prone to melancholy as the former. However, Antonio is not, as Murray suggests, a negative figure (1964, 225–27). His role resembles that of Horatio, who, like Hamlet, is a scholar, but unlike him, not prone to melancholy. Antonio's role in *The Revenger's Tragedy* is a little more complex: he has reason for revenge, like Vindice—his wife, after being raped by the Duke, commits suicide. Antonio also wishes, like Vindice, to achieve revenge, as the concluding scene in act 1 shows. Psychologically, however, he exists in the liminal stage between rationality and excessive melancholy, like Hamlet and Hieronimo, but unlike Vindice, who has made the transition into melancholy before the play opens.

Tourneur's play also includes every possible aspect of melancholy as discussed by Renaissance theorists. For example, both excessive and inadequate sexual activity are described by Burton as leading to melancholy (1927, 204–5). Tourneur at least suggests that Vindice's melancholy, although produced by grief and a desire for vengeance, springs from his total sexual abstinence for nine years since the death of his beloved over whose skull he's brooded; he seems to illustrate Burton's description of the man "that from his wife's death, abstaining, after marriage, became exceedingly melancholy" (1927, 204). Burton also talks of old age as a disease in itself, particularly to be condemned when accompanied by unbecoming sexual activity (183–184). The old Duke, therefore, presiding over the villainy of his court, provides a satiric portrait of melancholia, and the play features an ironic commentary on the conventional Elizabethan faith in the aristocracy as moral examples to be emulated. The Duke also illustrates Burton's claim that melancholy is a "hereditary disease" (184), for he at least partly takes responsibility for the villainy of his sons.

Burton voices the general belief of the time that malignancy and melancholy of the mind were discernible in countenance and exterior, and Vindice, when he disguises himself, immediately meets the approval of the conniving Lussurioso: "He's e'en shaped for my purpose." In fact, the whole play provides an exaggerated satiric analysis of the revenge tradition and the emotional condition of melancholia. Appropriately, therefore, its action takes place in Italy, the generally acknowledged seat of malancholy and vices, and all the characters exhibit the same psychological state; they are all motivated by the passions of revenge and lust. In other words, the triple pattern of revenge that we encountered in *Hamlet* has been multiplied in Tourneur's play to include almost every character.

Having established the insanity motif in the very first scene, Tourneur concentrates on Vindice's degenerative journey into greater mental and spiritual disorder, a parody of the medieval dramatic tradition in which figures take spiritual journeys through life toward spiritual growth, as in *Everyman*. Like *Everyman* or *The Castle of Perseverance* the play dramatizes psychological inclinations, but takes little interest in emphasizing Christian morality. This absence is even more conspicuous in Ford's tragedy, a factor that has led frequently to the charge of decadence made about his plays.

Tourneur's indebtedness to the medieval morality tradition has been pointed out by many critics since Leo Salingar first gave the idea elaborate treatment in his analysis of the play (208–24). The play is a medieval parading of Vices—the Ducal family interestingly has seven members, and the play opens with a procession, which becomes, like the masque of the concluding scene, a metaphoric equivalent for the dramatic action. All seven deadly sins are represented in the play—Ambitioso and Supervacuo embody both envy in their attempts to get rid of their brother and pride in what they assume is a successful manipulation of circumstances; the Duke, the junior Brother, and Lussurioso embody lust and covetousness, although Lussurioso is also prone to anger, which results both in his imprisonment and the enmity of Vindice whom he wishes killed; the Duchess embodies lechery; and all the characters by their inordinate indulgence in wine and feasting embody gluttony. None of the Vices are as neatly categorized as this description makes them out to be, for all the characters have more than one villainous aspect, but each has one or two predominant traits. Together they constitute a whole family of Vices. Ruled by their passions, primarily anger and lust, almost every character is finally an exaggerated study in melancholia. Almost every character is also motivated by the passion of revenge, and the play illustrates the contemporary belief that revenge destroys the mind. The characters move progressively toward greater villainies, which, in keeping with the revenge formula, ultimately rebound on themselves.

The familiar medieval theme of human life as a pilgrimage to the Holy City during which one is waylaid by the seven deadly sins provides the structural framework for *The Revenger's Tragedy*, although Tourneur converts it into a journey toward damnation in which the protagonist voluntarily courts the company of evils, represented by the symbolically named members of the court. The conventional pattern of Vice disguising itself as Virtue also is reversed, as the initially guiltless Vindice, by disguising himself as the evil Piato, gets morally converted to evil. The scene of Gratiana's fall thus modifies a familiar scene in the morality plays in which man succumbs to temptations offered by disguised tempters posing as virtues. In this scene, however, the once virtuous Vindice disguised as Piato convinces his mother to offer her daughter (and his sister), Castiza, to the lustful desires of Lussurioso. The skill with which he manipulates Gratiana's emotions in this scene is itself an indication of his propensity toward villainy.

The journey motif also coalesces with the metaphor of "entrance" used repeatedly in the play (Murray 1964, 242). Vindice's entrance into the court begins his transformation, and he tempts Castiza by promising her the same opportunity. The motif merges with the Renaissance belief that an initial succumbing to the lure of passion could lead to melancholy and progressive involvement in vice. The metaphor of entrance has both biblical and sexual connotations, and it thus concentrates the two major themes of lust and the consequent spiritual fall central to the dramatic action of the play.

That Vindice is a variation on the medieval Vice figure is clear in the role he plays as the satanic tempter who manages to convert his own mother to evil. It is worth noting that both Vindice and Castiza refer to their mother's conversion as an entrance or possession by the devil, thus making explicit the connection between Vindice and the medieval Vice figure or the archetypal tempter, Satan. Vindice also tempts his brother, drawing his pupil deeper and deeper into villainy. In this familiar role as corrupter of virtue, he reflects both the Duke, who poisons women who refuse to gratify his lust, and Lussurioso, who wishes to corrupt the chaste Castiza. That the Duke and Vindice are ultimately variations of a single vice is dramatically and symbolically expressed in the scene after the Duke's death, in which the disguised Duke is mistaken for Piato by Lussurioso.

Vindice's psychological disintegration, his passage from himself, is far more complex than Hamlet's, and forms the central focus of Tourneur's play. Contrary to Fredson Bower's claim that insanity in the later revenge plays is a minor theme usually confined to a minor character (1940, 157), *The Revenger's Tragedy* seems to be a concentrated study in insanity and the power of melancholy passion to corrupt the mind. The same might be said about Ford's tragedy. The very fact that Tourneur (and Ford later) has dispensed with the ghost is an indication, as Charles and Elaine Hallett point out, that the later plays, unlike the earlier ones, are concerned with exploring

origins of revenge in the human psyche (1980, 6). Vindice is not, as
Robert Reed suggests, a mere "pretender to madness" (1952, 109).
The motive of revenge is overshadowed, not merely by the play's
emphasis on situation and intrigue, as Bowers suggests (1940, 158),
but also by its essentially medieval theme of moral and psychological
disintegration represented by Vindice's succumbing to the worldly
lure of inordinate passion.

Vindice's first step in the journey from himself and toward
increased melancholy is the creation of Piato, the duplication of his
body. "What brother? am I far enough from myself?" he asks his
brother, whose response, "As if another man had been sent whole
/ Into the world, and none wist how he came" (1.3. 1–3),
metaphorically foreshadows the transformation that Vindice
undergoes in the course of the play. The duplication is so effective
that even his mother does not recognize him. The metaphor of the
journey is also used early in the play when Vindice uses the excuse
of having to undertake a "speedy travel" to explain his absence
to Gratiana. His loss of identity and the consequent search for self
are dramatically represented when Lussurioso hires Vindice to find
and kill Piato; Piato is not, however, to be found, a symbolic
dramatization of the fact that Vindice is now completely lost to
himself and to the world. The event is ironically paralleled in act 4,
scene 1, in Gratiana's house. Gratiana, newly converted to sin, tries
to force her daughter to give herself to Lussurioso, but the chaste
Castiza, appalled by the request, pretends not to see her mother as
she queries:

> I cry you mercy, lady, I mistook you;
> Pray, did you see my mother? Which way went she?
> Pray God I have not lost her.
>
> (2.1. 161–63)

The journey motif is superimposed on the typically Jacobean
contrast between the court and the country. Vindice's entry into the
world of the court is the beginning of his corruption. Once
corrupted, he takes his evil to the country, to the home of Gratiana
and Castiza. The mythic pattern of primordial corruption by Satan,
the fall, and the final redemption through grace is certainly present
in the play in the story of Gratiana's conversions, first by Piato to
sin and then by Vindice to virtue, and Tourneur uses this theme to
create what must have been a traditional doctrinal contrast between
the stories of man's and Satan's falls. Gratiana, like Adam and Eve,
is capable of remorse, but neither Vindice nor the satanic court is

capable of it, and, therefore, they forego redemption. Castiza's refusal to leave the country for the court is itself, therefore, a symbolic affirmation of virtue. The equation of tyranny with rape is made often in the drama of this period, as Ronald Wymer argues (1986, 104), and the attempt to lure Gastiza into sin by Lussurioso is a powerful depiction of the rape of the country by the city. The action is repeated later in the play by the old Duke who tries to rape what he thinks is a country lass, to find out only too late that it is the poisoned skeleton of one of his earlier victims. The glee with which Vindice plots this event indicates the now almost complete "rape" of his own mind by melancholia.

Fredson Bowers argues that "Tourneur created so many villains, each struggling against the others but none against Vindice, that Vindice is too often submerged, and the play lacks on occasion a controlling protagonist" (1940, 136). This may be true to a degree, but it is clear that there is, contrary to Bowers's claim, action taken against Vindice—Lussurioso wishes Piato killed, and thus provokes Vindice's vengeance against himself. Besides, as a tableau of vices and melancholia, the play focusses on Vindice as representing the ducal family whose members are all ultimately variations on him. Vindice is the central Vice figure, and although in action he does not indulge in the lustful behavior that characterizes the rest of the figures, he embodies their corruption in his language and in his desbelief in virtue. All the members of the ducal family show the same progressive deterioration that he shows in the course of the play and mirror through their fates the fate that awaits him in the final scene.

This complete merging of personalities, where one character becomes indistinguishable from the other, is metaphorically and powerfully represented in the double masque of the final act in which "the differences between one man and another dissolve into the similarities of choreographed movement" (McMillan 1984, 288). The disguising of the human body beyond all recognition is now complete, and all action is reduced in this scene to mere repetition, while everybody's appearance seems simply to mirror those around him. The scene concludes the series of earlier disguises: Vindice had disguised himself as Piato, his beloved's skeleton had been painted and disguised to convey the posture of a country lass, the Duke's youngest son had undergone a substitute execution, the bastard son had usurped the body of the father by sleeping with his mother, and all characters had merged finally into mere variations of each other.

In this sense, as beings in continuous transformation, the characters in the play become "grotesque" representations of the body, instances of deliberate demystification. Mikhail Bakhtin defines the grotesque body as more than simply ugly or repulsive; the grotesque body presents a state of constant change:

> The grotesque image reflects a phenomenon in transformation, an as yet unfinished metamorphosis, ... the grotesque images preserve their peculiar nature, entirely different from ready-made completed being. They remain ambivalent and contradictory; they are ugly, monstrous, hideous from the point of view of "classic" aesthetics, that is, the aesthetics of the ready-made and the completed. ... Life is shown in its twofold contradictory processes; it is the epitome of incompleteness. And such is precisely the grotesque concept of the body. (1968, 24–26)

This sense of the fluid self is dramatically represented in *The Revenger's Tragedy* though the multiplication of the human body, a multiplication that desanctifies and reduces the body to the level of the grotesque and the unrecognizable. Characters such as Vindice acknowledge their lack of self and attribute this loss directly to their fluidity of being, to their frequent disguises. The play thus dramatizes the Augustinian notion of evil as incompleteness or lack of essence.[7]

In its anatomy of revenge, melancholy, and ultimately, human nature itself, Tourneur's play also evokes a sense of the many popular medical anatomies of the sixteenth and seventeenth centuries. As Devon Hodges points out, anatomies were a fad in sixteenth-century England, and the last of the great anatomies is Burton's *Anatomy of Melancholy* published in 1621. (1985, 1). Tourneur's play may be viewed in conjunction with the best known medical anatomies of the Renaissance such as Andreas Vesalius's *De Corporis Fabrica* (1543). Tourneur illustrates on the stage what Vesalius's drawings of the human anatomy do through pictorial representation. In the eight plates by Vesalius, a "muscle man" is presented in a variety of dancelike poses suggesting extreme agony. A paring down takes place thereafter in each plate until we are left in the last plate with only the man's skeleton with the bones still "poised to retain signs of human suffering" (Hodges 1985, 5). A similar movement takes places in Tourneur's play, and Vindice (like several of the other characters) transforms gradually from the human sufferer mourning the death of his beloved to an unrecognizable and grotesque abstraction, a representation of revenging death. Our reaction to the transformation resembles our reaction to Vesalius's drawings of the body; we move from involvement in the suffering to a distanced horror, for while we recognize the truth of the final picture which had after all been implicit even in the first, we do "find it hard to privilege this collection of bones" (Hodges 5).

In its grotesque reenactment of the conventions of the revenge plays, and through its exclusive concentration on the degeneration of the melancholy mind, Tourneur's tragedy presents a concentrated moral satire. In conception, it provides an exaggerated representation of the outcome of succumbing to the passions of lust, anger, or vengeance, and, as such, the play looks back both in form and in implication to the morality tradition. As Somerset argues, the morality plays are often "vividly grotesque portrayals of deformity and torment which horrify the viewer by showing him the results of sin" (1975, 57), a statement equally applicable to Tourneur's play. Even the idea of degressive degeneration into vice through an initial indulgence owes its origin to the morality tradition where one sin leading to another was frequently represented and often took the conventional symbol of the tree with branches (Somerset 57). William Archer's perception of the farcical elements in the play is not, therefore, as far-fetched as it would seem at first (Murray 1964, 256). Incidents containing elements of grim humor can be found throughout: Lussurioso's unsuspecting confidence in hiring Vindice to taint Hippolito's sister, Vindice's given task to find and kill himself, the Duke's interpretation of the silence of the disguised skull as the shyness of a country lass, the ironic thwarting of Ambitioso's and Supervacuo's plans by the Duke, the death of the younger brother, and the consternation of the real masquers when confronted with the task of murder already accomplished. Incidents such as these contribute to "the tone of comedy that runs throughout this tragedy" (McMillan 1984, 285). The ingredients for such grotesque humor exist in earlier revenge plays in such incidents as Pedringano's death in *The Spanish Tragedy* and Hamlet's manipulation of circumstances to lead Rosencrantz and Guildenstern to their deaths, but Tourneur's more intensified use of the element points to the satiric nature of the play, its most significant departure from other plays in the tradition.

In fact, "grotesque" might even be an appropriate generic description for the play. Describing the fluid nature of Renaissance tragedy, Jeffrey Rayner Myers argues that the "dynamics of canon" in the period might best be understood within the context of Renaissance iconographic traditions. He cites Michaelangelo's *Pieta* as an example of such a mercurial genre that often evoked images of the *Madonna* and vice versa. Tourneur's intensified mingling of tragedy and humor, his depiction of Vindice as both villain and moral scourge, and his multiplication of bodies beyond recognition so that his characters become indistinguishable from each other, makes *The Revenger's Tragedy* a unique extension of the revenge genre, and "antic" in the original sense of that expression. The play seems ultimately to insist that evil behavior springs from fragmented psyches, from the absence of a stable core of being.

Like *The Revenger's Tragedy*, Ford's *'Tis Pity She's a Whore* analyzes the state of melancholia, and may be regarded as a grotesque extension of the revenge genre. The influence of Burton on Ford has been discussed often and his most original creation, Giovanni, in *'Tis Pity* is immediately recognizable as a melancholy figure. One is not prepared, however, for the play's simultaneous elevation of the melancholy man into a hero by his language and stance and his denigration into a morally diseased and obsessed maniac by his actions. Because Ford provides the boldest and richest culmination of the tendencies I have been describing, however, I reserve discussion of his carnivalesque and subversive play, which provokes conflicting and contradictory responses from the reader, to a later chapter.

The Fragmented Self: Essence and Non-Being

The multifaceted and fragmented protagonists in the later plays ultimately raise questions about the self as a recognizable and definable entity even more fervently than their melancholy counterparts in the earlier tragedies. Hamlet posits the theory that the self is impenetrable in his notorious baiting of Guildenstern:

> *Hamlet.* Will you play upon this pipe?
> *Guildenstern.* My lord, I cannot.
> *Hamlet.* I pray you.
> *Guildenstern.* Believe me, I cannot.
> *Hamlet.* I do beseach you.
> *Guildenstern.* I know no touch of it, my lord.
> *Hamlet.* 'Tis as easy as lying: govern these ventages with your finger and thumb, give it breath with your mouth, and it will discourse most eloquent music. Look you, these are the stops.
> *Guildenstern.* But these cannot I command to any utterance of harmony; I have not the skill.
> *Hamlet.* Why, look you now, how unworthy a thing you make of me. You would play upon me; you would seem to know my stops; you would pluck out the heart of my mystery; you would sound me from my lowest note to the top of my compass; and there is much music, excellent voice, in this little organ, yet cannot you make it speak.

'Sblood. do you think I am easier to be played on than a pipe? Call
me what instrument you will, though you can fret me, you cannot
play upon me.

(3.2. 350–72)

Several points in Hamlet's analogy are worth noting. Hamlet
ironically implies that playing on the instrument is as easy as lying;
the play repeatedly insists, however, that lying and deceit ultimately
expose themselves. Second, Guildenstern's simplistic view of
Hamlet's character produces Hamlet's piqued tone and indignation
as he insists first that he be regarded as a more complex being, and
that, unlike a musical instrument, he is impenetrable. It is precisely
this impenetrability of character that the play emphasizes throughout. Hamlet himself remains ambiguous and beyond grasp to the
end. The same, however, might be said about Claudius, or Gertrude,
or Ophelia. The play, in other words, presents character as unstable
and impenetrable (although fascinating), and like all the characters
in the play, the audience repeatedly tries throughout to penetrate this
mystery of the self. But the play goes so far as to suggest that "at
the center of Hamlet, in the heart of his mystery, there is, in short,
nothing" (Barker 1984, 37). Hamlet's (and other Shakespearean
protagonists') insistence on the analogy between the world and
theater might be seen as yet another exposition of this idea, for if all
the world is a stage and all its men and women merely actors, then
they lack an essential core of being. Human life itself, as Hunt
argues, becomes a " 'thing . . . of nothing,' an existence constructed
around a void" (1988, 34). The same nothingness seems to be at the
center of being for many figures on the early Stuart stage; Iago, De
Flores, Bosola, Vindice, Malevole, and Giovanni are only a few
among many characters who defy conclusive analysis even while they
remain continually fascinating. Dollimore argues that these figures,
"made up of inconsistencies and contradictions," are prototypes of
"the modern decentered self" (1984, 50).

In these ambivalent figures of the Stuart theater, in the fascination
of the age with disguise and dissembling, in repeated depictions of
the fragmented body and the psyche, we have dramatic prototypes
for theories about the self articulated as coherent philosophies in the
writings of Thomas Hobbes and John Locke several years later. In
fact, Hobbes's and Locke's sociopolitical ideologies may have
originated in Stuart dramatizations of the fragmented body and
psyche.

In his political theories, Hobbes depicts both the physical and the
social body in "shockingly physical terms of anatomy and disease";

his vision resembles depictions of fragmentation in many Jacobean and Caroline plays (Barkan 1975, 115). On its title page, Hobbes's *Leviathan* pictures a huge king whose body consists of many individuals, thus evoking the theory about the kingdom as the extended body of the monarch used so frequently by James, but Hobbes goes on to describe the social body as an artificial mechanism. This reduces the whole notion of the dual bodies to a convenient political construct. Hobbes's depiction and analogies, contrary to being unthinkable before his time, as Barkan suggests (115), are the natural culmination of an evolution toward demystification that had begun several years earlier. This demystification of the social and political bodies leads naturally, as it had in Stuart drama, to a demystification also of the self. Hobbesian theory makes no provision for the self as a recognizable entity:

> But what then would become of these Terms, of *Entity, Essence, Essentiall, Essentiality,* ... and of many more that depend on these, applyed as most commonly they are? They are therefore no Names of Things; but Signes, by which wee make known, that wee conceive the Consequence of one name or Attribute to another: ... Therefore, *to bee a Body*, to *Walke*, ... and the like, that signifie just the same, are the names of *Nothing*. (Hobbes 1986, 691)

Hobbes goes on to characterize notions of "essences" and "entities" as a "false Philosophy"; in his writings, the self becomes an artificial although necessary philosophical construct. Interestingly, in the Restoration version of *Dr. Faustus*, we witness an artificial and conscious reconstruction of being; the play ends with a celebration in hell, where in the midst of song and dance the dismembered Faustus is reassembled as a unified subject.

Like Hobbes, Locke sees no essential core of being in man: "Let us then suppose the Mind to be, as we say, white Paper, void of all Characters, without any *Ideas*" (1969, 189). Experiences and sensations furnish the individual with his ideas, and presumably with his character. Virtue and morality represent traits acquired through proper education. What Greenblatt notes about the Renaissance, that identity in the age is not inherent but a "social fabrication," applies equally to the theories of Hobbes and Locke (1986, 215). Their ideologies provide theoretical elaborations of notions that had already been explored on the seventeenth-century stage.

The evolution of these radical ideologies immediately after the turbulent Stuart era argues for the validity of certain claims made by the cultural anthropologist, Clifford Geertz. Geertz argues that ideologies come into being during periods of cultural crisis and transition:

> It is when neither a society's most general cultural orientations nor its most down-to-earth, "pragmatic" ones suffice any longer to provide an adequate image of political process that ideologies begin to become crucial as sources of socio-political meanings and attitudes. (1973, 219)

This notion of ideologies proves especially relevant to the seventeenth century; the sociocultural crisis in the early half of the period manifested through powerful images on the Stuart stage probably contributed to the evolution of dominant ideologies such as Hobbes's or Locke's in the later half. Thus, Stuart theater that contributed to the sociopolitical temper of the mid-century also may have provoked an intellectual transformation that followed on the heels of political upheaval. Indeed, Stuart depictions of the self, of the body in transition, may have contributed directly to the intellectual environment of the post-Restoration period.

3

Evil as Corruption and Decline: Ritual Parricide on the Stage

Patriarchal Authority and Effective Theater

Another kind of violence, parricide, also draws power from its evocation of King James's theorics. Two concepts mentioned earlier are relevant in this context. James's patriarchal theories—specifically, the notion of the king as head over the social and domestic bodies—receives ironic treatment as Stuart tragedies depict corrupt or declining patriarchal systems. Artaud's "theatre of cruelty," concerned with patriarchal power, also illumines essential functions of Stuart theater. Commenting on Artaud, Jacques Derrida insists that "cruelty" should not be confused with violence: "certain products are perhaps violent, even bloody, but are not, for all that, cruel" (1978, 239). He argues that

> there is always murder at the origin of cruelty, of the necessity named cruelty. And first of all, a parricide. The origin of theatre, such as it must be restored, is the hand lifted against the abusive weilder of the logos, against the father, against the God of the stage subjugated to the power of speech and text. (1978, 239).

Stuart drama provides on instance of the theater of cruelty directed at the patriarchal figure. Depictions of parricide and a general undermining of patriarchal authority are essential aspects of several Stuart plays. Dramatic concern with declining patriarchal power may be related to a gradual undermining of existing authority in the age and indicates the positive power of drama as it contributed to the sociopolitical transformation that occurred in seventeenth-century England. Stuart dramatic reaction "against the abusive weilder of the logos," against the patriarch and monarch, ultimately had creative effects, but these effects differed somewhat from those that Derrida and Artaud envision for the modern theater of cruelty.

An important distinction needs to be made, therefore, between Derrida's and Artaud's discussions of parricide in the theater, on the one hand, and the manner in which the same is represented in seventeenth-century drama, on the other. Derrida and Artaud see patriarchal murder as entirely liberating; in the plays that I will be considering, however, parricide emerges as an ambiguous act. Stuart theatrical depictions of parricide ultimately may have had a liberating effect on society as a whole, as I hope to suggest in the course of this chapter, but dramatists depict parricide (or the general undermining of patriarchal authority) as a disaster. The plays depict the undermining of patriarchal authority primarily as the subversion of a desirable norm. Thus, Stuart depictions of the patriarchal system in decline may be regarded as evil in the Ricoeurian sense, as representations of corruption in that which was once good.

Rene Girard's theories about violence against patriarchal figures, because they emphasize the inherent ambiguities of such violence, provide an interesting gloss on Stuart dramatic violence. In his study of the scapegoat mechanism in society, Girard focusses especially on collective violence that takes the form of scapegoating.[1]

Girard's theory about the origin of culture and society in a single act of real violence recalls Freud's similar claims in *Totem and Taboo*; but Girard repeatedly emphasizes what he sees as fundamental and important differences between the two philosophies. Unlike Freud, Girard does not situate this original violent act in the sexual impulse, but in a more general desire. To Girard, the object of desire is less important than the mimetic effect that all desire produces. When one desires an object, the very act of desiring it makes the object desirable to others; thus, by desiring the same object, others imitate the original desire and mimetic rivalry evolves. Mimetic rivalry in turn erases the differences among rivals, because when rivals desire the same objects, they become mirror images of each other, and the rivalry culminates in violence, for rivals invariably turn against each other. Often, however, mimetic rivalry in large communities results, not in general violence and chaos, but in the scapegoat phenomenon, in which violent impulses are redirected collectively toward a single individual who is held responsible for the crisis in the community. Mimetic rivalry then transforms into collective action as crowds redirect their passion against a scapegoat of unanimous choice; thus, by choosing a surrogate victim, the community redirects violence away from itself and toward an outside object. The sacrificing of the scapegoat results in two drastic transformations: mimetic rivalry becomes mimetic unity, and the victim transforms from a criminal into a benefactor who averts social calamity by participating in the sacrifice. Thus, Girard insists that the scapegoat phenomenon functions as a defensive and self-regulatory act by which communities return to and reemphasize social stability.

Girard sees traces of these original events in myth and ritual, which camouflage rather than reveal the violent act and mimetic rivalry to emphasize the unity that results from these events. In written rites, on the other hand, in literary works, one glimpses these original events most vividly; Girard insists that in literature, violence and mimetic rivalry are not subsumed by the need to reaffirm social unity, as in religious rites and myths. Literature thus acquires a privileged status over myth, ritual, or religion in Girard's writings as most directly exposing the relationship between mimesis and collective violence. Girard regards drama, especially tragedy, as a form in which the scapegoat phenomenon and mimetic rivalry are repeatedly reenacted. Tragedy, he argues, reenacts society's violent beginnings and itself flourished during periods of social crisis when those origins become most vivid in the collective memory. Thus, the cathartic effect of tragedy does not differ from that of ritual or religion; in all cases, purification and cultural unity result through a sacrifice enacted to evoke the original violence. Artaud's claims about the cathartic effects of "the theatre of cruelty" might be recalled in this context.

How exactly is the surrogate victim chosen by communities? How does mimetic rivalry transform into mimetic unity? And, most importantly, what relationship exists between the scapegoat phenomenon in society and in literary drama? Girard points out that scapegoat victims are often outsiders (Oedipus, for example, or the Jews in medieval Europe); sometimes they are marked by physical deformities, they are often figures who either hold or are perceived as holding exceptional power over their eventual victimizers (thus, kings and witches are always potential scapegoat choices). Invariably, "victims are chosen not for the crimes they are accused of but for everything that suggests their guilty relationship with the crisis" (Girard, *Scapegoat* (1986, 24). The monarch, therefore, is particularly vulnerable as a potential victim. What Girard notes about the sovereign authority in Shakespeare holds true for the sovereign authority in all drama, both social and theatrical: he is "always a sacrificial figure, ... a potential scapegoat" (1978, 152). Scapegoat sacrifices are frequently enacted during periods of crisis, and the victim is perceived as the source of the crisis; he is often presented as violating the codes of differentiation basic to society. Thus, parricide and incest, crimes that "signify the dissolving of even the most elemental cultural differences—those between father, mother, child," are often attributed to the victim (1978, 146). Finally, natural calamities such as the plague, a phenomenon which also erases differences, are frequently ascribed to the victim's social crimes.

The classic and most obvious example of scapegoating, one that Girard uses frequently and one central also to Freud's theories about cultural origins, occurs in the Oedipus myth and its best known version, Sophocles's play. As king, Oedipus holds exceptional power over society; his difference from his community is accentuated by his deformed foot; he enters Thebes as an outsider; the image of the plague dominates the play, and Oedipus bears responsibility for this social calamity; his transformation from savior to criminal to savior takes place as a result of his social significance.

But if Girard's paradigm provides an accurate account of the scapegoat phenomenon, his theories should illumine other and entirely different contexts. Girard himself suggests a connection between the scapegoat ritual and the events of the French Revolution. Marie Antoinette, because of both her royal blood and her Austrian origins, was a potential scapegoat; charges of an incestuous relationship with her son surfaced frequently during her trial. Although Girard does not wish to reduce the events of the Revolution to a single paradigm, he argues for a strong relationship between those events and the scapegoat phenomenon.

His theories would certainly apply to seventeenth-century England, which witnessed a similar revolution. The Stuart monarchs seem to have been appropriate scapegoat choices for many reasons. Although technically heirs to the English throne, as Scots, James and Charles were outsiders to English society. Plagues recurred during the period, especially during changes in monarchy; major plagues occurred in London in 1603, 1625, 1649, and interestingly, in 1659, during the time of Cromwell's death. Connections between the plague and Stuart monarchy were made frequently by critics of the latter; the tables were turned in 1659, to the obvious relish of the Royalists. Although incest did not figure in Charles I's trial as it did later in Marie Antoinette's, rumors about parricide were certainly current. Long after the revolution, a supporter of the Puritan cause, John Cook in *King Charles His Case*, alludes to the charge which had surfaced even in 1625 that Charles and Buckingham poisoned James during his illness: "Was he fit to continue a father to the people, who was without natural affection to his own father!" (quoted in Davies 1983, 165). Discussing the function of the sacrifice itself, Girard notes that "a sacrificial action or immolation is generally found, frequently interpreted as the re-enactment of a divine murder supposed to be the decisive event in the foundation of culture'' (1978, 147). In this sense, Stuart claims about the divinity of the monarch became a double-edged weapon that asserted power and at the same time made the monarch particularly vulnerable to the scapegoat process. Like the image of the king's dual bodies, claims about the inherent divinity of the king were calculated to ensure the perpetual acceptance of monarchical authority; but like that image, claims about divinity actually permitted the communal murder of the monarch. Thus, the Oedipus myth and the early Stuart story are not quite as dissimilar as they might first appear.

In medieval Europe, two groups had frequently been targets of scapegoat practices—Jews and witches. But Jews had been expelled from England in the thirteenth century and were not readmitted into the kingdom until 1665; similarly, historians have noted a diminishing interest in the period in witches and witchcraft. Perhaps the absence of both traditional victims added momentum to the choice of the monarch as a scapegoat, because the idea of Charles's execution seems to have developed abruptly and was carried out, although not without opposition, with a remarkable degree of acquiescence. Even the transformation of Charles from criminal to victim to divine benefactor takes place at the moment of the sacrifice—the *Eikon Basilike* published in 1649 presents the portrait by which Charles was to be remembered by many for a long time. The pose of the Christ-like sufferer invokes most vividly a traditional image of the scapegoat. Thus, Charles bears all the marks of a conventional scapegoat, and he is presented as one throughout the *Eikon Basilike*.

If Girard is right about the relationship between social and theatrical violence, Stuart tragedy should yield interesting parallels to the scapegoat ritual, which was certainly invoked by the events of the mid-century. Is there a relationship between the sociopolitical drama of the mid-century and early Stuart theater?

Ritual Parricide in Some Stuart Tragedies

The theory of the dual bodies of the monarch embraced by the Stuarts was calculated to ensure authority; theatrical depictions of the fragmented body, therefore, necessarily questioned and reevaluated this authority. But this reevaluation of monarchical and patriarchal authority took a variety of forms in Stuart drama; a frequent form seems to have been the metaphoric or literal scapegoating of the patriarch. Renaissance theoretical equations between patriarchy and monarchy made it possible for drama to present the destruction of both systems simultaneously. Many Stuart plays explore the question of patriarchal authority, often representing it in a state of decline. Metaphorically, these plays invoke a sense of declining monarchy itself.

In fact, the notion of metaphoric scapegoating may not have been at all alien to the seventeenth century; Neil Rhodes describes how the anti-Marprelate pamphlets, directed by a group of satirists (among them, Nashe and Lyly) against the Puritan, Martin Marprelate, indulged in immediately recognizable figurative scapegoating. In these satires, Martin Marprelate was "ridiculed in prose as a May-game scapegoat and figuratively purged with the apparatus of medical and judicial torture" (1980, 4). Dramatists probably intended to provoke a similar effect through their depictions. In Ricoeur's terms, once more, Stuart depictions of patriarchy and monarchy in decline present evil as a corruption of that which had once been good.

In Shakespeare's *King Lear* (1605), which quite explicitly depicts patriarchal and monarchical authority, Lear relinquishes his throne and thereby loses much of his patriarchal power. His initial loss is voluntary, but the consequent psychological displacement is unexpected and imposed on him by Goneril and Regan. This is not a unique instance in Shakespeare, and the father silenced and made powerless (even if this is not always the central issue in a play, as it is in *Lear*) occurs in several of his plays, both in the comedies and tragedies. Brabantio in *Othello* provides another instance. Rendered powerless before the Senate by his daughter, he, like Lear, dies conveniently, by the end of the play, and is thereby spared knowledge of Desdemona's tragedy. But both *Othello* and *King Lear* (and I do not know of any of Shakespeare's plays that would not fit into this category) have what I will call a "closed structure," in which a level of reconciliation takes place in the concluding scene, and characters better understand the events in which they have participated. The closed structure reemphasizes the patriarchal system that had been disrupted during the play, and the error of the disruption is apparent to the characters on stage and the audience. In *Lear*, Lear and Gloucester have recognized their mistakes and have reconciled themselves to the consequences; Goneril and Regan have suffered for their brutality and Edgar will succeed to the throne. Although Lear dies of a broken heart, he does so after being reconciled with Cordelia, after resolving to a degree the conflict that had started the play. In *Othello*, even if Iago's actions remain ambiguous at the end of the play, some explanation has been provided, and Othello dies recognizing his mistake; the Senate likewise has some understanding of the course of events that culminated in the tragedy. Besides, the play insists that Brabantio himself has been spared knowledge of the tragedy.

The same might be said of *Hamlet*, a tragedy concerned with patriarchal authority, parricide, and regicide. Hamlet faces an impossible dilemma: to correct an unnatural regicide, he has to commit greater transgressions, kill Claudius, his king and stepfather. In other words, he has to commit regicide and parricide. His act of revenge, therefore, can never be wholly corrective; thus, Hamlet's own death is already inscribed within his role as revenger. Hamlet's test of Claudius thus manifests itself as a test of the authenticity of the father; but the authenticity of one patriarch, Hamlet senior, involves the deposition of the other, Claudius. From the very beginning, therefore, Hamlet's dilemma involves questions about patriarchal authenticity and authority. The tragedy that Claudius precipitates ultimately damages the innocent Danes most of all, because it damages the patriarchal system on which social stability depended, and all the actors in the tragedy (and the audience) recognize this by the end. The analogy between the fall of the patriarch and the fall of the state had been made explicit in the speech about Priam's slaughter rendered by the player at Hamlet's request. In that speech, the player recounts how Pyrrhus's blow directed at Priam destroys Illium even before it hits his victim. Hamlet's desire to hear that tale indicates his early awareness of the immensity of his actions. However, the murder of the patriarch, although successful temporarily, does not completely destroy patriarchal power: Hamlet's father remains a controlling figure throughout and precipitates the central actions and patriarchal authority reasserts itself also through Fortinbras's succession to the throne. Thus, patriarchal authority, first undermined by the murder and then reasserted through successful revenge, becomes a crucial issue in the play.

Macbeth (1606–7) also explicitly concerns itself with declining patriarchal and monarchical power. Critics have often noted the characterization of Duncan as weak and effeminate: "this father king seems strikingly absent even before his murder. Heavily idealized, he is nonetheless largely ineffectual" (Adelman 1987, 94). In fact, Janet Adelman attributes even the presence of demonic evil to weakened patriarchal authority: "The presence of the witches suggests that the absence of the father that unleashes female chaos has already happened at the beginning of *Macbeth*; that absence is merely made literal by the murder" (96). Adelman's argument gains potency considering that questions about masculinity are crucial to the play: Macbeth's actions are prompted by his desire to prove his manhood, and man's weakness increases in proportion to the appropriation of power by women. The play ultimately insists that woman's attempt to usurp power, represented both in the witches and Lady Macbeth, is doomed to failure. Moreover, the unsexing of either male or female renders them frightening; thus, the effeminate Duncan transforms at his death into a "gorgon" in his son's eyes, and Lady Macbeth increasingly resembles the witches on the heath. The closed structure of the play is apparent in its insistence on the restitution of patriarchal power. As Adelman argues, "the reconstitution of manhood becomes the central problem of the play" (96). Thus, things can be set right only by the man "not of woman born," one "torn untimely from his mother's womb," and saved from the damaging influence of womanhood. As in *Hamlet*, by the end of the tragedy, both Macbeth and the audience acknowledge the damaging effects of parricide.[2]

Jonson's Roman tragedy, *Sejanus* (1603), similarly reveals a closed structure. Set in the corrupt court of Tiberius, the play focuses not on Tiberius's frailities, but on Sejanus's treachery in seeking to usurp the kingdom. The "Argument" preceding the play emphasizes Jonson's vision of traitors and the punishment they deserve:

> This do we advance as a mark of terror to all traitors, and treasons; to show how just the heavens are in pouring and thundering down a mighty vengeance on their unnatural intents, even to the worst princes: much more to those, for guard of whose piety and virtue, the angels are in continual watch, and God himself miraculously working. (1966, 40–45)

The play thus focuses on monarchical authority and represents its thwarting as likely to end in disaster. In the play, Tiberius initially appears as weak and easily manipulated. Sejanus manages to persuade him to leave matters of governing to him; seduced by visions of a life of ease, Tiberius retires from the capital, and Sejanus seems to be entirely in control. But despite this illusion of weakness that Tiberius creates during the early part of the play, thus evoking Sejanus's desire to usurp power, the concluding scene constitutes a clear reassertion of monarchical authority even during the Emperor's physical absence from court. In a dramatic grand finale during which Sejanus expects to be recognized and elevated in rank, Tiberius's letter accusing him of treachery and condemning him to death is read before the full Senate. Shortly after, he is beheaded by order of the

Senate, and the multitude who wooed him earlier during his years of power turn against him and now vent their fury on his body. Terentius describes vividly the extent of their rage and the degree of dismemberment to which Sejanus's body is subjected:

> ... th' unfortunate trunk were seized
> By the multitude; who not content
> With what the forward justice of the State,
> Officiously had done, with violent rage
> Have rent it limb from limb.
>
> . . . .
>
> These mounting at his head, these at his face,
> These digging out his eyes, those with his brain,
> Sprinkling themselves, their houses, and their
> friends;
>
> . . . . .
>
> These with a thigh; this hath cut off his hands;
> And this his feet; these fingers, and those toes;
> That hath his liver; he his heart:
>
> . . . .
>
> The whole, and all of what was great Sejanus,
> And next to Caesar did possess the world,
> Now torn, and scattered, as he needs no grave,
> Each little dust covers a little part.
>
> (5.6. 810–34)

Their fury abates only after Sejanus's entire family, including his virgin daughter who is first deflowered, have been subjected to similar violence. Thus, like Shakespeare, Jonson depicts attempts to usurp monarchical authority as doomed to failure. And even as Lady Macbeth's transgressions had rendered her a frightening grotesque, so too Sejanus increasingly evokes horror and fear from his followers. His frightening aspect is metaphorically captured in the fate of his statue erected in Pompey's theater. Shortly before the scene in the Senate, Terentius describes how people have gathered to view the statue as it sends forth "smoke, as from a furnace, black and dreadful" (5.1., 30). He goes on to describe how, when the head was taken off so they might investigate the source of this smoke, "a great and monstrous serpent" leapt out. Clearly, Sejanus is being depicted here as a fearful grotesque, visible to the entire community as half serpent and half human. The description anticipates the impending failure of his plans and the horrible fate that awaits him. The play itself closes with clear assertions of Tiberius's power and monarchical authority in general. Sejanus himself seems to acknowledge his sins during the scene in the Senate, and his muted tone and weary acceptance of defeat suggest that he dies after recognizing the folly of his desires.

These early plays differ from later Stuart tragedies in their "closed structure"; despite the enormity of the tragedy, some reconciliation takes place at the conclusion. The later Stuart tragedies, however, in which such reconciliations prove tenuous, have what I will call an "open structure." Their open structure, with its total deconstruction of patriarchal power, demonstrates the darker vision of familial and social relationships in the later Stuart era.

Interestingly, in their open-endedness, these later tragedies recall Greek and Roman tragedy, especially those plays most intensely concerned with questions of patriarchal and monarchical authority. Sophocles's *Oedipus Rex* ends with the patriarch still alive to face the consequences of his action; his *Antigone* ends with Kreon (the king and patriarchal figure who has promised to be father to Antigone and Ismene) on stage alone and aware of his mistakes, left to face the consequences of his actions. In Euripides's *Medea,* Jason, bereft of wife and children, remains on stage dazed by the enormity of the tragedy, the consequences of his action. Many of Seneca's reworkings of Euripides's tragedies end similarly, with the full effect of the tragedy yet to be felt. In *Phaedra*, for example, based on Euripides's *Hippolytus*, Theseus remains on stage in the last scene with the mangled body of Hippolytus, unable to comprehend the tragedy. All these plays are concerned with kingship and its relationship to social order.[3]

In some later Stuart plays, a reconciliation is likewise either missing or unsatisfactory both for the audience and for the characters. The fathers in these plays are rendered powerless by their children, and no real reconciliation occurs at the end. In many plays, the tragic action affects the father figures most of all; in others, patriarchs bear direct responsibility for the tragedy through their inability to exercise authority or through their abuse of power. Tragedies thus deconsecrate, question, and reevaluate patriarchal authority and responsibility.

Middleton's *The Changeling* (1622), for example, seems ultimately to be directed against the patriarch, Vermandero, who though often on stage, remains ignorant and misled throughout the play, voiceless, guilty, and metaphorically dead. Middleton's tragedy depicts a metaphoric parricide, for at the end of the play, Vermandero, Beatrice-Joanna's father, is simply divested of all patriarchal authority through her death. Although the same might be said about

Florio, father of Giovanni and Anabella, in Ford's *'Tis Pity She's a Whore* (1633), Florio really dies as a direct result of the tragedy involving his son and daughter; moreover, because Giovanni, the instigator of the tragedy, expresses no regret, the final tragedy in Ford's play seems to be Florio's. In any case, both plays depict the patriarch throughout as essentially weak and powerless, unaware of the actions of his own children. And both plays have an "open structure", ending on a note of disquiet. Although these plays are not concerned with actual parricide, as *King Lear, Macbeth,* and *Hamlet* had been, the devaluation of patriarchal power by children in them constitutes metaphoric parricide and proves as unsettling as the literal murders in earlier tragedies.

Although not all Jacobean and Caroline plays end with the patriarch on stage yet to suffer the consequences of the play's actions, many have a similar inconclusive and open structure. Perhaps this change in tone reflects the greater pessimism of the later years and dramatic inability to envision an entirely successful restitution of patriarchal authority, an image that earlier tragedies such as *Hamlet, Macbeth,* and *King Lear* had insisted on.

Our introduction to Vermandero in *The Changeling* occurs in the opening scene. His guarded reaction in this scene to Alsemero, a stranger in town, is important. Inquiring about Alsemero's country, he explains his caution thus:

> we use not to give survey
> Of our chief strengths to strangers; our citadels
> Are plac'd conspicuous to outward view,
> On promont's tops; but within are secrets.

> (1.1 163–66)

Vermandero's castle is referred to several times in this scene, a seat of patriarchal authority of which he is very proud. The irony of his speech to Alsemero here lies in his conviction that the secrets of his castle are *his* secrets; as it turns out, the murder of Alonso Piracquo, his daughter's fiance, takes place in the dungeons of his castle and has been masterminded by his own daughter and servant. The details of the murder are "secrets" he uncovers only in the final scene of the play. As he searches for the murderer throughout the play, and, as he reiterates his claim about his and his household's innocence, he generates an irony not unlike that evoked in the opening and central scenes of *Oedipus Rex,* for example. Ultimately, as in *Oedipus,* Vermandero is the last person to learn the truth about his own family.

The images of citadel, castle, and temple, seats of patriarchal authority, are important in the play. In each of these places, however, we see the patriarch powerless or oblivious to the course of events. Before Alsemero's meeting with Vermandero, we have had several references to the temple at which Alsemero first saw Beatrice-Joanna and where he fell in love with her. The conventional scene of sanctity, however, regarded as such by Alsemero, proves to be the beginning of his (and Beatrice-Joanna's) undoing; Beatrice-Joanna gains power over him here, as she quickly changes her affection from Alonso Piracquo to Alsemero. In this scene, by keeping Vermandero ignorant of her new feelings for Alsemero, Beatrice-Joanna subverts her father's authority over her, and by using the pretext of having been at her devotions to woo Alsemero, she treats the temple, a conventional scene of patriarchal authority, with irreverence. Her sudden change of affection from Alonso Piracquo to Alsemero, a complete stranger, and Alsemero's immediate infatuation with her beauty become a parody of conventional depictions of love at first sight. This parody, together with the desecration of the temple where they meet, already indicates the potential failure of their relationship.

Vermandero, however, remains entirely ignorant of these developments and the events that follow. His bewildered cry at seeing his wounded daughter and De Flores in act 5 is revealing in its choice of image:

> An host of enemies enter'd my citadel
> Could not amaze like this: Joanna! Beatrice!
> Joanna!
>
> (5.3. 147–48)

After discovering that his daughter and De Flores had engaged in an adulterous relationship and that they had murdered Alonso Piracquo and Diaphanta in his own castle, he says little except to respond to De Flores's statement, "now we are left in hell," with "We are all there, it circumscribes us here" (164, 165). Alsemero's concluding speech promises consolation for himself and Alonso Piracquo's brother, but about the heart broken Vermandero, he can only say:

> To dry a child from the kind father's eyes.
> Is to no purpose, it rather multiplies.
>
> (5.3. 222–23)

Critics have for the most part been oblivious to the immensity of Vermandero's tragedy in this play. Summarizing the action of the entire tragedy, N. W. Bawcutt, for example, dismisses it as one would dismiss a bad dream: "The normal tenor of life has been interrupted by a sudden crisis; at the end of the play, the crisis has been resolved, and normality finally asserts itself"(Middleton, 1958, lxviii). Yet, the open structure of the play and the concluding lines emphasize, on the contrary, that the permanent effects of the tragedy are to be felt only by the patriarch who has remained entirely ignorant of the course of events throughout the play. The play, in other words, concludes on the verge of the true disaster—the father's knowledge of the extent to which he has been, throughout the play, a powerless figure working under the illusion of being in control. The tragedy is disquieting and unlike any Elizabethan depiction of patriarchal authority in its final effects.

Middleton's rather ambiguous title, which has been a point of critical contention for some years, may be especially relevant to the play's depiction of patriarchal power.[4] It may, of course refer to Beatrice-Joanna, the changeling child "carried away" by the deformed De Flores. Such a reading proves problematic because Beatrice-Joanna's function hardly can be reduced to that of an innocent victim; neither can De Flores simply be dismissed as the arch-villain solely responsible for the turn of events. Confronted by such ambiguities, some critics have seen the term *changeling* as referring simply to the several drastic transformations that take place in characters in the main and subplots. If this is the meaning intended by the title, the ultimate irony is that it may refer as easily to Vermandero. The patriarchal position, after all, undergoes the greatest degree of transformation. Vermandero, at the beginning, proud of his castle and his beautiful daughter (in short, of his patriarchal authority), is in the last scene divested of both and thus "changed" beyond recognition. His silence at the end itself metaphorically suggests the total annulment of his authority. Read thus, the title may even include the larger social context of the play—it may refer to the changing role of the patriarch in seventeenth-century England, in a society less inclined to acknowledge him as the arbitrary center of power.

Florio's predicament in *'Tis Pity She's a Whore* is similar to Vermandero's in Middleton's play. Like Vermandero, he is immensely proud of his children, and he often prefaces his addresses by praising one or the other, Giovanni and Anabella. Written later in the Caroline period, however, Ford's play differs markedly in tone from Middleton's; patriarchal deconsecration, rendered through vocabulary (especially in Giovanni's speeches) that borders on the festive and anarchic, is far more emphatic in tone.

The play dramatizes a crime even more transgressive than adultery, the incestuous relationship between Giovanni and Anabella, about which Florio remains entirely ignorant until the concluding scene. During the play, Anabella, who becomes pregnant, is forcibly married to Soranzo, a wealthy gentleman who has wooed her for a long time. Soranzo gradually realizes the truth about Anabella's pregnancy and holds a feast during which he plans to revenge his shame by murdering Giovanni. Giovanni, driven to jealousy by Anabella's marriage and aware of Soranzo's schemes, also decides to use the feast as a cover for revenge. In the concluding scene, he murders Anabella in her bedchamber and is himself killed shortly after by banditti hired by Soranzo.

As in the concluding scene of *The Changeling,* the strongest effects of the tragedy are registered by the father. The others seem to dismiss the tragedy as unfortunate as they turn their attention to immediate matters. The effects on Florio, however, are profound; he seems first to lose his mind, continues to disbelieve Giovanni's claims, and then dies when he realizes the immensity of the tragedy. The parricide in this case is a double one; Florio's death only reiterates his mental destruction already accomplished by Giovanni's presence and actions in this scene. Both deaths, in turn, the mental and the actual, symbolically reiterate the subversion of patriarchal authority already accomplished and begun even as early as Act I through the collusion of Anabella and Giovanni in incest. The parricide is explicitly acknowledged by Giovanni himself at the end:

> now survives
> None of our house but I, gilt in the blood
> Of a fair sister and a hapless father.
>
> (5.6. 67–69)

The Cardinal, himself a weak and ineffectual figure, also emphasizes the undermining of partriarchal authority but, speaking presumably for all those present and to a degree for the audience, blames both Anabella and Giovanni for Florio's death:

> Monster of children! see what thou hast done,
> Broke thy old father's heart.
>
> (5.6. 62–63)

Despite Giovanni's insistence that he is solely responsible for his father's death, the Cardinal's view seems more accurate, and the image of the collusive parricide, the responsibility for which lies with both Anabella and Giovanni, dominates our final response to the play. In fact, all the patriarchs in the play are presented either in their weak or corrupted state; the Cardinal emerges as monetarily rather than spiritually inclined; and the Friar, Bonaventura, uses his authority to threaten and frighten Giovanni and Anabella, although with little success. The play's treatment of patriarchal authority, because it differs so markedly in intensity from earlier treatments, lends credence to Martin Butler's claim that "the drama of the 1630s, perhaps more than any earlier drama, did persistently engage in debating political issues of its day" (1984, 1–2).

Ford's more emphatic devaluation of patriarchal power becomes most apparent, therefore, when we compare his play with an earlier Stuart tragicomedy concerned with similar themes, Beaumont's and Fletcher's *A King and No King* (1611). In that play, Arbaces's love for his sister, Panthea, provides the central conflict, but because Arbaces is king of Arabia, the play explores questions of both patriarchal and monarchical authority. An intensely emotional and temperamental character, Arbaces may have been a prototype for Giovanni, in so far as both are involved in an incestuous relationship wiht their sister. Arbaces's dilemma, however, resolves when Gorbaces proves at the end of the play that Panthea is not really his sister.

The play opens with emphatic assertions of monarchical authority by Arbaces, who has just captured a royal prisoner, Tigranes, king of Armenia:

> Should I then boast? Where lies that foot of ground
> Within this whole realm that I have not past
> Fighting and conquering? Far then from me
> Be ostentation. I could tell the world
> How I have laid his kingdom desolate
> With this sole arm propp'd by divinity
>
> (1.1. 123–28)

These claims of divine support, repeated several times by Arbaces, are undercut by our recognition of his boastfulness and by his friend, Mardonius, who frequently cautions Arbaces against false pride and exaggeration. Tigranes, his prisoner, also recognizes the discrepancy between Arbaces's words and actions. Arbaces's claim of divine sanction for his actions rests, of course, on his mistaken belief that he is son to the king; but even his exercise of royal authority, such as it is, is undercut by his repeated attempts to force his sister into incest. In other words, rather than using divine authority to establish and maintain order and distinctions, Arbaces uses the authority invested in him to break down order and to blur familial distinctions between him and his sister. Thus, Arbaces both undercuts his claims to divinity and monarchy and devalues patriarchy; metaphorically, the play insinuates even in the early scenes that he is "no king." [5]

The reassertion of patriarchy and monarchy in the concluding scene is emphasized by the closed structure of the play. The play concludes with the revelation that Gobrius, Arbaces's rightful father and Lord Protector of Iberia, had planned the entire action, including Arbaces's love for Panthea. In the concluding scene, Arbaces acknowledges this manipulation: "Draw near, thou guilty man, / Thou art the author of the loathed'st crime" (5.4. 65–66). He recognizes that his affection for Panthea had been evoked long before he had even seen her:

> Thou know'st the evils thou has done to me
> Dost thou remember all those witching letters
> Thou sent'st unto me to Armenia
> Fill'd with the praise of my beloved sister,
> Where thou extol'st her beauty? What had I
> To do with that? What could her beauty be
> To me? And thou didst write how well she lov'd me—
> Dost thou remember this?—so that I doted
> Something before I saw her.
>
> (5.4. 84–92)

These accusations are directed at Gobrius when only half the truth has been revealed, and because Arbaces still thinks that Panthea is his half-sister. Gobrius acknowledges his deliberate manipulation of events, but goes on to prove that Panthea is the Queen Mother's daughter and rightful heir to the throne. Arbaces, he proves, has no royal blood in him. Arbaces's recognition that he does not belong to the royal line frees him from charges of incest, but in the process he can, as Panthea's husband, take the throne anyway. Ironically, Arbaces regains the throne precisely when he recognizes that he has no lawful claim to it.

The play, thus, toys throughout with incest, which, as I pointed out earlier, undermines patriarchal authority by blurring familial lines. At the end, however, we learn that all the events had been managed and resolved by the patriarch, Gobrius. Of course, no such reassertion occurs at the end of 'Tis Pity. On the contrary, Ford's play emphasizes that the patriarch, Florio, had remained entirely ignorant of the central actions involving his son and daughter. 'Tis Pity deconsecrates patriarchal authority emphatically and completely; Girard's claim that "between patricide and incest, the violent abolition of all family differences is achieved" may thus be especially appropriate to Ford's tragedy (1972, 74). In fact, Giovanni's knife, which he uses to kill his sister in a highly ritualistic scene and which he himself obviously perceives as carrying symbolic overtones, "is made into an instrument and sign of his impious assault on the very foundations of patriarchal order and power," as Michael Neill argues (1988, 172). And Giovanni himself, who dies with no regrets whatsoever, claims our attention as one who has defied, denied, and ultimately forced a reevaluation of such authority.

Another Stuart tragedy, Massinger's *The Unnatural Combat* (ca. 1624–25), also involves potential incest, an attempted parricide, and the eventual devaluation of patriarchal authority. Only one contemporary edition of the play exists, printed in 1639. Although critics have praised the tragedy for its execution and style, many others such as W. Gifford have been reluctant to give it much prominence within the canon of Stuart tragedies. Gifford, in fact, in his introduction to the play, calls it "a noble performance, grand in conception, and powerful in execution" but, unwilling to acknowledge its thematic concerns, goes on to make the following somewhat puzzling qualification: "but the passion on which the main part of the story hinges, is of too revolting a nature for public presentation; we may admire in the closet what we should turn from on the stage" (124).

The tragedy focuses initially on quarrels between Malefort senior and his son. The enmity culminates in their physical combat during which Malefort junior is killed. The rest of the play concentrates on Malefort's incestuous desire for his daughter, Theocrine, and his attempt ot avoid acting on this desire by entrusting her to Montreville, a false friend. Montreville, who has long desired Theocrine himself, rapes her and then throws her out of his house. Malefort arrives to witness his daughter's death, the shame of her rape having been too much for her to bear. The psychologically tormented Malefort is himself struck by lightning shortly thereafter, and the wicked but unrepentant Montreville yields himself to the state for punishment.

However, despite this seemingly neat resolution, the play remains ambiguous in its final implications and shares much with later tragedies such as Ford's. The tragedy again involves familial strife, and a calculated, although unsuccessful, attempt at parricide by Malefort junior. The play does not present us with the reasons for Malefort junior's "unnatural" hatred of his father until the last scene, so we initially perceive him as being in the wrong. But immediately after his son's death, as Malefort senior glories in his triumph, we perceive his guilt and begin to suspect that perhaps the initiating act in this enmity sprang from the father:

> there's now no suspition;
> A fact, which I alone am conscious of,
> Can never be discover'd, or the cause
> That call'd this Duell on, I being above
> All perturbations, nor is it in
> The power of Fate, againe to make me wretched.
>
> (2.1. 219)

We learn at the end of the play that the combat springs from Malefort junior's attempt to avenge his mother's murder by Malefort senior, who had committed the crime so he might marry again; thus, his father's initial disavowal of familial ties has evoked a similar attitude from his son. The play clearly establishes that the father holds full responsibility for this disruption of natural order. But, although the "unnatural" physical combat between father and son ends early in the play, the combat within Malefort's mind as he debates whether to act on his lustful desire for Theocrine continues. Initially disinclined to commit incest, he entrusts her to Montreville in order that temptation might be removed, and he thus inadvertently causes her rape and subsequent death. Ironically, he divests himself of the patriarchal power he had insisted upon early in the play during his encounter with his son:

> Have I so far lost
> A fathers power, that I must give account
> Of my actions to my sonne? or must I plead
> As a fearefull prisoner at the bar, while he
> That owes his being to me sits a Judge
> To censure that, which onely by my selfe
> Ought to be question'd?
>
> (2.1. 217)

Ironically, too, he arrives at Montreville's house seeking his daughter not to save her, but determined to carry out his incestuous desires. Thus, although the play toys with incest as *A King and No King* had done, it offers no convenient solutions; on the contrary, Massinger implies that Theocrine is doomed to physical violation and death and that patriarchal authority as manifested in Malefort is wholly abusive and self-destructive. Although the earlier play, *A King and No King*, ends in a restitution of patriarchal authority, *The Unnatural Combat* depicts the dire consequences of carrying such power to arrogant extremes.

Another interesting Stuart tragedy, attributed by some to
Chapman and by others to a minor playwright, Henry Glapthorne,
also debates parricide and regicide. *Revenge for Honour* was first
entered in the Stationer's Register by R. Marriott on 29 November
1653 as *The Paraside or Revenge for Honour* by Henry Glapthorne.
It was published in the following year by Marriott but attributed to
Chapman. Critics have identified this play with one licensed in 1624
under the title *The Paracide*. The question of authorship itself is less
important than the thematic concerns of the work. Not simply an
instance of decadent Stuart drama, the play explores questions of
patriarchal and monarchical authority and contributes to our
awareness of the ongoing public debate on these issues that
characterizes the Stuart era.[6] If it does date to around 1624, its
depiction of a weak and powerless monarch overruled by his two
sons carries interesting resonances. James, despite all his claims
about patriarchal authority, was overruled in his last years on most
matters of state by his son and Buckingham (Ashton 1979, 110). In
1653, of course, the play's theme of parricide and regicide by
poisoning would have carried other powerful associations. Rumors
that Charles murdered his father by poisoning him recurred during
the Commonwealth and figured frequently in arguments made by
Puritans to justify the king's execution.

Revenge for Honour, like many plays of the period, is not set in
England, although it depicts very clearly the English court of
political intrigue and sycophancy. The play's depiction of the Caliph
of Arabia, Almanzor, as weak, old, and naive is elaborate and
pointed. Several scenes present him variously swayed by the
arguments of his ministers and his sons. In act 2, scene 1, Simanthes
first convinces him to keep his son, Abilqualit, at home rather than
send him to the Persian wars. He takes immense pride in Abilqualit's
recent successes at war and his popularity among the people:

> 'Tis not the least
> Among the blessings Heaven has shower's upon us,
> That we are happy in such loving subjects,
> To govern whom, when we in peace are ashes,
> We leave them a successor whom they truly reverence.
> A loving people and a loving sovereign
> Makes kingdoms truly fortunate and flourishing.
>
> (2.1. 13–19)

Shortly after Simanthes leaves, the conniving Mura, a supporter of
Abrahen, Almanzor's younger son, uses the same arguments to insist
that Abilqualit should go to war and that Abilqualit's popularity
should be curbed lest it eclipse his father's:

> I relish not your son
> Should (as if you were in your tomb already)
> Engross so much the giddy people's favours.
> 'Tis neither fit for him nor safe for you
> To suffer it.
>
> (2.1. 64–68)

Almanzar's change of heart is immediate; he condemns Abilqualit in terms as extravagant as the ones he had used earlier to praise him:

> Black now and horrid as the face of storms
> Appears all Abilqualit's lovely virtues
> Because to me they only make him dangerous,
> And with great terror shall view those actions
> Which with delight before we view'd, and dotage.
>
> (2.1. 153–57)

As in *Macbeth,* the regicide that occurs later merely duplicates the mataphoric murder already accomplished by these opening scenes. Later in the same scene, Abrahen, aspiring to his father's throne, articulates his vision of the patriarch as powerful only through outmoded custom:

> He's our father,
> And so the tyrant custom doth enforce us
> To yield to him that which fools call natural,
> When wise men know 'tis more than servile duty,
> A slavish, blind obedience to his pleasure,
> Be it nor just, nor honourable.
>
> (2.2. 218–23)

His vision of the patriarch as powerful only by custom does not extend, however (as it logically should) to the monarch. Earlier, as he formulates his plan to murder his brother and father, Abrahen muses on his ambition without, however, recognizing any contradiction in his attitude:

> He is my half-brother
> Th' other's my father; names, mere airy titles.
> Sovereignty's only sacred;
>
> (1.1. 435–37)

Later, after poisoning his father and believing his brother, Abilqualit, to be dead, Abrahen dwells on his clever acquisition of the throne with an overconfidence that later causes his undoing:

And who can say now Abrahen is a villain?
I am saluted king with acclamations
That deaf the heavens to hear, with as much joy
As if I had achiev'd this sceptre by
Means fair and virtuous. . . .
My worst impiety is held now religious.
'Twixt kings and their inferiors there's this odds,
These are mere men; we men, yet earthly gods.

(4.1. 315–29)

Of course, the play insists that once patriarchal power is dismissed as mere custom, monarchical power also loses its aura of divine sanction. At the play's conclusion none of the royal family remains to rule; the serious effects of the tragedy are yet to be felt by the state now bereft of its leaders. Tarifa, an old general, expresses his concern for the state when he turns to the dying Abilqualit and asks, "My dear lord, / is there no hopes of life? Must we be wretched?" (5.2. 301–2). Abilqualit, as he entrusts the kingdom to Tarifa, insists that the welfare of the state depends ultimately on the strength and virtue of the monarch himself. As in many other Stuart tragedies, the play ultimately posits that patriarchal and monarchical power, when weakened and ineffectual, has damaging sociopolitical effects. Thus, like many plays of the period, *Revenge for Honour* presents a powerless monarch and father but insists that regicide and parricide, although inevitable results of this weakness, are nevertheless, "unnatural" solutions.

Another play of disputed date and authorship, *The Bloody Banquet*, depicts the loss of patriarchal authority by the old King of Lydia and clearly attributes the deaths of his children to his weakness and lack of leadership. No entry exists in the Stationer's Register for this play, and the only known edition of it was printed in 1639. However, because of several "ghost" editions, critics have suggested a date as early as 1620. Its authorship, also a matter of dispute, has been variously attributed to a Thomas Barker, about whom nothing is known; to Thomas Dekker, either alone or in collaboration with Middleton; to Thomas Drewe, who acted for Queen Anne's men; and to Robert Davenport. Although a play of mediocre merit, it proves interesting for its overt assault on patriarchal weakness, a stance it shares with many plays of the period. But unlike some of the plays discussed so far, a degree of restitution occurs in this tragedy, and patriarchal power is restored at the end; but the playwright still suggests that successful exercise of such authority might be impossible.

The play opens with a dumb show that enacts a truce between the
King of Lydia and the King of Lycia. But the truce proves
temporary, for the King of Lydia's nephew, Lapyrus, enticed by the
enemy, turns traitor against his country. Fresh wars ensue between
the monarchs, and the King of Lydia, with the aid of the King of
Cicilia, manages to repel his enemies. Strangely, the King of Lycia
and his son and daughter who are listed among the dramatis
personae, never appear again on stage.

The dramatic action begins with the usurpation of the throne of
Lydia by the King of Cicilia, who receives support for his actions
from the cunning Maseres, his favorite. The old king, surprised by
the treachery of his ally, flees the country with a few loyal
supporters. His wife, the queen, forewarned of danger to her young
sons, has already fled with the two babies. Tymetheus, the king's
oldest son and friend to Zenarchus, the usurper's son, remains at the
new court. But Tymetheus, although betrothed to the King's
daughter, Amphridote, is seen by the new queen, who immediately
desires him. With help from her servants, she manages to arrange
several clandestine meetings between them, but, afraid of discovery
by her jealous and violent husband, she withholds her identity from
Tymetheus. During one of their meetings, however, Tymetheus
discovers his secret lover; the young queen, angry at his audacity,
first promises to continue their affair and then kills him. Meanwhile,
Maseres, who wishes to see Tymetheus punished because he desires
Amphridote himself, already has conveyed news of the young
queen's treachery to her husband. The king, therefore, intending to
surprise his wife during her adulterous meeting, arrives to see
Tymetheus killed. Infuriated by the treachery of his queen, he vows
to make her consume Tymetheus's flesh completely. Tymetheus's
limbs are thereafter hung up for all to see, and the young queen is
imprisoned. In the meantime, Zenobarbus revenges his friend's
death by murdering Maseres; in turn, his sister, who had recently
shifted her affections from Tymetheus to Maseres, revenges her
lover's death by poisoning Zenobarbus. She also consumes poison
and dies. The old king and his followers, hoping to regain the
kingdom, arrive at court shortly after disguised as pilgrims. The new
king prepares a lavish feast for them; moved to pity and horror by
the plight of the young queen at the feast as she consumes the flesh
of her beloved, the old king asks for a reprieval of her punishment and
requests to know the identity of the person whose flesh she is eating.
When he discovers that it is his son's, he throws off his disguise and
kills the usurper. The tragedy closes with the old king's reacquisition
of his throne and the opportune return of the old queen with one of

her babies, the other having died of starvation in the forest. The
tragedy thus seems to end with the restoration of power to the old
king and with an assurance of lineal inheritance through the safe
return of his youngest son.

But when the action of the play is perceived in light of the opening
dumb show, this seemingly complete restitution appears problematic. The play emphasizes throughout that the King of Lydia
is old, easily manipulated, and readily trusting of those around him.
His relationship to the King of Lycia in the dumb show almost
parallels his later relationship with the King of Cecilia. Thus, the
dumb show serves to establish the king's weakness and his complete
reliance on his followers and friends. Despite his early lesson in
treachery at the hands of both his nephew, Lapyrus, and the King of
Lycia, he allows himself to be manipulated in a similar fashion again
by the King of Cecilia, who perceiving his ally's weakness, usurps the
throne from him very easily. In fact, this usurpation comes as a
complete surprise to the old king, who does little to question or
condemn it. He makes a feeble attempt to invoke guilt in the usurper
by referring to virtue, trust, and friendship, but the new king
repulses such attempts easily by referring directly to the old king's
weakness and Lydia's reliance on others for its own safety.

We soon perceive, however, that the new monarch is no more
resiliant or authoritative a figure than the old one. In fact, even his
usurpation of the throne is manipulated by his favorite, Maseres. In
the usurpation scene, we perceive him waver and almost change his
mind when his son questions the propriety of his action. But Maseres
easily convinces him about his right to the throne of the country for
which he has fought. Ironically, he argues that the king should not
allow himself to be captivated by the power of words:

> ... the dukedom, the Kingdome, Lydia.
> All pant under your Scepter; the sway's yours,
> Be not bought out with words, a Kingdome's deare
> Kisse fortune, keepe your minde, and keepe your state
> Y're laught at if you prove compassionate,
>
> (1.1. 103–7)

In this scene Maseres makes all the major decisions: he suggests that
the old king be banished and that Tymetheus be permitted to remain
at court because he presents no threat. Similarly, he plans the young
queen's discovery and thus brings about the central actions of the
play. After his murder by Zenarchus, the usurper, unable to exercise
power with authority or restraint, is easily surprised and killed by the
disguised pilgrims. But in the conclusion of the play little difference

shows in the old king's manner or power. Earlier he had relied on the support of neighboring kings; now he relies on the newly converted Lapirus, his nephew, for his reinstatement to the throne. The play concludes with a clear suggestion that although the throne has been won back, the situation at court is little different than at the beginning of the play, and that the old king's dependence on Lapyrus is no different from the usurper's earlier reliance on Maseres. In fact, our recognition of the dire consequences of such reliance mitigates the relevance of his reinstatement. The play's action may be regarded as a preface to further turmoil; the tragedy itself thus functions similarly to the dumb show with which it had opened.

A similar pattern occurs in Shirley's tragedy, *The Traitor* (1631). Alexander, Duke of Florence, is repeatedly presented as a weak patriarch and governor, easily manipulated by those around him. But his death, already inscribed within his ineffectuality at the beginning of the play, becomes an unnatural parricide to be punished by death. Amidea, the maid whom the Duke wishes to rape, emphasizes the essential sanctity of the ruler's body despite his corruption. When Sciarrha, her brother, reveals his plans to murder the duke, Amidea condemns her brother's plans as treachery of the worst degree and offers to kill herself rather than have her family suffer from the parricide. Her attempt to convert the duke from his villainous intentions also takes the form of a speech that emphasizes his divinity:

> Oh, think but who you are,
> Your title speaks you nearest Heaven, and points
> You pout a glorious reign among the angels;
> Do not depost yourself of one, and be
> Of the other disinherited.
>
> (3.3. 69–73)

The duke's conversion in this scene to virtue and his reconversion to villainy a few scenes later by the villainous Lorenzo, like Almanzar's conversions in *Revenge for Honour*, and the usurper's in *The Bloody Banquet*, serve only to emphasize the ineffectuality of this patriarch. In Chapman's play, however, some hope for the welfare of the state had been presented through Tarifa, whose noble and virtuous son is to suceed to the throne after his death. In Shirley's tragedy, the duke's death at the hands of Sciarrha later does little to change the welfare of the state, and the play closes, as *The Bloody Banquet* had done, with the clear suggestion that similar tragedies will reoccur.

The final scene, in which both the duke and Lorenzo are murdered, leaves the State in Cosmos's hands. But Cosmos is a weak character himself. During the play, he has been manipulated by his friend, Pisano, even as the duke had been by Lorenzo. In fact, the play insists on the similarity between these two relationships. The duke had treated Lorenzo as a brother and companion, valuing their friendship above everything else; in the opening scene, Cosmos gives up his beloved Oriana to Pisano claiming the value of friendship above love—"I were not worthy to be called his friend, / Whom I preferred not to a mistres" (1.1. 133–34). Cosmos's weakness, in fact, has been responsible for some of the tragedy. Thus, violence against one patriarch, Alexander, although inevitable, provides little relief to his subjects, because it leaves them at the mercy of another equally weak figure, Cosmos. This late Caroline play thus undercuts patriarchy even as it reasserts it through Cosmos's succession to the dukedom; but its open structure emphasizes that patriarchy itself has declined and that the state will necessarily suffer as a result. Like many other Stuart plays, *The Traitor* closes with the suggestion that the greatest tragedy is yet to come.

The Maid's Revenge (ca. 1624–25) also makes a similar point. The play centers on Asper de Vilarezo's children—his daughters, Catalina and Berenthia, and his son, Sebastiano. Antonio, Sebastiano's friend, falls in love with the younger daughter, Berinthea; unfortunately, Catalina also desires him and plots to poison her sister. Antonio discovers the plot in time and manges to save Berinthea by taking her away from her father's house. The enraged Sebastiano follows them, determined to rescue his sister; he and Antonio engage in a duel during which Antonio is killed. Berinthea, enraged by her lover's death, vows revenge, stabs her brother in his sleep, and then poisons Catalina before taking her own life. At the end of the play, Vilarezo arrives to find all three of his children murdered by intrigues about which he had remained totally unaware. His dismay and condemnation of his own ignorance regarding the events recall Vermandero's similar horror at the end of *The Changeling*:

I am Planet struck, a direfull Tragedy, and have
I no part in it: how do you like it, ha? Was't not
Done toth' life? they are my own children.

(5.3. 25–27)

The play closes with an emphatic assertion of his responsibility: "'Tis false, he lies that says Berinthea / Was author of their deaths, 'twas Villarezo'' (5.3. 8–9). Like many plays of the period, the tragedy closes with an acknowledgment of guilt by the patriarch for his earlier weakness and inability to exercise authority. Ironically, by the time of such realization, he can no longer exercise his patriarchal power rightly, for he has lost such authority through the deaths of his children.

Indeed, the decline of patriarchal authority provides one of the central thematic concerns in Stuart drama. Dramatists repeatedly lay responsibility for the tragedies on weak and ignorant patriarchal figures who fail to exercise power, especially over their own children. These depictions certainly encapsulate a recurring concern about the welfare of the body politic; many of these plays function as "a provident council" to the monarch, a body whose task Antonio describes to Delio in *The Duchess of Malfi*:

> And what is't makes this blessed government
> But a most provident council, who dare freely
> Inform him the corruption of the times?
> Though some o'th' court hold it presumption
> To instruct princes what they ought to do,
> It is a noble duty to inform them
> What they ought to forsee.

> (1.1 16–22)

However, unlike in earlier tragedies which also were concerned with similar issues, these later plays do not conclude with an emphatic reinstation of authority. Whatever restitution exists serves only to emphasize and accentuate the circularity of events. Their "open" structures testify to an increasing cynicism regarding both patriarchal and monarchical authority in seventeenth-century England.

Socio-Cultural Effects: Subversion and Reassertion

These symbolic depictions of the patriarch as powerless, therefore, may be related to seventeenth-century political, and social theory. They are, partly at least, a subversion of King James's beliefs in patriarchal authority. Renaissance theoretical equations between patriarchy and monarchy, equations central to James's and Charles's political rhetoric, made it possible for drama through allusion and suggestion to undermine both institutions simultaneously. That is, by depicting the father as essentially weak and powerless, plays could subvert both patriarchal and monarchical authority.

Foucault's discussion of the creative function of power, discussed earlier, is especially relevant in this context. To Foucault, the positive function of power is intimately related to a destruction of patriarchal and monarchical authority. In other words, the devaluation of patriarchy in the drama, in the popular imagination, is important to an understanding of the positive power of drama and the radical changes in society that were taking place during this century. "All violence," Girard argues, "is modelled on earlier violence and in turn serves as a model" (1978, 94). Violence against the patriarch in plays such as *The Changeling* and *'Tis Pity* may have acted as a model for the violence against patriarchy and monarchy during the 1640s. In any case, *King Lear, Macbeth, The Maid's Tragedy, The Changeling, 'Tis Pity,* and *The Traitor,* in which patriarchal authority is shown in a state of decline, could only have added some force to this deconsecration.

But, although "the roots of theatre ... are in social drama," as Victor Turner insists, theater is also a "hypertrophy, an exaggeration, of jural and ritual processes; ... it is not a simple replication of the 'natural' total processional pattern of social drama" (1982, 12). Theater reflects the processional pattern in society, and at the same time, it exaggerates and magnifies this pattern. As I have insisted, the relationship between drama and society is essential to our understanding of the social drama of the mid century; but I would now like to go a step further in my statements about the relationship between society and theater. Previously, I have discussed both as separate entities reflecting, informing, and modifying each other. I would now like to suggest that devaluation of patriarchal authority goes beyond a simple reflection of reality or an anticipation of political events. It actually forced those events. I would now like to propose that theater and society constitute a single (and complex) entity, an entity we might call "socio-theatrical ritual."

Seventeenth-century drama, probably more than any other drama, lends itself to scrutiny in terms of the rite or ritual. Mary Douglas asserts, "ritualism is most highly developed where symbolic action is held to be most efficacious" (1970, 8), and, as I have already shown, the king, court, and public were particularly prone to elaborate public symbols. In other words, I am not merely suggesting the ritual origins of drama or the manner in which our understanding of ritual clarifies our perception of drama; on the contrary, it is together, as a unified entity, that drama and society function as a "socio-theatrical" transformation ritual in seventeenth-century England.[7]

In this sense, the plays of the early Stuart periods may be characterized in Artaud's terms as "real"; "a real stage play," Artaud notes, "upsets our sensual tranquility, drives us to a kind of potential rebellion, calling for a difficult heroic attitude on the part of assembled groups" (1970, 19). Such a play provokes an active response from the audience and thus functions as a transformation ritual. In discussing the power of these plays, therefore, we have to consider both the emotional response they provoked in the audience and the communal act that became the culmination of this response. Regicide (and the general social acquiescence in it) was just a communal act.

I find Girard's study of the scapegoat mechanism to be especially relevant to seventeenth-century ritual as defined. The scapegoat pattern, as I have already suggested, consists of three stages: the intimations of a social crisis, the attribution of the crisis to some individual, and the collective murder of that individual (1978, 187). If we regard drama (or all artistic activity, for that matter) and society as a single entity, and highly charged political actions as a conjunctive result of drama and society, we can perceive the scapegoat mechanism at work in the first half of the seventeenth century. Drama creates the sense of a crisis and repeatedly attributes this crisis to the weakness at the head of the hierarchical system—to the patriarch; together with other factors which, however, fall outside the precincts of this study, it thus activates the scapegoat mechanism in society and permits the collective murder of the patriarchal figure—the monarch. Drama, in other words, did more than reflect and anticipate the cultural crisis of the mid-century; it actually helped to create that crisis. It "reactivate[d] the scapegoat mechanism for the benefit of society" (Girard 1986, 140).

Other interesting parallels exist between the social events and the literary drama of this period. Images of the plague or disease in general permeate seventeenth-century tragedies (Shakespeare's *Hamlet* and *King Lear*, Beaumont's and Fletcher's *The Maid's Tragedy*, Middleton's *The Changeling*, and Ford's *'Tis Pity She's a Whore* are only a few examples). Interestingly, too, masques of death, variations perhaps on the medieval dances of death, which were said to have been inspired by the plagues of the fourteenth century, recur in these plays. In *Hamlet* and *'Tis Pity*, incest is a dominant issue; in *The Maid's Tragedy* and *The Changeling*, adultery precipitates the tragedy. The paradigm that Girard has provided thus opens up interesting possibilities when applied to a period of social crisis such as seventeenth-century England.

Generally, we might say that what Erich Neumann categorizes as the "scapegoat psychology" operated in seventeenth-century England. Neumann describes this psychology as a factor in all nations and social groups:

> The unconscious psychic conflicts of groups and masses find their most spectacular outlets in epidemic eruptions such as wars and revolutions, in which the unconscious forces which have accumulated in the collective get the upper hand and "made history." The *scapegoat psychology* is in fact ... an attempt to deal with these unconscious conflicts. This psychology shapes the inner life of nations as much as it does their international relationships. (1972, 43–44)

Seventeenth-century drama contributed to the activation of the scapegoat ritual by "making evil conscious," by solemnly parading evil (violence and melancholia, for example) before the eyes of the populace so that by this projection, society might be purified (Neumann 1972, 44).

But as with everything else in seventeenth-century tragedy, depictions of patriarchal power (or powerlessness) cannot be reduced arbitrarily to a matter of subversion and criticism. After all, parricide in these Stuart plays is ultimately depicted as unfortunate, disquieting, and disastrous. In *The Changeling*, probably written in 1622, Middleton's characterization of Vermandero as disempowered patriarch may reflect the actual state of things at court during this time. Historians have noted that during the last years of James's reign, Charles and Buckingham virtually governed the country and made all the important decisions. This was an ironic turn of events, considering James's general reliance on the concept of patriarchal authority; Middleton may simply be capturing the tension between Renaissance hierarchical theory and actual Stuart practice. In any case, what David Underdown notes about Puritanism in the seventeenth century applies equally to theater and its subversion of orthodox Renaissance patriarchal and monarchical theory: "In the long run mainstream Puritanism did as much to reinforce as to weaken patriarchal theory" (1985, 99). The break with paternalism reflected in many Stuart plays was part of a general social debate on the issue, but this debate, as Barry Reay argues, was "conducted within a conservative framework," which in the long run reinforced rather than weakened paternalism (1985, 20). Leonard Tennenhouse's recent statement that Jacobean tragedies "maintain the patriarchal principles despite extravagant assaults on the monarch's natural body" (1986, 124) holds true for most plays of the early Stuart era.

Even a treatment of drama as ritual heightens the ambiguities at the center of theater's relationship to its audience. It should be remembered that the English stage saw no drama during the years immediately preceding the events of 1649. The theaters were closed under the Puritans and remained so until 1660. Even though I have insisted that the deconsecration of monarchy in early Stuart drama provided the precedent for the actual decapitation of the monarch in 1649, it must be noted that there are inherent problems in so categorizing the power of early Stuart theater. In fact, it is equally likely that tragedy may actually have held regicide at bay. If, as Girard suggests, ritual and the scapegoat mechanism in particular function as a self-regulatory aspect of society, intended to keep violence in check by redirecting it into acceptable channels, then seventeenth-century tragedy (in which monarchy and patriarchy are frequently devalued) functioned in a manner similar to ritual. As Girard insists, "the objective of ritual is the proper reenactment of the surrogate victim mechanism; that is, to keep violence *outside* the community" (1972, 92). As long as collective violence against the patriarch was ritually reenacted in the theaters of the seventeenth-century, violence remained under control. Absence of such an emotional outlet caused by the closing of the theaters may indeed have added momentum to and perhaps even made possible the social violence of the English revolution. In other words, despite its criticism of monarchy, Stuart drama, through its increasingly graphic images of violence, may have had a ritualistic and cathartic effect on society.

Thus, in the final analysis, theatrical destruction of patriarchal power in the drama emerges as both subversive and revertive. The plays simultaneously depict and denounce parricide. Jean-Christophe Agnew has said: "Events repeatedly showed the capacity of ritual drama to reconcile social conflict, or ... to inflame it" (1986, 40). The particular power of seventeenth-century drama lies in its simultaneous ability to reconcile and inflame conflicts, to subvert and assert hierarchical and patriarchal theory. Social relationships yield to the historian not a coherent image, but a heightened awareness of the cultural contradictions inherent in society. The same might be said of drama as it registers, reflects, destroys, and partly even creates these sociocultural systems. Richard Burt's warning against arbitrarily reducing the power of

Stuart drama to either authority or subversion might be kept in mind here (1987, 552). Plays such as *The Changeling* and *'Tis Pity* explicitly reveal these contradiction; their ambiguous depictions of patriarchal authority emphasize the dialectical and complex interplay between theater and court and between literature and society in seventeenth-century England.

In these depictions of violence in the drama, we encounter a vivid representation of the protean nature of seventeenth-century society, a society "in which conventional signposts of social and individual identity had become mobile and manipulable reference points" (Agnew 1986, 9). And it is precisely this that made theatrical enterprise in the age a dangerous one; the early Stuart theater, probably more than other literary forms, exhibited a variety of heterogenous and even conflicting desires. It imitated, condemned, acknowledged, and ultimately celebrated the decentering of authority that was taking place everywhere in English society at this time. In a sense, theater, because of its protean allegiances, "became sufficiently threatening in these respects to bring on its own destruction in the mid-seventeenth century, both as an institution and as a figure of thought" (Agnew 12). In the end, however, not only radical reassessments but even "enlightened social conservatism ... proved to be potentially revolutionary" (Heinemann 1980, 17). Although John Denham, in the following lines, seems to be laying the blame for the closing of the theaters on the Puritans alone, his vision of monarchy and the theater as essentially related is entirely valid:

> They that would have no King, would have no Play:
> The Laurel and the Crown together went,
> Had the same Foes, and the same Banishment.
>
> (1928, 94)

As Lyssipius warns at the conclusion of *The Maid's Tragedy*, "on lustful kings / Unlook'd for sudden deaths from God are sent; / But curs'd is he that is their instrument" (5.3. 295–97). Drama in the seventeenth-century seems to have functioned as just such an "instrument." And when monarchy returned, considerably weakened, theater too returned, but stricter censorship caused the gradual shifting of political debates from the theatrical arena to the newly created and as yet less strictly defined genre of the novel.

4

Evil as Deviations from the Norm: Subversive Images from the "Little Tradition"

Drama and the "Little Tradition"

Peter Burke, in his influential study of popular culture in early modern Europe, distinguishes between what he describes as the "Great Tradition" and the "Little Tradition" (1978, 28–29). The former refers to the ideologies and activities shared by the patrician class, and the latter to such events as the carnival and the Riding or Skimmington indulged in by the plebian class. Of course, as Burke indicates, and as we have increasingly begun to recognize, the line between these two cultures in seventeenth-century Europe was not clear-cut, and much interaction occurred between the two groups. In England, the gentry often participated in charivaris, ridings, and morriscos, and, for the most part, the plebian class believed firmly in the patriarchal and hierarchical ideologies of their social superiors.

But the distinction that Burke draws is nevertheless useful and valid. Both patriarchal theory and the sanctification of the monarch's body, discussed earlier, were ideologies rooted within the Great Tradition. As we have seen, dramatists both reemphasized and subverted these ideological bases of the Great Tradition through their depictions of the fragmented human body and psyche in plays such as *The Changeling, 'Tis Pity She's a Whore,* and *The Revenger's Tragedy*. But they also used factors drawn from plebian culture, the Little Tradition, to subvert and reassert existing social systems. Carnival, the dance of death, which was related to carnival, the Skimmington or charivari, and other communal forms of festivities influenced seventeenth-century drama as much as theories about patriarchy and hierarchy. Many plays use images drawn from these primarily plebian activities to voice their discontent with

106

existing systems. Moreover, images of the world-upside-down and the woman-on-top, central to these plebian activities, dominate many Stuart plays.

Popular festivals such as the carnival and the Skimmington are relevant to seventeenth-century drama for several reasons. As historians have proven, drama in the period catered to a very wide audience comprising both the gentry and the plebian class. Dramatists themselves were often drawn from the lower ranks of society, but successful playwrights could reap the advantages of a social climate in which chances of upward mobility were increasing rapidly. In other words, dramatists themselves occupied a middle group somewhere between the patrician and the plebian class; their plays thus drew from both the Great and the Little traditions in seventeenth-century culture.

To talk about carnival and festival within Renaissance contexts, one must refer to Mikhail Bakhtin's treatment of the subject in his highly influential study of Rabelais. Bakhtin emphasizes the carnivalesque elements in Rabelais and rightly argues for the importance of carnival in medieval and Renaissance Europe. But as Tzvetan Todorov in his critique of Bakhtin points out,

> In his evocation of the two stylistic lines, turned into two forms of culture, Bahktin does not act like an impartial historian; his sympathies for ... "popular" culture are obvious." (1984, 79)

Todorov goes on to argue for the need to recognize the complex interlacing between these two cultures in the best artistic productions: "art and literature, forms of representation, will work better the truer they are, that is, the more they resemble their object, heterogenous human existence" (80). Carnival was, of course, an essential aspect of the Little tradition in medieval and Renaissance culture, but writers such as Rabelais and the seventeenth-century dramatists whom I will be discussing, were, as I have already suggested, products of *both* the Little and the Great traditions. Therefore, it is necessary to discuss the convergence of these two traditions in the works of the medieval and Renaissance periods; to privilege one over the other is necessarily to present a partial or distorted picture.

Thus, even the image of the human body, although rooted in monarchical ideology, could become a potent symbol on the stage only because of its general relevance to plebian society. In fact, the image of the human body was an integral aspect of many plebian affairs. Referring to the importance of the image in popular culture, Mikhail Bakhtin notes,

> This image of the body acquired a considerable and substantial development in the popular, festive, and spectacle forms of the Middle Ages: in the feast of the fool, in charivari and carnival, in the popular side show of Corpus Christi, in the diableries of the mystery plays, the *soties*, and farces. (1968, 27)

He contends that the image dominated this culture throughout the Middle Ages and the Renaissance; during the seventeenth-century, however, it watered down and was ultimately absorbed by the rationalistic movements of the eighteenth-century.

Thus, in Jacobean and Caroline stage reliance on the image of the human body, we have an instance of the level of interlacing between the dominant and subservient cultures of the period. Theater had patronal obligations, but it also catered to a large and heterogenous audience; even the distinction between private and public theaters was not a clear-cut one, and dramatists often wrote for both. In the image of the human body, dramatists found a symbol meaningful to both the patrician and the plebian classes. Most importantly, the image could simultaneously reassert traditional hierarchies even as it could convey obliquely but vividly the general dissatisfaction with the corrupt influence of the court.

Popular festivals prove relevant to the seventeenth century also because they share characteristics with scapegoat ceremonies (Welsford 1962, 8). In many cultures, festivals culminate with the sacrifice and ritual death of the mock king who perished in reality or pretense. In England, the ceremonial decapitation scene (of the mock king or queen) formed the climax of the sword dance and mummers' plays. But in these festivities, death was always followed by revivial; the theme of death and resurrection functioned as an essential part of these celebrations. In a play such as *The Revenger's Tragedy*, which concludes with a sacrifice performed through the course of a double masque (performed like the morrisco, by eight masked figures), we have a parody of the death and resurrection theme; death is followed here by more deaths as agents ultimately become victims of others' villainy. Vindice and his masquers mutilate bodies already murdered by four masquers. The first set of masquers are then attacked and murdered by the second, and shortly after, the latter, discovered in their villainy, also are condemned to die.

Dramatic invocation of the festive mode in scenes such as this may have activated the scapegoat mechanism that culminated in the "social" and public drama of 1649. The ceremonial decapitation of the monarch on the public social stage may be regarded as a culmination of these ritual festivities enacted in the Stuart theaters. Mary Dahl argues the "theatrical images of political killings" in twentieth-century drama "reveal themselves as analogous to the psychological and sociological mechanisms in ancient rite or sacrifice" (1987, 3). The claim may be even truer for seventeenth-century drama.

Another aspect of the festival, its temporary and "revolutionary" nature, is also important to the transformation of society effected by seventeenth-century drama. Festivals in medieval and Renaissance England were revolutionary in that they disrupted normal patterns, but they also reemphasized the order that had first existed. Thus, even as images drawn from the Great Tradition had reaffirmed the need for return to social harmony, so too images drawn from the Little Tradition often asserted rather than negated social order. Jacobean and Caroline drama thus may be characterized as simultaneously orthodox and revolutionary in its festivity. Leah Marcus, arguing for the revisionist and normative aspects of festival in seventeenth-century England, makes the point about the "politics" of mirth in the period (1986, 7). She explores this phenomenon especially in the court masques; as I hope to show, the simultaneously conservative and revolutionary aspects of celebration become apparent also in Stuart dramatic invocations of the festive mode.

Finally, dances often were a part of festivals; they were closely related to festivals in spirit and in their function as temporary lapses from normal social restraints. They are, therefore, equally important influences of the Little Tradition on the stage drama of the seventeenth-century.

Plebian culture—carnival, Skimmington, and popular dances and sports—thus exercised great influence over the drama and literature of early modern England. Only recently have we begun to recognize the extent of this influence.[1] But our forays into the complexities of seventeenth-century drama as it drew from both patrician and plebian culture seem only to have begun. The plays of this period ultimately elude any theoretical straitjacketing precisely because of their dual roots in patrician and plebian society, and the latter influence has for the most part been ignored until recently. Ultimately, Stuart drama only reinforces that "in the ideological horizon of any epoch and any social group, there is not one, but several mutually contradictory truths, not one but several diverging ideological paths" (Bakhtin and Medvedev 1978, 19).

I will first discuss ritualized and regularized events such as the carnival, festival, and dance of death and then deal with the Skimmington, an occasional rather than a regular event. Many plays, among them *'Tis Pity She's a Whore* and *The Maid's Tragedy*, invoke the spirit of festival and carnival; the morrisco, the sword dance, and the dance of death seem especially relevant to *The Revenger's Tragedy, The Changeling,* and *'Tis Pity She's a Whore*. Radical differences emerge in the manner in which the image of the woman-on-top, central to the Skimmington, is invoked in an Elizabethan comedy such as *The Taming of the Shrew* and a Jacobean tragedy such as *The Maid's Tragedy*. Dramatists depended on images of things gone awry drawn from these plebian activities to emphasize and reassert social norms. The corrective purpose of these images of topsy-turviness, these representations of carnivalesque deviations from desirable social norms in Stuart drama, makes them instances of evil in the Durkheimian sense.

Festival and Tragedy

The festive nature of the comedies of the sixteenth and seventeenth centuries has long been acknowledged. As C. L. Barber points out in his seminal study, many of Shakespeare's comedies function as festivals in which all bounds are broken and disorder reigns through the major part of the plays. This extreme chaos, however, serves to heighten the need for order in society, and thus asserts and vindicates the order to which society returns at the end of the play. The notion of festival might be extended to the best tragedies of the seventeenth century; such a claim might seem radical, but the violence in many Jacobean and Caroline plays can be explained in terms of the cultural phenomenon of the "festival."[2]

Rene Girard points out that festivals exist in all societies in some form or another, and that they always retain a highly ritualistic character (1972, 119). Elizabethan and Stuart revenge plays, in which the protagonists finally triumph in their private revenge, may be regarded as one such form of festival. Despite Elizabethan taboos against private revenge, the plays could enact and re-enact successful revenge within the closed and artificial realm of the theater, within the confines of ritual spectacle or "festival." "The fundamental purpose of the festival," Girard argues, "is to set the stage for a sacrificial act that marks at once the climax and termination of the festivities" (119); the protagonists' success, therefore, is necessarily accompanied by their own death at the end of the revenge plays, at the close of the spectacle. Girard defines festival as a social phenomenon in which "family and social hierarchies are temporarily suppressed or inverted" (119). Thus, for example, children determine the course of events while fathers remain silent in *The Changeling, The Maid's Revenge,* and *'Tis Pity,* or women govern their husbands in *Macbeth, The Maid's Tragedy,* and *Women Beware Women*. Girard posits that "for the duration of the festival unnatural acts and outrageous behavior are permitted, even encouraged" (119). Thus in *'Tis Pity,* in which familial and social transgression in the form of incest verges on celebration, we have an intense example of the carnivalesque-festive genre. The intensely festive nature of this play emerges in radical differences between its treatment of incest and earlier depictions of the subject.

Such intense festive liberation was, of course, an essential aspect of carnival celebrations, which were sanctioned extremes in riotous merrymaking before men submitted to the rigors of Lent. And the element of the carnivalesque, as many writers have pointed out, was "surprisingly strong in early modern England" (Reay 1985, 8). The origin of the practice has been a subject of much speculation, but many regard carnival as a version of the Roman saturnalia recontextualized within a strictly Christian setting. At any rate, during carnival disorder reigned and traditional hierarchies were either ignored or inverted. Wherever it occurs, carnival, as Umberto Eco argues, is a time

> when the upside down world has become the norm. Carnival is revolution (or revolution is carnival): kings are decapitated (that is, lowered, made inferior) and the crowd is crowned. (1984, 3)

In essence, the festivity of carnival in seventeenth-century England was the converse of the court masque. While the masque elevated the persons to whom it paid homage by raising them to the stature of the gods, a "downward movement" and debunking occurred during carnival, when everything was "desanctified and made common" (Bristol 1985, 22–23).

A similar tendency to desanctify and make common does characterize the *dramatized* masques in many Jacobean and Caroline plays such as *The Maid's Tragedy* and *The Revenger's Tragedy*. These dramatized masques draw on the court tradition of eulogy, but at the same time, they mock the court form by incorporating aspects of the carnival. The persons for whom the masque is being performed in these plays become victims of the masquers' desire for revenge and are attacked or killed at the culmination of the performance. These dramatic masques are carnivalesque and subversive celebrations, recognizable parodies of the court masques from which they draw their name.[3] Although court audiences differed radically from those at the theaters therefore, these dramatized masques deserve to be seen within the context of the court form whose title and mode they appropriated so blatantly.

A final aspect of the carnival that Bakhtin ignores, and which proves relevant to my concept of tragedy as festival, is its constant potential for violence. As Bakhtin argues, carnival was festival, and the carnivalesque was linked with the comic, with laughter. But there was another side to carnival; it also involved a liking for "dismal and macabre sensations" (Rector 1984, 39). The dance of death and grotesque images related to bodily decay were often part of carnival celebrations. Like most festivals, carnival was always potentially violent; gradually, the traces of violence inherent in the celebratory and anarchic tone of carnival seem to have disappeared, but those who participated in carnival in medieval and Renaissance Europe must surely have been aware of its underlying menace. Festival could even provide a cover for violence. For example, in the early fifteenth century, a group of English courtiers devised a Twelfth Night mumming play supposedly to amuse King Henry IV, but actually to stage his assassination. The plot was discovered and those involved were punished, but the event suggests the inherent danger of festival as a cover for covert and violent activities (Christian 1966, 32). The inherent dangers of extreme festivity must have been universally recognized in Europe; the famous incidents at Romans in the sixteenth century, documented recently by Le Roy Ladurie, provide yet another example of violent carnival festivities.

A movie of the sixties, *Black Orpheus*, captures this dual mood of carnival, its festive and its violent aspects, most vividly. A carnival provides the background for this retelling of the Orpheus and Eurydice story, and the entire movie is carnivalesque, comic, and anarchic in spirit. The celebration, however, culminates in both violence and restoration; Eurydice is carried away by a figure dressed as a skeleton and representing death, while Orpheus, after a futile attempt to recover her, is stoned by the women of the town who had previously desired him. The movie does not, however, culminate with his violent death as he falls down a cliff with Eurydice in his arms. Instead, after this event, two village boys play on Orpheus's guitar as they reverse the carnival spirit of the preceding scenes and herald the dawn. Something of this mood of festivity and danger characterizes the carnivalesque tragedies of the early Stuart eras, which explore the concept of evil as topsy-turviness in the familial, social, and political worlds.

Carnival and the Dance of Death

Certain aspects that Bakhtin denotes as basic to carnival are relevant to a large number of Jacobean and Caroline tragedies. I will now concentrate especially on two factors: depictions of the grotesque and reliance on images of games.

Bakhtin regards "the flowering of grotesque realism," a basic element in carnival festivity, as reaching its summit in the Renaissance. Jacobean and Caroline plays offer a vast array of images drawn from the realistic grotesque. Bakhtin's unique definition of the term *grotesque* provides a comprehensive account of certain aspects of popular festivity that have for the most part been ignored by critics. The most important characteristic of the grotesque to Bakhtin is its essential incompleteness of being; in medieval and Renaissance depictions of the grotesque,

> there was no longer the movement of finished forms, vegetable or animal, in a finished and stable world; instead the inner movement of being itself was expressed in the passing of one form into the other, in the ever incomplete character of being. (*Rabelais* 1968, 32)

In the grotesque world of continuous change, death loses all its tragic and terrifying overtones (Bakhtin 407). Critics have often noted that Jacobean and Caroline dramatists depict death thus; characters such as De Flores and Giovanni embrace death with joy and regard it only as yet another state of being to be savored for joys similar to those offered by life. Earlier critics often characterized these depictions as instances of moral decadence in seventeenth-century drama; others have attributed Stuart attitudes toward death to the evolution of the baroque movement in the seventeenth century.[4] They may as easily have been the legacies of popular culture, of such activities as the carnival.

The grotesque world also juxtaposes images of life and death; feasting and disease coexist. Bakhtin regards feasting and drinking as images closely interwoven with images of the grotesque body, because both represent the body in change. Almost all the major Stuart tragedies take place in the midst of celebrations; bodies are dismembered even while others indulge in feasting, drinking, or sex.

Middleton's *The Witch* (ca. 1609) opens with a wedding during which the Duke toasts the bride and groom in a skull that is then passed around among the guests. In *The Revenger's Tragedy*, Vindice pins the Duke's tongue down with his dagger as they witness the incestuous sexual exchanges between the Duchess and her step-son, the "bastard." In *The Maid's Tragedy*, Evadne runs a dagger through the king's body while he assumes that she is indulging in love play and eagerly awaits her next move. In *'Tis Pity She's a Whore*, Giovanni is shown in bed with his pregnant sister, whom he then murders, and after digging out her heart, he carries it on his dagger to Soranzo, his sister's husband, and guests in the middle of their feast. The announcement with which he enters shocks more than his manner:

> You came to feast my lords, with danity fare;
> I came to feast too, but I digg'd for food
> In a much richer mine than gold or stone
> Of any value balanc'd; 'tis a heart,
> A heart, my lords, in which is mine entomb'd.

(5.6. 95)

In *Women Beware Women*, a series of murders takes place in the midst of celebrations; the masque presented to the Duke and Bianca at their wedding leaves a number of dead bodies on the stage, but the duke and his friends mistake people's deaths for ecstatic and drunken celebration. When Livia throws flaming gold upon Isabella, thus killing her, Febritio, Isabella's father, explains her fall to the concerned duke thus:

> As over-joyed belike.
> Too much prosperity overjoys us all,
> And she has her lapful it seems, my lord.

(5.2. 120–23)

By the end of the nuptial ceremonies, the duke and Bianca are themselves murdered. Ironically, in an earlier scene, Bianca summarized this natural juxtaposition of death and celebration as she noted, "In times of sports death may steal in securely" (5.1. 63). In a similar scene in Fletcher's Roman tragedy, *Valentinian*, Eudoxia murders Maximus, whom she is to marry, in the midst of a banquet and a dance presentation, and at first those present mistake his dying for drunkenness. In Shirley's *The Cardinal*, the Cardinal is stabbed as he tries to rape the Duchess; in a similar scene in *The Bloody Banquet*, the Queen shoots her secret lover, Tymethes, during one of their secret encounters. In all these plays, copulation, death, and feasting occur simultaneously.

Bakhtin's description of the grotesque body also provides a context in which several figures in Jacobean and Caroline drama might be viewed:

> The grotesque body ... is a body in the act of becoming. It is never finished, never completed; it is continually built, created, and creates and builds another body. ... This is why the essential role belongs to those parts of the grotesque body in which it outgrows its own self, transgressing its own body: the bowels and the phallus. These two areas play the leading role in the grotesque image ... This is why in the main events in the life of the grotesque body, the acts of the bodily drama, take place in this sphere. Eating, drinking, defecation, and other elimination ... as well as copulation, pregnancy, dismemberment, swallowing up by another body—all these acts are performed on the confines of the body and the outer world, or on the confines of the old and the new body. In all these events the beginning and the end of life are closely linked and interwoven. (1978, 317)

In Ford's Giovanni and Anabella in *'Tis Pity*, we have just such representations of the grotesque body. Our initial vision of them as complete beings proves wrong in the course of the play, and they transform gradually into the carnival-grotesque. The phallus, because of Giovanni's incestuous relationship with his sister, and the womb, because of Anabella's consequent pregnancy, perform primary functions in the play. In the middle sections of the play, we have only fragmented visions of Giovanni and Anabella: Giovanni's initial (and seemingly complete) role as brother has changed to that of lover and father; Anabella's seeming completeness also has been likewise split through her pregnancy. Giovanni draws his sister into villainy, and we tend to view Anabella as a victim and Giovanni as the initiator of incest. Metaphorically, this enticement may be regarded as a swallowing of body by body; Anabella's pregnancy, which precipitates much of the later action, emphasizes the opposite function, the evolution of body from body.

Evadne, Amintor's wife, in Beaumont's and Fletcher's *The Maid's Tragedy* transforms, like Anabella, from seeming completeness into the carnival-grotesque body. The metaphoric representation of bodies swallowing bodies recurs in this play: the king draws Evadne into immorality by instigating their secret relationship and by arranging her subsequent marriage to Amintor, a nobleman, who discovers the truth about his wife only after their marriage; Evadne, by marrying Amintor to hide her relationship with the king and to find a legal father for her child, forces Amintor into silent acquiescence in the matter, and thus draws him into immorality; Amintor confides in Melantius, his friend and Evadne's brother, who has just returned from the wars to celebrate his sister's wedding, and thus provokes Melantius's wrath and precipitates revenge; and Melantius forces Diphilus, his weak and easily manipulated brother, to become an accomplice in his revenging actions. As in *'Tis Pity*, the phallus and the womb dominate our impressions of the play through the adulterous relationship between the king and Evadne, and through Evadne's pregnancy, which we are told about at the very beginning of the tragedy.

Similarly, Vittoria Corombona, another Jacobean heroine, suggests the carnival-grotesque by her designation as the "white devil" in Webster's tragedy: she is both angel and devil at once. Lady Macbeth in *Macbeth*, Bianca in *Women Beware Women*, and Beatrice-Joanna in *The Changeling* provide other vivid examples of the carnival-grotesque on the Stuart stage; however, I will reserve discussion of some of these female-male grotesques to a later section in this chapter.

In *The Bloody Banquet*, however, we have a vividly literal image of body swallowing body. The young queen of the tyrant, Armatrites, despite jealous guarding by her husband, manages secretly to meet with the handsome and lustful Tymethes, son to the old king who has been deposed by Armatrites. Fearing that Tymethes will boast about his conquest of her to his male friends, the queen takes care to meet him in veils so that her identity might be withheld. During one of their meetings, Tymethes manages to discover her identity, for which she murders him. The young queen's secret, however, has already been revealed to her husband, who arrives to discover her act of murder. He punishes her by making her eat Tymethes's flesh. The last scene of the play (on which the play is titled) presents a generous banquet given by Armatrites to the old king and his followers who have arrived at court disguised as pilgrims. Tymethes's bloody flesh is served in his skull to the queen, who consumes the flesh even while the others, including Tymethes's father, feast. And the tyrant king derives much vicarious pleasure from witnessing this macabre cannibalism: "The Letcher must be swallowed rib by rib, / His fleshe is sweete, it melts and goes down merrily" (5.2. 1976–78). The tragedy visibly relates feasting, bodily decay, aduleterous sex, and death in this vividly dramatic concluding scene.

Bakhtin also argues that "the theme of madness is inherent to all grotesque forms" (1978, 39); but he sees madness in folk grotesque as entirely liberating and festive:

> In folk grotesque, madness is a gay parody of official reason, of the narrow seriousness of "official" truth. It is a festive madness. In Romantic grotesque, on the other hand, madness acquires a somber, tragic aspect of individual isolation. (1978, 39)

But folk grotesque, like carnival in general of which it is a part, was likely to have been inherently dualistic and simultaneously suggestive both of the liberating and the tragic aspects of madness.

The dual moods of festivity and danger, essential aspects of folk festival forms such as the carnival, surface also in most Stuart depictions of madness. Hamlet's madness offers at once a bold travesty of the official attitude (as represented by Claudius's reaction of banishing him), and an instance of "tragic isolation" (as represented by his frequent internal musings to which the audience alone are privy). Precisely this ambivalence makes his "madness" fascinating. The dual nature of madness, its liberating and its threatening aspects, is captured most vividly in *The Changeling*. A stint in the madhouse during which Antonio and Franciscus single-mindedly pursue Isabella, ultimately liberates them from their fixation; but De Flores's similar pursuit of Beatrice-Joanna (which resembles the madness of the other characters in its fixed nature) proves fatal to him and to Beatrice-Joanna. The contrast between liberating and grotesque madness is emphasized also in *The Cardinal*. Alvarez's murder is preceded by the servants' preparation for a play in honor of his wedding to the duchess. In the comic scene, the "mute" makes several references to losing his head, that is, the headpiece he should wear in the performance. Carnival celebrations often culminated with the decapitation of the central character, and this scene is followed by Alvarez's murder and the duchess' subsequent metaphoric loss of her head, her madness. The references in the underplot to losing the head and the duchess' madness a few scenes later appear finally as comic and tragic variations on a single theme.

Bakhtin also argues for the importance of games in the carnivalesque genre and insists that "games are also closely related to time and to the future." He goes on to comment on the general significance of this imagery:

> It is needless to dwell on the roots of the imagery representing feasts and games. What is important is not their generic relationship but their *related meaning*. ... There was in those days [Rabelais's time] a vivid awareness of the universalism of this imagery, of its link with time and the future, destiny, and political power. ... The images of games were seen as a condensed formula of life and of the historic process: fortune, misfortune, gain and loss, crowning and uncrowning. Life was represented as a miniature play. (1978, 235)[5]

This healthy attitude toward games in the Renaissance later underwent a change when, "having been absorbed by the sphere of private life, the images of games lost their universal relationship and were deprived of the meaning they formerly conveyed" (Bakhtin 1968, 236). The transition that Bakhtin sees in sixteenth-century France seems to occur in England a century later. The tensions that resulted in this change are apparent in the controversies that raged throughout James's and Charles I's reigns regarding the importance of games. In his *Declaration of Sports* (1617), James supported popular pastimes as necessary outlets for group tensions; he regarded them as activities that ensured rather than disrupted communal order. If people could not engage in healthy and lawful sports, they would "in place thereof" set up "filthy tiplings and drunkennesse" which would in turn breed "a number of idle and discontented speaches in their Ale-houses" (*Declaration* 1981, 195). The *Declaration* was reprinted in 1633 by Charles with a new preamble and a directive drawn from the concluding paragraph in James's work, but by this time the controversy over sports had increased in intensity. On 13 November, the House of Commons issued an order that

> The Book concerning Injoining and Tolerating of Sports upon the Sabbath-Day be forthwith burnt by the Hands of the common Hangman, in the usual places. (quoted by Craigie 1981, 229)

This was followed by several more instances in which the book was ordered to be burnt.[6] The controversy over sports culminated finally during Cromwell's rule in laws which banned many of the traditional pastimes that had accompanied such plebian affairs as Shrove Tuesday. This change in public attitudes toward games, which seems to have occurred in England during the seventeenth century, took place simultaneously with changes in the sociopolitical structure.

But in plays of the Stuart era, we encounter images of games in their carnivalesque form, as "condensed formulae of life."

Middleton's *The Changeling* is an expanded version of barley-break, a popular sport of the time; chess, a primarily patrician sport, is reduced to carnivalesque travesty and becomes a metaphor for central action in his *Women Beware Women* and in his political satire, *A Game at Chess*. Ironically, Middleton, the "Puritan's favourite dramatist," seems to have used the metaphor of games frequently to illumine the central actions of his plays.

Although little is known about how it was actually played, barley-break or the "Last Couple in Hell" was a popular sport in England during the sixteenth and seventeenth centuries. Iona and Peter Opie suggest that it was played by six players, three boys and three girls, who divided into couples. The couples took three different positions, two pairs going to either end of the ground, and one pair taking the middle position known as hell. The two pairs on the ends would then attempt to "break" and exchange partners, while the pair in the middle tried to intercept them and draw them into "hell." The catchers in the middle could not catch unless they were joined together, and the outside players were safe once they linked with their new partners. After a few such "breaks," during which positions changed, the couple that ended in the middle became "the Last Couple in Hell" (1969, 129–30). *The Changeling* seems to have been envisioned as a variation on this game.

References to barley-break occur twice in the play, first in the subplot by a Madman and then in the concluding scene by De Flores; "I coupled with your mate at barley-break," he tells Alsemero shortly before he dies. And the game seems to provide an apt metaphor for the actions in the play. Both the main plot and the underplot of the play involve adulterous seduction. Three men and three women participate: Beatrice-Joanna, Diaphanta, and Isabella, Alsemero, De Flores, and Alibius.[7] The play opens with Beatrice-Joanna's love for Alsemero and thus establishes them as the first couple; but Beatrice-Joanna changes places shortly after with Diaphanta: Beatrice-Joanna couples with her servant, De Flores, while Diaphanta, her maid, couples with Alsemero. Later (1.2.), what appears at first to be a vivid representation of hell, the madhouse, turns out to be a sanctuary from evil, because the characters who enter it are converted and learn the error of their ways. On the other hand, Vermandero's stately castle ensnares its victims; Alonso is murdered in its dungeons, and Alsemero becomes a victim of the villainies initiated by De Flores and Beatrice-Joanna. The last scene establishes that Beatrice-Joanna and her accomplice, De Flores, the central figures in the tragedy, having held fast together, are the "Last Couple in Hell." They are also versions of

"Love" and "Folly," the characteristics John Suckling some years later places in Hell in his lyrical account of barley-break:

> Love, Reason, Hate, did once bespeak
> Three mates to play at Barley-break;
> Love, Folly took; and Reason Fancy;
> And Hate consorts with Pride; so dance they:
> Love coupled last, and so it fell
> That Love and Folly were in hell.
>
> They break, and Love would Reason meet,
> But Hate was nimbler on her feet;
> Fancy looks for Pride, and thither
> Hyes, and they two hug together:
> Yet this new coupling still doth tell
> That Love and Folly were in hell.
>
> The rest do break again, and Pride
> Hath now got Reason on her side;
> Hate and Fancy meet, and stand
> Untouch'd by Love in Folly's hand:
> Folly was dull, but Love ran well,
> So Love and Folly were in hell.
>
> (1971, 18–19)

In fact, references to several games and popular sports—bull and bear-baiting, morris dancing, push-pin—occur in *The Changeling*. These together with images of copulation and defecation, which occur especially in the underplot, emphasize the play's links with the carnivalesque genre.

Similarly, the game of chess provides the metaphor for a central event in *Women Beware Women*. The play represents the rape and subsequent corruption by the Duke of Florence of the initially chaste Bianca during her husband Leantio's absence from the town. Bianca's rape occurs during a chess game initiated by Lady Livia (who is in collusion with the duke) to divert the attention of Bianca's mother-in-law, left by Leantio to watch over his wife during his absence. The patrician and supposedly intellectual game of chess is Leantio's mother's favorite pastime, and yet the match between her and Livia, which Livia wins easily, only emphasizes the mother's stupidity and obtuseness. The "downward movement" or carnivalesque debunking that the game of chess receives in the play resembles Stuart dramatic travesty of the lofty masque.

Scenes of the chess game are interposed among ones in which the duke courts Bianca, and thus Middleton emphasizes the close relationship between the two. As the "black king makes all the haste he can" on the board, we are to envision the duke's successful advances. The game reaches its most intense point a few minutes later; "The game's even at the best now: you may see, / Widow, how all things draw to an end," Livia notes, and Bianca walks onto the stage shortly after, now converted to adultery with the Duke:

> I've made bold now,
> I thank my treachery; sin and I am acquainted,
> No couple greater.
>
> (2.2. 339–41)

Bianca's rape by the duke and her conversion almost immediately from innocence to immorality resembles Beatrice-Joanna's similar relationship with De Flores and subsequent transformation in the earlier tragedy. Thus the chess game between Livia and the mother is more than a device calculated to divert the mother while the duke rapes her daughter; it functions as a systematic metaphor for the cunning manipulation of subjects by those in power. But even more important, the game has undergone carnivalesque travesty: chess becomes not an intellectual pastime but its very opposite—a means of physical and sexual manipulation. And women, traditionally associated with nurturing and protection, become, during this travesty, agents of destruction and corruption instead. Thus, in Middleton's major tradgedies, the carnivalesque genre surfaces through references to games that frequently function as metaphors for the plays's central actions of adultery, rape, and murder.

'Tis Pity She's a Whore, written later in the Stuart period, may be regarded as even more wholly festive and carnivalesque in spirit; the play draws the audience into its festive anarchy only to reassert the need for order at the end. This manipulation of our emotions, the play's ability to draw us into participating in or condoning its actions, makes it both intellectually exciting and emotionally disturbing. As Donald Anderson points out, the play has "explosive energy at the beginning and maintains it whenever the central plot ... holds the stage" (1986, 37). A remark that the narrator makes in Charles Maturin's gothic novel of the nineteenth century, *Melmoth the Wanderer*, seems to me to offer a succinct summary of the effects of the language and action in Ford's play: "The drama of terror has the irresistible power of converting its audience into its victims" (1977, 345).

In fact, *'Tis Pity* is festive in the extreme; to a degree at least, it is a celebration "in which sexual proximity is not only tolerated but prescribed or in which incest becomes the required practice" (Girard *Violence* 119). Despite our moral compunctions about incest, while we listen to Giovanni, we are often drawn by the rhetoric of his language, by the intensity of his emotions. His words echo not only conventional protestations of love, but also the language of great lovers such as Romeo, Othello, and Mark Anthony. Giovanni, in fact, dies declaring to his father and the citizens of Parma that this cruel love has been noble and holy:

> Here I swear
> By all that you call sacred, by the love
> I bore my Anabella whilst she lived,
> These hands have from her bosom ripped her
> heart.
>
> (5.6. 57–60)

And there is ample evidence that Anabella's conversion is only half-hearted; after all, we see her last in bed with Giovanni. Because of its characterization of love as noble and elevating, the play has frequently been compared with some of Shakespeare's tragedies, especially *Romeo and Juliet*. But in this play the love is incestuous, and, unlike in earlier depictions of incest, no divine intervention occurs to label the act as a moral violation as in *Pericles*, and at no point do the characters express any genuine regret, as in *A King and No King*.

This dual effect of the play, both to horrify and fascinate, is particularly evident in the concluding and much discussed scene in which Giovanni is killed. Two important events take place in this scene: Giovanni, with obvious disquieting relish, first presents Anabella's heart on a dagger to Soranzo and other noblemen, including the Cardinal and his father, while they are in the middle of a feast. This is followed by an attack of banditti, against whom Giovanni struggles, and is finally killed. His first action evokes horror, although Giovanni seems to present it as an act of valor. His suicidal self-defense seems also to have been intended as heroic. We see Giovanni earlier preparing himself mentally for the act:

> Shrink not, courageous hand, stand up, my heart,
> And boldly act my last and greater part.
>
> (5.6. 104–5)

In other words, his greater and final act of valor after killing his sister is to commit virtual suicide. Like his actions throughout, his death evokes a mixed response and is only partially heroic, because he is cheated of the valiant act by the attack of the banditti. This thwarted suicide, like everything else in the play, reveals the constant tension between conception and actual action.[8]

A similar tension exists between action and speech in this scene. Through rhetoric, Giovanni woos us into considering his dilemma sympathetically, but the violence of his actions (a violence directed against father, sister, those present on stage, and the audience) evokes horror and negates any sympathy we may have felt. In other words, the dilemma in which the central characters (Giovanni and Anabella) are involved throughout the play, a dilemma which is caused by their simultaneous desire to stop at and to transcend all social barriers, is similar to our own emotional responses to the play.

Contrary to being decadent in comparison to earlier plays, as early critics of Ford's tragedies insisted, Ford's play thus affords an instance of carnival liberation at its most intense. Recent criticism of Ford, who seems to be suddenly in the forefront of critical interest, has sought to modify earlier claims of decadence, and to establish that the context of the Caroline age differed greatly from the Jacobean, and that the drama reflects this difference.[9] But I do not wish merely to emphasize the difference in social contexts between Jacobean and Caroline England; I believe, like Artaud, that, "if one is to look for an example of total freedom in rebellion, Ford's *'Tis Pity She's a Whore* provides it" (1970, 20). I believe, moreover, that the intertextuality between Ford's plays and the earlier drama makes his best tragedies the most intensely individual and the richest plays of the Caroline age. In Ford's play we encounter a total deconstruction of all systems that had hitherto fascinated the Jacobean audience. The most striking factor about Ford's tragedy is our inability to sympathize with Giovanni or Anabella as we had done with earlier protagonists. The issues are more muddied and more complicated in *'Tis Pity* than in any previous plays. In effect, therefore, Ford's play differs markedly from other plays of the period; it evokes a heightened sense of carnival and festival. As I hope to show, this heightened festivity functions as a central ingredient in the liberating effects of Stuart tragedy.

The festive combination of horror and fascination is not exclusive to Ford, of course. We can assume that spectacles of torture and punishment on the stage probably provoked a response not unlike that which Nashe describes in *The Unfortunate Traveller* in a crowd eager to witness a public execution:

Herwith, all the people, outragiously incensed, with one conjoined outcry yelled mainly: "Away with him, away with him! Executioner, torture him! Tear him, or we will tear thee in pieces if thou spare him!

The executioner needed no exhortation herunto ... At the first chop with his wood-knife would he fish for a man's heart, and fetch it out as easily as a plum from the bottom of a porredge-pot. He would cracke neckes as fast as a cooke cracks eggs. ... Bravely did he drum on this Cutwolfe's bones, not breaking them outright, but, like a saddler knocking in of tacks, jarring on them quaveringly with his hammer a great while together. ... no limb of his but was lingeringly splinter'd in shivers. (1954, 327)

The tone of festive savagery, marked by the use of culinary images to describe violence, by the celebratory drumming on the bones, and by the relished prolonging of the torture, recalls the juxtaposition of feasting and death, festive celebration and bodily decay, in many Stuart plays.

The power to shock, disturb, and fascinate, central to the carnival-grotesque, dominates another image related to carnival, and of considerable importance in seventeenth-century drama—that of the dance of death or the dance macabre. Monica Rector suggests that "medieval macabre dances" were an aspect of carnival celebrations (1984, 39). Fascination with this theme is said to have originated during the fourteenth century in France as a direct result of the plague; the earliest recorded date of the dance of death is slightly before 1376 (Kurtz 1939, 178). Records indicate the performance of a masque of death during Edward VI's reign. The sudden arrival and departure of the plague, the vast numbers killed by it unexpectedly, and its undiscriminating nature perhaps inspired the image. Popular superstitions about the midnight dancing of the dead in graveyards (we might recall that the superstition is referred to in *Hamlet*) may have added validity to artistic representations of the image. (Warthin 1931, 5).

But the sense of dance does not seem to have been central to all representations of the dance macabre. James Clark argues that

In the Middle Ages, the word "dance" was often used figuratively. The dance is a symbol of death, nothing more. Poet and artist intended to portray in allegorical form the inevitability of death and the equality of all men in death. (1950, 111)

Some critics even surmise paradoxically that the motif of dancing entered the dance of death only later (J. Clark 1950, 99; Spinrad 1987, 6). "Dance" seems to have signified only advent, journey, or presence, and some pictures of the dance of death do not involve any suggestions of dancing. Thus, "dance of death" or "the dance macabre" functioned as a "a generic term for dancing skeletons as well as pictorial representations, murals, broadsides, and single prints" (Eichenberg 1983, 14). The use of dialogue seems even to have been central in many representations. The pictures of the dance macabre at St. Paul's, for example, included dialogue. John Stowe in his chronicle describes their creation:

> John Carpenter, town-clerk of London in the reign of Henry the Fifth, caused with great expense to be curiously painted upon board, about the north cloister of Paule's a monument of death leading all Estates, with the speeches of Death and answer of every state. (1945, 42)

John Lydgate, the poet, and Sir Thomas More also saw the same monument, which was destroyed some time later.[10]

The dialogue in these so-called dances of death may have had its origin in Lucian's representation of death in *The Dialogues of the Dead*, a work known to the seventeenth century. Lucian is often cited as a probable source for images of death in the Toten Tanz or Dance Macabre in the Middle Ages and the Renaissance (Kurtz 1939, 9). His work is important in considerations of the theme in the seventeenth century because it introduces death, not within the context of the dance as many medieval European depictions did, but within the dramatic context of the dailogue. Another source that unites the sense of theater with the image of death is Cervantes's *Don Quixote*, also popular in seventeenth-century England. During one of his adventures, Don Quixote encounters a group of strolling players who are playing *The Parliament of Death* (1930, 509–11). Thus, the general transference of the image from dance to the theatrical arena had classical and Renaissance precedents.

The relationship between the plague and a general fascination with the image may be crucial. The dance of death probably reemerged as a popular social phenomenon in seventeenth-century England during the plague years, and dramatists may have capitalized on this general interest. Interestingly, Artaud draws a quite definite connection between effective theater and the plague. Does the frenetic energy and the highly experimental nature of seventeenth-century drama have any connection with the phenomenon of the plague that did after all begin (1604), demarcate (1625), and terminate (1665) the age? Does the plague have anything to do with the activation of the scapegoat mechanism in the period? It was customary to draw connections between the plague and the arrival of a new monarch and to regard the coincidence of their occurrence (in both 1603 and 1625) as an evil premonition. The delight of the Cavaliers at the plague of 1654 soon after Cromwell became Protector, noted by Anthony Wood, takes on new relevance in this context (Slack 1985, 19). An interesting relationship between mass epidemics and the scapegoat psychology is drawn by Erich Neumann: "Often the outbreak of mass epidemics and the scapegoat psychology are interconnected psychological reactions which stem from a single unconscious conflict" (1972, 44). I would like to suggest that a tantalizing connection links the following apparently discrete factors in seventeenth-century England: the two Stuart rules, the several instances of the plague, dramatic fascination with the dance of death, and the scapegoat psychology that culminated in the events of 1649. In a society which drew elaborate connections between the conduct of the monarch and the social situation, these apparently discrete factors coalesced to convey a distinct sense of things gone awry.

The dance of death shares with festivals in general its dual mood of celebration (of death's impartial disregard of the social importance of its victims) and horror (at the degree of bodily decay and erosion it could cause). What seems to us a bewildering conjunction of opposite feelings (fascination and horror) seems to have been an inherent aspect of the image. Sir Thomas More remarks on this dual response as he describes the drawings at St. Paul's:

> We were never so greatly moved by the beholding of the Dance of Death pictured in Paul's, as we shall feel ourselves stirred and altered by the feeling of that imagination in our hearts. And no marvel. For those pictures express only the loathly figure of our dead, bony bodies, bitten away the flesh; which though it be ugly to behold, yet neither the light thereof, nor the sight of all the dead heads in the charnel house, nor the apparition of a very ghost, is half so grisly as the deep conceived fantasy of death in his nature, by the lively imagination graven in thine own heart. (I:467–68).

"The phenomenon of grim humor," the mood of comedy and horror, seems also to have been "intrinsic to the dance of death" (Kurtz 1939, 9). The satiric-comic overtones of literary representations of the dance have received much attention recently (Spinrad 1987, 21). The combination of horror and comedy also surfaces in works about the plague. Thomas Dekker's "The Wonderfull Yeare," written after the plague of 1603, for example, is essentially comic in temper. On the one hand, Dekker represents the power of death by describing it as an invading conqueror, but the work combines awe and humor, fascination and parody:

> Imagine then that all this while, Death (like a Spanish Laeger, or rather like stalkihng *Tamburlaine*) hath pitcht his tents, (being nothing but a heape of winding sheetes tackt together) in the sinfully-polluted Suburbes: the Plague is Muster-maister and Marshall of the field: Burning, Feauers, Boyles, Blaines, and Carbuncles, the Leaders, Lieutenants, Serients, and Corporalls: the maine Army consiting (like Dunkirke) of a mingle-mangle, viz. dumpish Mourners, merry Sextons, hungry Coffin-sellers, scrubbing Bearers, and nast Graue-makers: but indeed they are the Pioneers of the Campe, they are imployed onely (like Moles) in casting vp of earth and digging of trenches; Feare and Trembling (the two Catch-polles of Death) arrest eueryone. (1925, 31–32)

In the passage just cited, Dekker simultaneously undercuts and glorifies the power of death. This dual tone holds true for the entire work; Dekker's account consists of a variety of little tales. Some are comic, such as the one about the housewife, who believing that she was on her death bed, confessed her many affairs to her husband, and then recovered of the plague. Some are horrifying, such as the one about the dying man thrown into a pit with corpses only to be heard groaning three days later. Dekker's description, which combines comedy and horror, suggests the image of the grinning skeleton, the figure of death in the dance macabre (McGhee 1987, 77).

This image also is invoked in Webster's *The White Devil* in the scene in which the Duke of Brachiano, Vittoria Corombona's lover, dies. Poisoned and dying, he bursts into laughter as he surveys those around him, and not surprisingly, when he sees Vittoria, his thoughts turn to copulation:

> Ha, ha, ha. Her hair is sprinkled with arras powder,
> That makes her look as if she had sinn'd in pastry.
>
> (5.3. 118–19)

He becomes a version of the grinning skeleton in the dance macabre, and those around perceive him as one who might draw their lives from them. Flamineo, for example, is troubled by his talk:

> I do not like that he names me so often,
> Especially on's death-bed: 'tis a sign
> I shall not live long: see he's near his end.
>
> (5.3. 127–29)

The scene effectively combines comedy and menace.

The Tyrant's thoughts at the end of the *Bloody Banquet*, when he is confronted with death, similarly turn to copulation. He stabs his adulterous queen and gloats in the act that prevented further adultery between her and his murderers: "I had left her to your lust, the thought is bitterness, / But she first falne; ha ha." The others stab him together even in the midst of his laughter. And he embraces death with eagerness, glorifying its pleasures as more intense than sex: "So laugh away this breath, / My lust was nere more pleasing than my death." Like Brachiano, he recalls the grinning skeletons in the medieval dances.

The most conspicuous figures of death in these medieval dances were the decomposed corpse and the grinning skeleton, but Phoebe Spinrad points out that other figures exist; she notes the instance in a late fourteenth-century poem where death is an old ugly crone (1987, 2). Thus, in *Macbeth*, the three witches who summon Macbeth and Banquo with their strange messages, which strike the hearers as at once frightening and alluring, may be seen as symbols of death. And their presence on the barren heath together with their ritualistic incantations suggest that they may be performing yet another variation of the dance macabre. Even in the opening scene, at their encounter with these strange creatures, Macbeth's and Banquo's deaths seems already inscribed within the action of the play.

Central to the dance macabre was the notion of the indiscriminating power of death. Pictorial representations often showed death leading a group of people belonging to various social levels. All differences between them are erased by the presence of death, and each is reduced to a skeleton. In *The Dialogues of the Dead*, Mennipius captures this sense of equality and the total effacement of individuality: "I can only see bones and bare skulls, most of them looking the same" (1913, 23). The idea recurs as a basic ingredient in all subsequent treatments of the subject. In a sense, death's equalizing power inverts and comments on the hierarchical and hence complex social and political systems. The dance of death therefore functions as a carnivalesque reduction of structured society.

Nicholas Brooke's claim that *The Spanish Tragedy* is "stylized" and "in the end, a kind of dance of death," seems to be even truer of a Jacobean play such as *The Revenger's Tragedy* (1979, 5). Images central to the dance of death are, in fact, explicitly evoked at several points in the play. For example, iconic images of the dance juxtaposed youth with age and beauty with death. Medieval representations of the theme often pictured young lovers in a garden in an embrace during which one is summoned by death. This iconographic tradition receives an ironic representation in Tourneur's play. In the garden scene in which the old Duke tries to woo the beautiful "country lass," we have a parody of the conventional representation. All the essential elements in the original picture are present, of course, although they have been transformed drastically. The meeting in the play is supposed to consummate lust, not love, it takes place in a garden, an image that normally conjures up images of the original garden, a place of purity and sin, but which here is an entirely negative world, a place where the Duke had arranged several such encounters in the past and in which several deaths and treacherous intrigues have taken place. The young country lass is a painted skeleton, thus at once both youth and death, a beautiful maid and a decaying skeleton (death is thus metaphorically presented as at once attractive and horrible); what is more, death occurs literally as the direct result of a kiss.

The masques of the play's last scene capture the image of the dance of death even more vividly. They serve as a dramatic metaphor for the play's actions thus far. The masquelike action of the play ends with Vindice's accomplishment of his avowed revenge in the third act during which he kills the Duke. What follows is the antimasque, a grotesque mimicking of the earlier action; here Vindice transgresses all bounds of justice and decorum. The actions after the murder of the Duke are intensified symbolic metaphors for the now complete degeneration of his mind. Similarly, the second masque of the last scene simply repeats the action of the previous one; Vindice and his masquers come prepared to kill those already murdered by the first set of masquers. In appearance and action, the masquers are indistinguishable from each other. In this masque, which in its artistic ingenuity parallels Hamlet's and Hieronimo's dramatic creations, Vindice's role is that of the masque magician, traditionally a grotesque character, a creator of chaos and disharmony (Traister 1984, 158). The metaphor of the masque emphasizes once again Vindice's alliance with evil, for, as Traister points out, in the masque, magician and demon were "associated in voluntary partnership" (169), and the magician was usually represented as a deformed figure with no human features (153). Thus, Vindice's performance of the masque is an apt metaphoric equivalent for his role in the play as a whole, because by this time he has completely succumbed to his passions and is no longer recognizable as human. If his disguise as Piato symbolically ushers his transition into vice, his role as a masquer suggests his psychological disintegration and complete lack of personality, having now become indistinguishable morally from those around him.

Vindice actually functions as an agent of death and justice; this can be seen most vividly in the opening scene. While the parade of the Ducal family passes behind him, Vindice stands in the foreground with the skull of his beloved in his hand, gloating about his future plans. The scene clearly suggests the dance macabre in form and movement. This opening image may be regarded as an apt metaphoric rendering of the actions of the drama to come.

The anatomy of body and psyche in this play and in other Stuart tragedies itself becomes a sort of dance of death as it evokes medical anatomies such as Vesalius's.[11] The masques in most Stuart tragedies, which parallel or comment on the central actions of the plays, may similarly be treated as dances of death. Plays such as Webster's *The Duchess of Malfi* especially, which Enid Welsford describes as "infected with the spirit of the masque," metaphorically suggest the stylized dance macabre (1962, 296). In fact, dramatists explicitly conceived of their dramatic masques in terms of this pictorial genre. Thus, in *The Traitor*, the masque presented by Sciarrha to Alexander, the Duke of Florence, is quite literally a dance of death. We recognize immediately that the masque metaphorically enacts the Duke's impending murder by Sciarrha, but the Duke himself remains oblivious of its import. The masque begins with a dance by Lust, the Pleasures, a Young Man, and Death until the Young Man is whisked away by Death. During the dance, Sciarrha describes Death's grotesque form with obvious fascination to his sister:

> does not
> That death's head look most temptingly? the worms
> Have kissed the lips off.
>
> (3.2. 42–44)

Similarly, the dance of madmen in *The Duchess of Malfi*, shortly before the Duchess is murdered, the dance of women in *The Maid's Tragedy*, which also culminates in murder, and a host of other Jacobean and Caroline masques evoke the dance of death in manner and action.

The ritualistic nature of the death summons in many plays itself suggests the stylized dance of death. Bosola's role in *The Duchess of Malfi* as he plots and executes the death of the Duchess provides a case in point.

Images of the "Woman-on-top"

Thus, both carnival and the dance of death, an image inherently carnivalesque because it inverts and thus comments on life, are important influences on seventeenth-century drama. These are not, however, the only influences of plebian culture on seventeenth-century drama, and the extent to which theater shared in both patrician and plebian culture remains to be explored. Carnivals and festivals took place regularly and at appointed times of the year. They differed, therefore, from irregular and occasional plebian activities such as the Skimmington. As sanctioned festivity, the carnival was potentially less dangerous and less violent than the charivari or Skimmington, although the two shared certain characteristics. More threatening in aspect than the carnival, the Skimmington with its central image of the "woman-on-top" became a powerful metaphor to describe topsy-turviness in society as a whole.

The Skimmington (or the charivari as it was known in Europe), a form of communal protest against social deviations (especially sexual) from the norm, was prevalent all over Europe in the medieval and Renaissance periods. The protest was usually characterized by a procession consisting of neighbors of the offending party, and the journey, which culminated at the doorstep of the offenders, was always accompanied by rough music and mocking laughter. Effigies of the offenders were mocked and subjected to general public abuse. In England, where it was a fairly common practice, it was known by a variety of names, among them Skimmington, Ridings, and Rough Music (Underdown 1985, 127). Although not officially authorized, authorities generally overlooked the practice except when the violence that it sometimes precipitated resulted in lawsuits. While in Europe it was directed against all kinds of offenses, mismatched couples, second marriages, and sexual excesses of any kind, in England, "the more elaborate forms of charivari ... were nearly always directed against couples of whom the wife had beaten or abused the husband" (Underdown 1985, 121). "Recorded instances of this form of charivari," Underdown tells us, "nearly all date from the later sixteenth and seventeenth centuries" (121). Records may not provide an accurate index to the prevalence of the charivari or Skimmington; because of its unofficial status, it may have reached the record books only rarely. But, in the context of increasing social turbulence during this period, it may be reasonable to assume that seventeenth-century English society indulged fairly frequently in such social protests. That it was a fading, although generally accepted, form of social protest may be seen in the following lines, in which Andrew Marvell seems to approve of this form of primitive justice:

> The court as once of war, now fond of peace,
> All to new sports their wanton fears release.
> From Greenwich (where intelligence they hold)
> Comes news of pastime martial and old,
> A punishment invented first to awe
> Masculine wives transgressing Nature's law,
> Where, but the brawny female disobeys
> And beats the husband till for peace he prays,
> No concerned jury for him damage finds,
> Nor partial justice her behaviour binds,
> But the just street does the next house invade,
> Mounting the neighbour couple on lean jade,
> The distaff knocks, the grains from kettle fly,
> And boys and girls in troops run hooting by:
> Prudent Antiquity, that knew by Shame,
> Better than Law, Domestic crimes to Tame,
> And taught youth by spectacle innocent.
>
> (Marvell 1972, 373–89)

The crowds that made up the Skimmington processions were mostly men "drawn from the middling and lower elements of society" (Underdown 1985, 133). In certain kinds of Skimmingtons, the crowd was led by a masked figure sometimes in a terrifying horned devil mask (130). The offending shrew was often represented by a pole in a chemise or by a man dressed up as a woman. The primitive justice of the Skimmington, which openly mocked and parodied the offending parties, often drove them out of the community for shame. Like carnival in general, the Skimmington was a festive activity undertaken in "merriment," but it also had its violent side. It shared with carnival a derisive mocking tone and a depiction of the topsy-turviness in society that it wished to revert. Thus, it was often accompanied by images of the "world-turned-upside-down," such as riding backwards or the shrewish wife beating her husband. The ride backwards became, as Ruth Melinkoff argues, a powerful and frequent symbol of evil, and pictorial representations of evil often included the motif because of its pervasive significance (1973, 164).

The Skimmingtons in England were usually directed at shrewish wives. Martin Ingram points out, however, that in England especially, while the termagant wife and her abject husband were ... pre-eminently the target of ridings, lesser forms of female insubordination and related offenses sometimes provoked demonstrations involving some of the characteristic symbols of the charivari. (1985, 169)

Thus, many Jacobean and Caroline plays that focus on the "woman-on-top" archetype and the potential threat that this posed to hierarchical and patriarchal society may be said to echo "rough music." The theater as an arena for Skimmington seemed especially appropriate, because Elizabethan and Jacobean actors, like the participants in a riding, were all males.

The woman-on-top image depicted in many Stuart tragedies coalesces also with depictions of the monstrous and the grotesque. In a recent study of Shakespeare's plays, Leonard Tennenhouse argues that grotesque transformations in the bodies of aristocratic women occur as they take over the domain of men, and that these plays ultimately reassert patriarchy by showing this usurpation as having disastrous effects. Desdemona's assertive interest in court dealings and war, for example, "makes her sexually monstrous according to the Jacobean understanding of power" (1986, 126). This view of Desdemona might seem farfetched, but Jacobean tragedy certainly teems with such monstrous women whose usurpation of patriarchal authority proves disastrous for all involved; Evadne, Beatrice-Joanna, and Lady Macbeth are but a few cases in point. True, the "woman-on-top" archetype appears in several plays of the sixteenth and seventeenth centuries, and it does not always have disastrous effects. In earlier comedies especially, women's usurpation of masculinity becomes a temporary release within the festive realm, calculated ultimately to reassert masculine authority. Portia's disguise as a judge is a case in point. Male garb gives her a powerful voice through which the problems in the play might be resolved. Yet her usurpation of masculinity, as in all Shakespearean comedies in which we encounter the female-male, is temporary and reinforces the patriarchal order to which society returns at the end of the play. To what extent was this festive treatment of the woman-on-top in Elizabethan England a result of having a female monarch on the throne? It is hard to tell, but the carnivalesque inversion certainly turned bitter after 1603, and in later plays, the woman-on-top almost always emerges as grotesque and monstrous.

The potency of the woman-on-top archetype depended, of course, on its symbolic relevance to the corresponding familial, social, and political order. Victor Turner describes a symbol thus: "Symbols instigate social action ... they condense many references, uniting them in a single cognitive field. In this sense, ritual symbols are 'multivocal'" (1976, 117–18). The woman-on-top image may be regarded as just such a "ritual symbol"; equally relevant to patrician and plebian society, it could represent (and question) inversions in both private and public bodies. Thus, invariably the image of the woman-on-top in Stuart plays invokes a sense of disruption in patriarchal, hierarchical, and monarchical order.

In a recent essay on changing gender norms during the Elizabethan and Stuart periods, Phyllis Rackin rightly argues that the

> theater provided an arena where changing gender definitions could be displayed, deplored, or enforced and where anxieties about them could be expressed by playwrights and incited or repressed among their audiences. (1987, 29)

She goes on to discuss two concepts of androgyny prevalent during these periods, one that sees the androgynous as ideal and the other that regards it as monstrous. The former image dominated Renaissance depictions of androgyny, but, she argues, this image was gradually "replaced by the satirical portrait of the hermaphrodite, a medical monstrosity or social misfit, an image of perversion or abnormality" (29). James's ascension to the throne and his patriarchal theories may have had a great deal to do with this reassertion of gender distinctions in the Stuart eras. In the following pages, I would like to address the issue of feminine disguise and depictions of the male-female as they change from the Elizabethan to the Jacobean periods. The male-female grotesque in many Stuart tragedies, a symbol of topsy-turviness within the domestic and social realms, invariably becomes a source of evil and chaos. To trace this evolution in attitudes toward the male-female, I first consider the invocation of the Skimmington or Riding in an early comedy, Shakespeare's *The Taming of the Shrew*, and then in a sequel to the play written by Fletcher, *The Woman's Prize or the Tamer Tamed* (1611).

The very title of Shakespeare's play and its central action indicate its relationship to the Skimmington. As the Skimmington was accompanied by images of topsy-turviness, so Shakespeare's play seems to abound in grotesque inversions and parodies. The sun becomes the moon, an old man becomes a comely maid, the wealthy bridegroom is a man in rags, and so on. The man-woman of the outer plot, the page who disguises as a lady, mirrors a similar transgression in Kate, the young maiden who usurps the dominating manner of the male and thus becomes a shrew, a man-woman, the central figure in the Skimmington.

In fact, the whole play seems to resemble in structure a riding calculated to reform shrewish women. The frame of the play suggests the carnivalesque. The main plot, the story of Kate and Petruchio, is also a subplot, the frame within the frame; the outer frame ensures our recognition that the masquerades of the inner play are initiated and sanctioned by authority, by the lord who has devised a "flatt'ring dream or worthless fancy," "a pastime passing excellent, / If it be husbanded with modesty" (1.1. 43, 66–67). The norm is thus asserted long before the concluding scene, even at the beginning, in the masquerading of Sly as a nobleman. And as in all festivals, a mock lord and lady are chosen to preside over the festivities—Christopher Sly becomes the "Lord" and the disguised page becomes his "Lady." The series of inversions that follow must be viewed in the context of this overall and initial inversion. Degradation and inversion are the very means by which the shrew is tamed and made to conform.

Kate's taming begins during her first encounter with Petruchio in act 2, scene 1. Significantly, she commits a fault that victims of the Skimmington were almost always charged with—she strikes Petruchio during this first encounter. And her conversion actually involves a literal "riding": she is forced to ride on an old horse from her father's to her husband's and back, and much of her taming occurs during these ridings. Martin Ingram points out that one of the most common symbols associated with the Skimmington was the riding: "the centerpiece of these ridings was a horse and rider" and often, the offending woman (or couple) was made to ride (sometimes backwards). The horse was often old and feeble, and sometimes it was replaced by an ass so that the ignominy might be stressed. A series of degradations followed, and the woman was often pelted with mud and dirt and thereafter cleansed through a ducking in a pond (Ingram 1985, 168). Something similar happens to Kate in her journey from her father's house to Petruchio's. Mocking laughter was a basic ingredient in all Skimmingtons, and the tone of derisive mockery dominates Shakespeare's play. The Lord's prank on Sly is a form of mockery; Petruchio's wooing is conducted within the context of derisive laughter; the play closes with Petruchio's mockery of the other husbands after he has paraded Kate's newfound wisdom and subservience; Kate herself delivers a lecture that celebrates her superiority over the others. She had been the source of social disharmony in the early half of the play, and the general disruption of order caused by her "shrewishness" had been emphasized throughout by frequent images of disruption and inversion in society. For example, when Petruchio inquires after the wedding whether the horses are ready for their travel, Grumio replies, "Ay sir, they are ready; the oats have eaten the horses" (3.2. 204–5). The statement, although an inadvertent slip, nevertheless reflects what many of the characters in the play perceive as the topsy-turviness in Petruchio's and Kate's relationship. It is natural, therefore, that after her conversion, her speech to Bianca and the Widow, who refused to obey their husbands, stresses the relationship between familial and political order:

> Fie, fie. Unknit that theatening unkind brow,
> And dart not scornful glances from those eyes,
> To wound thy lord, thy kind, thy governor.
> . . . .
> Thy husband is thy lord, thy life, thy keeper,
> Thy head, thy sovereign; . . .
> Such duty as the subject owes the prince,
> Even such a woman oweth to her husband;
>
> (5.2. 139–58)

According to one of the actors in a riding of 1604, their purpose was not only that "the woman which had offended might be shamed for her misdemeanor towards her husband . . . but other women also by her shame might be admonished in like sort" (Ingram 1983, 174). Just so, Shakespeare's play concludes with this explicit statement delivered by Kate to the other wives in the play and by implication to all wives in the audience. Kate's speech signals the close of festivity, a supposed righting of the upside-down-world; it provides a stylized summary of the penal and reformative purpose of the Skimmington as a festival.

Kate's subservience in these lines has troubled many modern critics. The twentieth-century penchant for detecting irony in everything has prompted some to regard her stance as yet another step in the game of power between her and Petruchio. I find it hard to quite accept such a reading. The conclusion of the play is, I believe, troublesome, but for other reasons than Kate's antifeminist stand. The irony of Kate's conversion lies in our realization at the end of the play that distinct gender roles are still a male ideal. Bianca and the Widow, against whom we are to measure Kate's so-called reformation, are hardly the subservient wives they were supposed to be. The real threat to patriarchy, in fact, has always issued from them. The play ultimately highlights the discrepancy between ideals and reality; Kate, the reformed shrew, the ideal wife, proves to be the exception rather than the norm. The play thus suggests that, undesirable although it might be, the woman-on-top is the norm rather than the exception in society.

This ambivalence links the play with the Skimmington as a festival in yet another manner. We have seen how the Skimmington was both penal and festive in tone. But, as Martin Ingram insists, its frequency and ritual complexity point to its relevance as more than social criticism. He suggests that the charivari or Skimmington points to a "deeper unease" within those who participated in or sanctioned its festivity.

> Deep in the hearts of the organizers of ridings lay the knowledge that women could never be dominated to the degree implied in the patriarchal ideal. For that ideal was only too plainly in conflict with the realities of everyday life, and indeed with alternative ideals. It is clear that, in practice, the balance of authority between husbands and wives in marriage varied considerably, and husbands could by no means count on female submission. . . . In these circumstances, reactions to the dominant wife were bound to be ambivalent. (1985, 176)

Thus participants sensed the discrepancy between the ideal and the norm, something that Shakespeare's play seems explicitly to dramatize. *The Taming of the Shrew*, structured so closely on the form of the Skimmington, remains inherently ambivalent. And the theme of the world-turned-upside-down becomes through the image of the Skimmington an explicit reference to gender tensions caused by undesirable deviations from the norm in Renaissance society.

These gender tensions become more vividly apparent in Fletcher's sequel to the comedy, *The Woman's Prize or the Tamer Tamed*, written during the Stuart era. In this play, Kate has died, although without losing her shrewish nature. As a result of her aggressiveness, Petruchio has become very demanding and tyrannical. At the beginning of the play, he has just married the gentle and soft-spoken Maria. Maria, however, following instructions from Bianca, decides to assert herself on her wedding night. She locks Petruchio out of his house and torments him in a variety of ways until he gives in to several conditions laid out by her. Maria's act of resistence against patriarchal authority (she resists both her husband's and her father's pleas to reconsider her actions) makes her a heroine among the women of the village who decide to follow her example in their own relationships with their husbands. The play closes abruptly after Petruchio has gone through several trials and tribulations and presumably has learnt his lesson.

Despite its seemingly open sanction of women's demands for equality, however, Fletcher's play emerges as remarkably similar to Shakespeare's in its invocation of the Skimmington and in its decided emphasis on the inherent tensions within gender relationships. The play seems to argue overtly for equality between men and women; it even closes with such an injunction in the epilogue:

> The Tamer's tam'd, but so, as nor the men
>   Can finde one just cause to complaine of, when
> They fitly do consider in their lives,
>   They should not reign as Tyrants o'er their wives
> Nor can the women from this president
>   Insult or triumph: it being aptly meant,
> To teach both Sexes due equality;
>   And as they stand bound, to love mutually.
>
> (1966, 1–8)

But the events in the play register a more complicated message. Even the play's title may be perceived as ironic: Fletcher establishes early that the term *tamer* when applied to Petruchio is a misnomer, for Katherine had remained a shrew throughout her marriage to him. If anything, the victory in the power struggle between them had ended in her success, because Petruchio has supposedly developed a violent temper by having to put up with her shrewishness. This fact is stressed early in the play by Petruchio's friends as they discuss the plight of the "demure" Maria newly married to the violent Petruchio. Tranio points out that Petruchio still suffers from nightmares about his first marriage:

> For yet the bare remembrance of his first wife
> (I tell you on my knowledge, and a truth too)
> Will make him start in's sleep, and very often
> Cry out for Cudgels, Colstaves, any thing;
> Hiding his Breeches, out of feare her Ghost
> Should walk, and weare 'em yet. Since his first marriage,
> He is no more the still Petruchio,
> Than I am Babylon.
>
> (1.1. 31–38)

Indeed, all the women in the play emerge as similarly powerful. And the entire play may be viewed as a Skimmington; male actors crossdressing as women create a temporary pandemonium in the town by speaking presumably for women's equality, but their exercise of authority remains entirely comic. Such assertion of power also proves temporary and ends abruptly when they apparently decide to return to their conventional wifely roles. Maria's final attitude toward Petruchio symbolizes the end of the women's "merry sport" and indicates a general return to normalcy in the town:

> As I am honest,
> And as I am a maid yet, all my life
> From this houre since, since ye make so free profession,
> I dedicate in service to your pleasure.
>
> (5.4. 54–58)

Ironically, however, the normalcy suggested in this play seems no different from that in Shakespeare's. The women's rebellion actually emphasizes, not their revolt against an established system, but their reiteration of normal positions of power. And by emphasizing that Kate had never reformed, Fletcher's drama presents an even darker vision of gender relations; it insists, not as Shakespeare had done that the servile woman is an exception, but that she does not even exist. In fact, without exception, the men in the play seem entirely under the control of the women.

Although there is no literal riding, the play does present a march by the women in support of Maria's actions, and images of the world-upside-down recur throughout. Early in the play, Jaques describes the women's aggression to the men in mock-heroic terms, but his attitude establishes that such aggression is not a recent thing.

> The forlorn-hope's led by a Tanners wife,
> I know her by her hide; a desperate woman:
> She flead her husband in her youth, and made
> Raynes of his hide to ride the Parish, her plackett
> Looks like the straigts of Gibralter, still wider
> Downe to the gulphe, all sun-burnt Barbary
> Lyes in her breech; take 'em all together,
> They are a genealogy of Jennets,
> . . . .
> cry they can,
> But more for Noble spight, than feare: and crying
> Like the old Gyants that were foes to Heaven,
> They heave ye stoole on stoole, and fling main Potlids
> Like massive rocks, dart ladles, tossing Irons,
> And tongs like Thunderbolts, till overlayd,
> They fall beneath the waight; yet still aspiring
> At those Emperious Codsheads, that would tame 'em.
>
> (2.4. 42–60)

Jaques also manages to spy on their drunken activities during the height of their rebellion and reports thus to the bewildered men:

> They have got a stick of Fiddles, and they firke it
> In wondrous waies, the two, grand Capitanos,
> (They brought the Auxiliary Regiments)
> Daunce with their coats tuckt up to their bare breeches,
> And bid the Kingdom kisse 'em, that's the burden;
> They have got Metheglin, and audacious Ale,
> And talke like Tyrants.
>
> (2.6. 36–42)

Shortly thereafter, the women articulate the implications of their unfeminine activities even more clearly in a song:

> A Health for all this day
> To the woman that bears the sway
>   And wears the breeches;
> Let it come, let it come.
> Let this health be a Seal,
> For the good of the Common-weal
>   the woman shall wear the breeches.

The world they claim to license will acknowledge their position as rulers over men. Even the calling off of festivities springs from the women, while the men seem simply relieved at the resolution.

Thus, despite the moderate tone of the prologue and epilogue that stresses equality between the sexes, the women's actions throughout suggest that they do not want equality but a complete reversal of gender sterotypes. The play, as a Skimmington presented by male actors, provides a commentary on the actual state of male-female relationships in seventeenth-century England. Thus, despite the inversion of the Shakespearean format, the final point seems to be essentially the same as that in the earlier play. Like Shakespeare, Fletcher seems to be dramatizing discrepancies between Renaissance ideals and actual seventeenth-century practice.

The play's essentially festive and comic tone, however, contrasts sharply with images of the woman-on-top in some Stuart tragedies, in which we encounter the image with increasingly greater frequency. Greenblatt argues that in many Elizabethan plays, "the transformation of gender identity figures the emergence of an individual out of a twinned sexual nature" (1988, 91). Kate (and many Elizabethan heroines such as Portia, Viola, and Rosalind) may be regarded as undergoing just such a transformation and process of self-discovery.

In Stuart tragedies, on the other hand, the transformation of gender frequently figures the death of the individual through his twinned sexual nature.

One reason for this darker tone in later depictions of twinned sexual nature may be that women were becoming more powerful in society, so that the unreality of the patriarchal norm became increasingly apparent and male security became even more seriously threatened. David Underdown notes that between 1560 and 1640, "records disclose an intense preoccupation with women who are a visible threat to the patriarchal system" (1985, 119). He concludes that especially the early seventeenth century was a period of strained gender relations in England and that this strain lay at the heart of the "crisis of order" during the early Stuart monarchy. Even as James's and Charles's particular reliance on the patriarchal ideal points to its comparative decline in this period, so, too, dramatic concern with the image of the women-on-top points to a real crisis in seventeenth-century gender norms. The increasing dominance of women could no longer be treated comically; these plays in which the carnival turns bitter ultimately point (as do the court records of this time) to an increasing male insecurity.

The increasing bitterness of the later plays may also be explained in other sociocultural terms. As historians have noted, the early seventeenth century experienced continuing controversy about sports and festivities. As Puritan threat to these aspects of popular culture increased, the festivities themselves incorporated greater bitterness and violence. Martin Ingram, discussing Skimmingtons that turned violent, points out that "when refusal to take part in festivities (or worse still, attempts to suppress such festivities) were based on Puritan principles, such ridings were apt to become distinctly less light-hearted and more elaborate" (1985, 171).

Leonard Tennenhouse notes a similar difference even in depictions of festivals between these two periods. In Jacobean and Caroline plays festivals invariably degenerate into scenes of corruption; "the signs of festival become those of filth, disease, rape, and insurrection" (1986, 118). In the less threatening atmosphere of Elizabethan England, festive activities could remain essentially comic, but as the age progressed, carnival and festival turned bitter and more anarchic. A similar darkening of tone characterizes the plays of the seventeenth century as they mirror images from popular culture. In fact, as I pointed out earlier, many of the darkest tragedies are staged within the backdrop of excessive celebration. *The Changeling*, for example, starts with preparations for a wedding. We are constantly reminded throughout the play that further festivities are forthcoming, and the concluding scene discloses the full tragedy in the midst of festivity. *'Tis Pity She's a Whore*, also concerned with marriage, concludes, as *The Changeling* had, with feasting than turns tragic. A similar tone pervades *The Maid's Tragedy*; it, too, is replete with masquing and dancing as it celebrates a wedding.

The pervading tone of dark destivity and mirth in the later Stuart plays differentiates them even from Shakespeare's great tragedies, in which the opening scenes often convey not celebration but a sense of things gone awry. The opening scene in *Hamlet* conveys a definite sense of impending disaster; *Macbeth* begins with scenes of battle; even *Othello* begins with images of disruption. The later Stuart theatrical penchant for staging tragedy in the midst of celebration, however, reveals the essentially carnivalesque nature of the later plays. They begin at the point where comedy traditionally concluded; and while in Elizabethan tragedies the dark tone had mirrored tragic actions, these Stuart tragedies deliberately overplay and emphasize the sense of festivity and celebration. True, the sense of impending doom is not entirely absent in the opening scenes of these plays, but intimations of disaster are veiled by festivity. *The Maid's Tragedy* (c. 1610), for example, begins with a gloomy masque of darkness, during which Cynthia reveals her envy of Phoebus and Boreas breaks loose from his bonds. But because the masque is part of a wedding celebration, we miss or undervalue the associations of darkness, gloom, and things gone out of control.

In these later plays, the harmonious relationship between familial order and political order, invoked in Kate's concluding speech, modifies to depict crises in both these realms. In many Stuart tragedies, the female-male grotesque, a comic matter in *The Taming of the Shrew* and *The Woman's Prize*, becomes a hideous transvestite; the androgynous in the seventeenth century no longer functions as an ideal, but conveys a sense of grotesque transgression. In *the Maid's Tragedy*, for example, the image of the woman-on-top combines with the undermining of both patriarchal and monarchical authority, and thus the play presents a world-upside-down in its fullest sense.

Constant doubts are raised throughout about Evadne's claim to womanhood itself. In the opening scene, Lyssipius describes Evadne to her brother as

> A lady, sir,
> That bears the light above her, and strikes dead
> With flashes of her eye.
>
> (1.1. 73–75)

Based on the Petrarchan tradition of praise, the description at once suggests Evadne's beauty and coldness even as it links her with Cynthia, the moon goddess, shortly to be invoked in the masque that celebrates Evadne's marriage to Amintor. Evadne, in fact, shares a great deal with the masculine-feminine goddess of the hunt and childbirth, although she remains a grotesque version of her. Evadne's purpose in marrying Amintor is to find a father for the child she is carrying; she callously reveals on their wedding night that if she were to lose Amintor, she would have to find another "miserable one" to replace him. In response to her revelations, Amintor loses all desire for her and even expresses relief at having heard the news before he touched her. To him she remains throughout the play hideous but beautiful. Even in the last scene, when she offers herself to him after having murdered the king, he recoils from her, although partially moved to pity, as if from something hideous:

> Why, thou hast raised mischief to his height,
> And found one to out-name thy other faults;
> Thou hast no intermission of thy sins,
> But all thy life is a continued ill.
> Black is thy colour now, disease thy nature.
>
> (5.3. 131–35)

Blackness and disease have totally displaced the image of light with which she had been associated in the opening scene. Evadne herself had admitted to her husband, "I am hell, / Till you, my dear lord, shoot your light into me" (4.1. 228–29). Thus, the wedding masque of the opening scene had appropiately evoked both night and light, although images of pollution and darkness gradually displaced the early association of light.

Evadne even evokes an image of herself as huntress, another association with Diana, when she boldly reveals her intention to choose victims by their social standing:

> I swore indeed that I would never love
> A man of lower place; but if your fortune
> Should throw you from this height, I bade you trust
> I would forsake you, and would bend to him
> That won your throne. I love with my ambition.
>
> (3.1. 176–80)

She goes on to suggest in this scene that if she were disloyal to the king, she would be as one struck by leprosy. The audience recognizes, of course, that she has already undergone such a mutilation and transformation. A scene later Melantius describes her as "a whore, a leprous one" (3.2. 174–75). Interestingly, he also suggests a connection between sexual laxity and disease, a connection Evadne herself had evoked earlier, and which is repeated several times in the play. She suggests the relationship again when she later tells her husband, "My whole life is leprous, it infects / All my repentance" (4.1. 196). She also draws the association between a tyrant monarch and the plague when she tells the king

> Thou art a shameless villain
> A thing out of the overcharge of nature
> Sent, like a thick cloud, to disperse a plague
> Upon weak catching women; such a tyrant
> That for his lust would sell away his subjects
>
> (5.2. 89–93)

Thus, Evadne's transformation during the play into something monstrous is accompanied by frequent references to disfiguring diseases, especially leprosy and the plague. Bakhtin's point about the prevalence of images of disease in the carnivalesque genre certainly proves relevant to this tragedy.

The implication that her deeds have robbed her of her femininity is first suggested by Evadne herself, although others echo the idea later in the play. After her confrontation with her brother, during which she first expresses repentance, she notes,

> sure, I am monstrous;
> For I have done these follies, those mad mischiefs
> Would dare a woman.
>
> (4.1. 181–83)

A few lines later, she suggests her alliance with the female monster, Hydra:

> I do appear the same, the same Evadne,
> Dress'd in the shames I lived in, the same monster.
> But these are names of honor to what I am;
> I do present myself the foulest creature,
> Most poisionous, dangerous, and despised of men,
> Lerna e'er bred or Nilus. I am hell.
>
> (4.1. 224–29)

The degeneration from the chaste and beautiful goddess of the moon to a monster potentially dangerous to men and requiring domination by them is now complete. She exposes her complete transformation: to the king shortly before she murders him:

> I am not she; nor bear I in this breast
> So much cold spirit to be call'd a woman
>
> (5.2. 63–64)

Disbelieving the transformation, he only pleads, "I prithee speak not these things. Thou art gentle, / And wert not meant thus rugged" (5.2. 85–86); the implication is that she has usurped an essentially male quality, that of rugged boldness. This accusation of masculinity is echoed later when, in reaction to the murder, the gentleman of the bedchamber exclaims, "Who can believe a woman could do this?" (5.2. 128).

The murder scene itself captures vividly the image of the woman-on-top. Evadne first ties the king to his bed, and he, believing that her actions constitute preliminary love play, actually permits her to render him powerless. Unwilling to believe her claims that she intends to kill him, he goes to his death awaiting her next "sexual" move. Even the manner of his death (she stabs him with a dagger) suggests the sexual role reversal.

The play also dramatizes another usurpation of the male role. Evadne has the appearance of woman, but in the last scene, after her "rugged" act of murder, she is most fully the female-male grotesque. On the other hand, Aspatia, Amintor's former lover whom he had rejected to marry Evadne, usurps male attire in this scene to commit what is virtually a suicide by fighting her former lover, Amintor. The two women, mirrors of each other throughout the play, are thus most fully contrasted in this concluding scene. Although she bears the semblance of womanhood, Evadne has been transformed beyond recognition, while Aspatia, despite her usurpation of male attire, remains inherently feminine (Ophelia-like). Her male attire only reinforces her womanhood. Both usurpations, both inversions of the male-female hierarchy, however, prove disastrous, and both women die as a result of their usurpation.

As in the case of Aspatia, Lady Macbeth's usurpation of the male character in *Macbeth* only reinforces her feminine weakness. Shakespeare's play, written during the same period as Beaumont's and Fletcher's, similarly combines the theme of the woman-on-top with parricide and regicide. Lady Macbeth ushers her transformation into the female-male grotesque by an incantation that calls for a negation of her femininity:

> Come, you spirits
> That tend on mortal thoughts, unsex me here
> And fill me from the crown to the toe-to full
> Of direst cruelty. Make thick my blood;
> ... Come to my woman's breasts,
> And take my milk for gall.
>
> (1.5. 40–48)

As such, she mirrors the female-male grotesques of the opening scene, the witches whose bisexual nature puzzles Banquo and Macbeth:

> What are these
> So wither'd and so wild in their attire,
> That look not like th' inhabitants o' th' earth,
> And yet are on't? Live you? Or are you aught
> That man may question? You seem to understand me
> By each at once her choppy finger laying
> Upon her skinny lips. You should be women,
> And yet your beards forbid me to interpret
> That you are so.
>
> (1.3. 39–47)

Both fearful and fascinating, outsiders to the society that they change so drastically and insiders within the action of the play that begins with them, their ambiguous function mirrors Lady Macbeth's very closely. Like them, she remains technically innocent of the regicide, only initiating it with compelling reasons and leaving the carrying out of it to Macbeth. But Lady Macbeth differs significantly from Evadne and later female-male grotesques such as Middleton's Beatrice-Joanna. She usurps the male role by proxy and discovers during the play that the usurpation is doomed to failure. The conviction with which she describes her own masculine strength proves at the testing to have been a vain boast. Thus, she tells Macbeth early that she is capable of denying and negating even her motherhood:

> I have given suck, and know
> How tender 'tis to love the babe that milks me;
> I would, while it was smiling in my face,
> Have pluck'd nipple from his boneless gums
> And dash'd the brains out, had I so sworn as you
> Have done to this.
>
> (1.7. 55–60)

The conventional image of woman as nurturer thus undergoes a carnival inversion in which she becomes the source of death; Macbeth's murder of the king provides yet another instance of inversion during which the host murders his guest. The carnivalesque world is also invoked most vividly by Ross and the Old Man in act 2, scene 4, as they describe the aftermath of Duncan's murder:

> *Old Man.* 'Tis unnatural,
>   Even like the deed that's done. On Tuesday last
>   A falcon, tow'ring in her pride of place
>   Was by a mousing owl hawked at and killed.
> *Ross.* And Duncan's horses—a thing most strange and certain—
>   Beauteous and swift, the minions of their race,
>   Turned wild in nature, broke their stalls, flung out,
>   Contending 'gainst obedience, as they would make
>   War with mankind.
> *Old Man.* 'Tis said they eat each other.
> *Ross.* They did so, to th' amazement of mine eyes
>   That looked upon.
>
> (2.4. 10–19)

The scene implies a general topsy-turviness in the land and reinforces the unnaturalness of both the murder of Duncan by his kin (action that parallels that of the horses eating each other) and of the woman-on-top (typified by the witches and Lady Macbeth).

But, as I suggested earlier, Lady Macbeth's desire to be in control remains a dream. Only a few days after her bold rejection of familial ties, Lady Macbeth explains her inability to kill Duncan with an assertion of familial bonds that contrasts sharply with her earlier denial: "Had he not resembled / My father as he slept, I had done it" (2.2. 12–13). In essence, therefore, Lady Macbeth remains a grotesque only in potential and in her own imagination.

By contrast, Bianca in *Women Beware Women* and Beatrice-Joanna in *The Changeling* transform into frightening grotesques during the play. Their transformations become especially vivid because of radical differences between our first images of them and our concluding impressions. At the beginning of the tragedies, the playwrights clearly pattern their description of these heroines on Petrarchan ideals of beauty, even as Beaumont and Fletcher had done with Evadne. But dramatic changes occur by the end of the plays, and the other characters invariably voice their horror at the hideous transformations that have occurred. For example, after Beatrice-Joanna's villainies have been discovered, Alsemero recoils from her as she tries to explain her actions in terms of her love for him. Shortly after, however, when her surprised father tries to approach her, she acknowledges her own hideousness:

> O, come not near me, sir; I shall defile you.
> I was that of blood was taken from you
> For our better health; look no more upon't,
> But cast it to the ground regardlessly;
> Let the common [sewer] take it from distinction.
>
>   (5.3. 149–53)

Like Alsemero, Leantio, on discovering Bianca's adultery, recoils from her in horror:

> Why, here's sin made, and nev'r a conscience put to't
> A monster with all forehead and no eyes!
> Why do I talk to thee of sense or virtue,
> That art as dark as death?
>
>   (4.1. 91–94)

Although she flaunts her adulterous relationship here, in the concluding scene, Bianca, like Beatrice-Joanna, acknowledges her hideousness: "But my deformity in spirit's more foul: / A blemished face best fits a leprous soul" (5.2. 202–3).

These later depictions of the woman-on-top appear to be far more critical in spirit than earlier treatments. Interestingly, these later plays also combine the theme of the woman-on-top with suggestions about the general decline in patriarchal authority. These two themes seem to dominate in later Stuart tragedies. Significantly, in an earlier Elizabethan tragedy such as *Hamlet*, which also deals with parricide, despite the potential for doing so, Shakespeare refrains from depicting Gertrude in terms of the female-male grotesque. Despite her wrongs, Gertrude is etched with a sympathy that is lacking in later depictions of corrupt women. The social environment of Jacobean and Caroline England may have had a great deal to do with this difference.

Theatrical Festivity and Social Liberation

Thus, many Stuart tragedies seem to invoke the carnival spirit by depicting the woman-on-top and the world-upside-down. Concentrated depictions of the grotesque body in transition, as it succumbs to disease and death or indulges in excessive feasting and copulation, make these plays vivid examples of the carnivalesque genre. Many of the characteristics that writers denote as basic to the carnival provide central motifs for the actions of these plays. I would now like to consider the relationship between these expressions of the carnivalesque in seventeenth-century drama and the sociopolitical events of the mid-century. To do so, I would like to quote some theories about the liberating effects of carnival, developed in response to Bakhtin's celebration of the mode.

Umberto Eco insists that while "Bachtin [sic] was right in seeing the manifestation of a profound drive towards liberation and subversion in medieval carnival . . . the hyper-Bachtinian ideology of carnival as *actual* liberation may . . . be wrong" (1984, 3, italics added). As I indicated earlier, all festivals, including carnival, were subversive and revolutionary in spirit, but revolutionary in the seventeenth-century sense of the word; they functioned as *temporary* subversions calculated to reemphasize the status quo. Bakhtin (except in his introductory pages, where he recognizes the temporary nature of the subversive spirit in carnival) seems to perceive these subversive elements as a permanent and genuine threat to the dominant ideologies of the time. On has only to recognize that carnival was originally a church-sanctioned festival to realize that its subversive spirit worked *within rather than outside* the dominant culture. Carnival forms certainly parodied the rituals of the church, but they did not "belong to an entirely different sphere"; nor are they forms "systematically placed outside the Church and religiosity," as Bakhtin argues (1968, 7).

But this is not to say that there was nothing threatening about them; on the contrary, as I emphasized earlier, carnival and festival were always potentially dangerous activities. As Natalie Zemon Davies argues, "comic and festive inversion could *undermine* as well as reinforce . . . traditional systems" (1975, 131). And this is precisely what seems to have happened in the seventeenth century; the repeated invocation of festival inversion permitted and precipitated an actual inversion in society. Michael Andre Bernstein's recent modification of Bakhtin's theories in the essay, "When the Carnival Turns Bitter: Preliminary Reflections on the Abject Hero," may be especially useful in trying to understand the darker tone in Stuart tragedy, and more important, in trying to determine the relationship of Stuart dramatic carnivalesque to social liberation.

Bernstein argues that the literary carnival (as represented by Rabelais, for example) is bounded by its "celebration of language itself" (1983, 301). Although in actual carnival, which was always potentially dangerous and could result in violence, the spectator functioned as the moral authority, in the textualized carnivalesque of Rabelais's fiction, the reader becomes the authority. According to Bernstein, the ritual liberation that Bakhtin celebrates in Rabelais, and which Bakhtin treats as actual liberation, proves to be temporary. Bernstein goes on to argue that only "when the laughter turns bitter" can "Bakhtin's paradigm of all-inclusive ritual come closest to realization" (299). In textualized carnival "turned bitter," according to Bernstein, the reader is unable to function as authority. In the evolution of the literary carnivalesque, Bernstein sees this bitter carnival emerging much later than in the seventeenth century, in the writings of Diderot. I would like to argue that while it may be difficult to pinpoint an exact moment in the evolution of the "bitter" carnival as Bernstein does, "bitterness" was an aspect of the literary carnivalesque even in seventeenth-century England.

The dichotomy that Bernstein sees between gay and bitter carnival is similar to that between the plots in many Elizabethan and Stuart plays. Christopher Sly's elevation to the status of a lord in *The Taming of the Shrew* permitted a temporary "bottom's up" situation, recognizable to the audience as such. In *The Maid's Tragedy*, or *Macbeth*, or *'Tis Pity She's a Whore*, on the other hand, we encounter an unsettling world whose threat proves genuine. The transition that Bernstein sees as taking place in the later half of the eighteenth century in France— "a crucial turning point in the history of the Saturnalian dialogue, a moment of precarious equipoise after which the destructive forces inherent in the convention begin to dominate" (1983, 284)—surfaces in England in the Stuart tragedies of the seventeenth century. It is precisely this aspect of the carnival turned bitter that makes plays such as *'Tis Pity She's a Whore* unsettling. The audience is unable to exercise a stable moral authority; our emotional and intellectual response to the play remains ambivalent throughout. The carnival world, it would seem, turned increasingly bitter during the Stuart period, and this bitterness may have contributed to the social change of the 1640s, which many Englishmen saw as an actual liberation. The carnival upside-down world in many Stuart tragedies, versions of Durkheimian evil, thus dramatize and criticize social deviations from desirable norms, but the increasing bitterness in these dramatic invocations of the carnival, because it gradually annulled the moral authority of the spectator, may have made possible an actual sociocultural liberation.

5

Evil and Sociocultural Transformation

Jacobean and Caroline explorations of evil thus take various forms: all three versions of evil as defined by Augustine, Ricoeur, and Durkheim exist in Stuart tragedy. And this dramatic fascination with the darker world within may be linked directly to the sociopolitical changes of the mid-seventeenth century. Stuart England witnessed a variety of radical upheavals, not least among them the redefining of the state of England itself. But the political events culminating in the beheading of Charles I formed part of a series of related changes in politics, culture, literature, and society. In literature, the age witnessed a clear transition from oral to written transmission of ideas. Social mobility appears to have increased dramatically during the era. A redefinition of gender norms appears also to have been imminent. Alongside all these, the theater itself was subjected to intense scrutiny as both supporters and detractors of the mode argued vehemently about its effects on society. Stuart dramatists project their concern over these controversies by active and repeated engagement with contemporary issues in their work. It seems as if especially in the seventeenth century, "myth and custom, tragedy and state, are rooted together" (Nietzsche n.d., 329).

Many plays explore the Augustinian concept of evil as lack of essence through the dramatic device of the disguise, thus debating ideas about the self as an entity. Terry Castle's claim about disguise in eighteenth-century literature proves relevant to the earlier period as well:

> By making magically available the body of the other, ... costume collapsed the boundary between individuals. But this collapse in turn hinted at another, greater indiscretion: the collapse of ideological polarities, those divisions around which culture itself was organized. (1986, 77)

Stuart villains such as Vindice in *The Revenger's Tragedy*, Lorenzo in *The Traitor*, the Cardinal in *The Cardinal*, Bosola in *The Duchess*

151

of Malfi, and De Flores in *The Changeling*, by their multifaceted and inscrutable natures, become manifestations of the Augustinian concept of evil as lack of essence. Thus, as Dollimore argues,

> it seems more useful to talk not of the individualism of this period but of its self-consciousness, especially its sense of self as flexible, problematic, elusive, dislocated, and of course, contradictory: simultaneously arrogant and masochistic, victim and agent, object and effect of power. (1984, 179)

Thus, Stuart depictions of evil as lack of essence provide dramatic meditations on the concept of being itself. Most important, these meditations on the mutable and fragmented self prefigure and perhaps made possible the philosophical theories of Hobbes and Locke. Dramatic fascination with evil thus molded the philosophical and intellectual temper of the following era.

Plays such as *The Changeling, Revenge For Honour, The Traitor, The Maid's Revenge, 'Tis Pity She's A Whore* and *The Unnatural Combat*, which metaphorically represent patriarchy and monarchy in decline, also engage in a communal discourse which carried into the political arena. Vermandero and Florio, for example, disempowered and symbolically slain by their children, evoke sympathy from the audience; their sympathetic depiction, however, suggests that these plays do not reject the patriarchal ideal, but that they reaffirm it by depicting the damaging consequences of its decline. Many plays even suggest that ineffectual or corrupt patriarchs bear responsibility for the tragic events that occur. Increasingly, the later plays reveal an "open structure," which negates any possibility for the reconciliations that concluded earlier tragedies. Literal and metaphoric depictions of regicide and parricide together with a generally dismal vision of patriarchal authority make these plays important documents within a larger communal discourse that climaxed in the political violence of the mid-century. These depictions may even have provoked the political events of the mid-century; as Greenblatt insists, "Jacobean tragedy was in fact one of the decisive influences in the creation of a 'public' that for the first time in history assumed a right to bring a king to justice" (1982, 7). Thus, Stuart depictions of patriarchal decline may be classified under Ricoeur's category of evil: corruption and decay in that which was once healthy and morally sound.

Several plays such as *The Maid's Tragedy, Women Beware Women,* and *'Tis Pity*, by their carnivalesque tone and actions, depict a world turned upside down, a world that has deviated from desirable social norms. Images such as that of the woman-on-top and the carnival-grotesque, which dominate these plays, may be classified under Durkheim's category of evil. Many of the characteristics that Bakhtin denotes as central to the carnivalesque genre may also be found in these plays: death and decay occur in the midst of feasting and copulation, the phallus and the womb figure as prominent images, adultery and incest are dominant issues, and games function as metaphors for central actions. In fact, carnival celebration becomes so intense in a later tragedy, such as Ford's *'Tis Pity*, that the lines of demarcation between moral authority and carnival celebrant are deliberately blurred, and the audience almost participates in or at least condones the carnivalesque social transgressions depicted on the stage. The world-upside-down in Ford's tragedy and in many late tragedies indicates theater's transition into the "bitter" carnival. The carnivalesque and folk elements in many Stuart plays, instances of deviations from and inversions of social norms and thus of Durkheimian evil, may also have contributed to the sociocultural changes that accompanied the political upheavals of the mid-century.

Jacobean and Caroline plays, therefore, did more than merely reflect seventeenth-century society; they provoked cultural changes. Rene Girard's point about classical Greek tragedy perhaps provides an analogy for the great age of drama in England:

> Historians seem to agree that Greek tragedy belonged to a period of transition between the dominance of an archaic theocracy and the emergence of a new, "modern" order based on statism and laws. (1972, 42)

A similar transition seems to occur during the mid-century in England, and Stuart drama contributed to this social change. In psychological terms, Stuart dramatic fascination with the darker world within constitutes a delving by the social psyche into the chthonic, the underworld of evil within to confront it and thus to effect a sociocultural metamorphosis. "Theatre," as Artaud argues, "shakes off material dullness, and collectively reveals their dark powers and hidden strengths to men, urging them to take a nobler, more heroic stand in the face of destiny than they would have assumed without it" (1970, 22). English social fascination with evil in the seventeenth century had such a transformative effect.

Most importantly, however, this relationship between theater and society emerges as nonlinear, ambivalent, and complex. Neither social attitudes nor theatrical representations in the age can be described in monolithic terms, and the relationship between these two worlds emerges as equally fraught with contradictions and ambiguities. For example, despite the Stuart monarchs' insistence on their divine sanction, an argument can be made that they also contributed to an undermining of this position; both James and Charles contributed directly to theories about the king's and Parliament's mutual accountability, an issue which in the 1640s seems to have divided monarch and Parliament. In 1607, for example, John Cowell's *The Interpreter or booke containing the signification of words*, which argued for the absolute rights of the monarch, was suppressed by James himself. Cowell had argued that the king's power could not be questioned or restricted by any earthly authority or laws. The book was debated and condemned in the House of Commons, but the House of Lords seemed reluctant to do much about the issue. The incident might have petered out if James had not intervened to unequivocally denounce Cowell's pretensions to understanding the Law and the rights of king and Parliament. Charles I in 1642 in *His Majesties Answer to the Nineteen Propositions* even more emphatically described England's position as a "regulated monarchy" whose laws were made jointly by its tripartite governing body, the king, the peers, and the commons. Thus, Stuart pretensions to divine sanction coexisted with disclaimers about absolute power. The coexistence of such contradictions permeates all areas of seventeenth-century culture, and drama was no exception.

An interesting play, *The Tragedy of Mariam* (1603–4), may be studied as typical in its depiction of these contradictions. The only play of the period that we know was written by a woman, Lady Elizabeth Carey, the tragedy, like many plays of the period, debates the issue of patriarchal and monarchical authority. Interestingly, however, it presents this issue from the woman's perspective. Recently, Catherine Belsey has made much of the fact that this play, which explores a woman's right to speak, did not see publication until ten years after it was written, and then with its author's name withheld (1985, 175). These circumstances lend themselves easily to our contemporary tendency to read the "silenced" woman's plight into the evolution of this play. But it should be remembered that it was not uncommon for texts to be published several years after they were written. Nor was it unusual to print texts with only the author's initials on them. Much also might be made about its debate of patriarchal authority, but again, its representation of the debate appears to be little different from that in many Stuart plays. The issue remains ambivalent as in Ford's or Middleton's works on the subject.

The play centers on Mariam, wife of Herod, King of the Jews. To marry her, Herod had divorced his first wife, Doris, and rejected his children by her. Later, he secured his position as king by murdering Mariam's brother, an act for which Mariam has not quite forgiven him. Mariam has also learned that Herod has made arrangements for her death if he should be killed while away from his kingdom, a discovery that alienates her from him completely. The play opens with news about Herod's death reaching Mariam as she awaits his return from Rome. Uncertain about whether she should rejoice or grieve, she reminisces about Herod's intense love for her and his former cruelties toward her family. Even as she decides to rejoice in her freedom from the tyrant, however, news arrives that Herod is still alive. Meanwhile, the jealous Salome, Herod's sister, who wishes to divorce her husband, Constabarus, and marry Silleus, plots Mariam's ruin. Herod returns to find Mariam cold and distant, for she has vowed to stay away from his bed. Salome seizes on the opportunity to convince her brother that his wife has been unfaithful to him during his absence. The incensed Herod, convinced about Mariam's infidelity by her coldness toward him, orders her death. He discovers his mistake only too late and goes mad from guilt and pain at the loss of his beloved wife.

The play presents two revolts against patriarchal authority, and thus registers an ambivalent and even contradictory message. The viciously jealous and cruel Salome voices her discontent with patriarchal order several times in the play, as does the chaste and gentle Mariam. Early in the play, as Salome contemplates her new love for Sillius and her hatred of Constabarus, she compares her plight with that of men, who can more easily divorce their spouses:

> It is the principles of Moses lawes,
> For Constabarus still remaines in life,
> If he to me did beare as Earnest hate,
> As I to him, for him there were an ease,
> A seqarating bill might free his fate:
> From such a yoke that did so much displease.
> Why should such privilege to man be given?
> Or given to them, why bard from women then?
> Are men then we in greater grace with Heaven?
> Or cannot women hate as well as men?
> Ile be the custome-breaker: and beginne
> To shewe my sexe the way to freedomes doore.
>
> (1.4. 309–20)

Her denial of Constabarus's right to her bed parallels Mariam's renunciation of Herod's rights over her later in the play. Constabarus, amazed by Salome's audacity, envisions her as a male-female, a hermaphroditic monstrosity:

> Are Hebrew women now transform'd to men?
> Why do you not as well our battles fight,
> And weare our armour? suffer this, and then
> Let all the world be topsie turned quite.
> Let fishes graze, beastes, swine, and birds descend,
> Let fire burn downward while the earth aspires:
> Let Winters heat and Summers cold offend,
> Let Thistels grow on Vines, and Grapes on Briars.
>
> (1.6. 435–38)

Salome responds to this vision of the world upside down by emphasizing her historical position as a pioneer of women's rights:

> For me I am resov'd it shall be so:
> Though I be the first that to this course do bend,
> I shall not be the last full well I know.
>
> (1.6. 448–50)

The play itself presents Mariam, not Salome, as a figure to be emulated and admired, but even this vision remains muted. Shortly before her death, Mariam encounters Doris, who gloats over her rival's downfall in terms that recall Constabarus's description of Salome earlier:

> Your soule is blacke and spotted, full of sinne:
> You in adutry liv'd nine yeare together,
> And heau'n will never let adultery in.
>
> (4.8. 1854–56)

Herod, however, after his rash action, bemoans Mariam's death by comparing her beauty and virtue to Salome's evil. This vision of Mariam receives support in the concluding remarks of the Chorus and determines our ultimate attitude toward the heroine.

The play thus focuses on patriarchal and monarchical authority and attempts by women to subvert both, but the final message of the tragedy remains contradictory. It seems at once to endorse and condemn woman's assertion of power. Even the Chorus remains ambivalent as it debates this issue; it indicates its admiration for Mariam, but also suggests that a wife's duty involves obeying her husband. The play also presents the women who reject patriarchal power in contradictory terms; Salome emerges as a frightening carnival-grotesque, while Mariam is presented as saintly. This tragedy, written by a woman early in the Stuart era, may be regarded as typical in its ambivalent sanction and denunciation of female usurpation of authority. Stuart drama characteristically reveals such ambivalence as it debates not only women's roles in society, but also the monarch's, the dramatist's, and the theater's. Later tragedies such as *The Maid's Tragedy*, *The Changeling*, *Women Beware Women*, and *'Tis Pity She's A Whore* also participate in these communal discourses about patriarchal power and a woman's right to assert herself; but the ambivalence that marks this debate in *Mariam* appears more pronounced in the later plays. And, as we have seen, these intense communal debates within the theatrical arena may have contributed to the radical sociopolitical transformations that occurred in the mid-century.

Archetypes of Transformation: Proteus, the Masque Magician and the Trickster

If any particular image, therefore, may be designated as central to our perception of seventeenth-century drama, it is probably that of transformation or metamorphosis. In fact, Proteus, the sea god, a classical figure associated with metamorphosis, may be treated as a central archetype in the works of the Stuart era. The drama of the period abounds in protean characters; Hamlet, Vindice, and Malevole are only a few of those who crowd the Jacobean and Caroline stage. I would like to conclude this study of evil in Stuart tragedy by suggesting that Proteus, a figure of transformation (one who transforms situations for others and is himself capable of transformation), is an archetypal image central to seventeenth-century drama. Even in plays that do not explicitly refer to him, the protagonists invoke him through their manner and behavior. He dominates our perception of protagonists in many tragedies, of Stuart drama as a whole, and ultimately, of the dramatists themselves as agents of sociocultural transformation.

There are several classical literary sources for the story of Proteus (all probably known to the seventeenth century), among them Homer's *Odyssey* 4. 363–570 and Ovid's *Metamorphoses* 8. 731, 11. 231–65.[1] Homer narrates how Menelaus, king of Sparta, on his return from Troy, was detained on an island; he did not know why he was detained there or how he could obtain passage thence. Finally, with the aid of Proteus's daughter, Eidothea, he was able to force Proteus to answer questions about how he might leave the island. One day Menelaus and his men covered themselves with seal skins provided by Eidothea and lay in wait among the seals for Proteus, the old man of the sea. Menelaus narrates what happened thereafter:

> At midday the old man himself emerged, found his fat seals already there, and went the rounds to make the count. Entirely unsuspicious of the fraud, he included us as the first four in his flock. When he had done, he too lay down to sleep. Then, with a shout, we leapt upon him and flung our arms round his back. But the old man's skill and cunning had not deserted him. He began by turning into a bearded lion and then a snake, and after that a panther and a giant boar. He changed into running water too and a great tree in leaf. But we set our teeth and held him like a vice. (1946, 76)

Menelaus's determination paid off, and the weary Proteus was finally forced to answer Menelaus's questions about his return home.

Ovid modifies Proteus's nature somewhat and describes the rape of Thetis, the sea goddess, by Peleus, who succeeds only after he consults Proteus. Thetis, like Proteus, can change shape at will, and thus resists Peleus's advances several times. But Peleus consults the gods of the sea, and Proteus advises him to hold on to Thetis despite her many transformations, until she becomes her original self again; Peleus thus "attained his desire and begat on her the great Achilles" (264–65). In this story, Proteus figures as an agent of violence, but he also makes possible the birth of the great Achilles (he had prophesied earlier that Thetis would beget a son who would surpass his father in greatness).

Ovid's description of Glaucus, another sea deity, very similar to Proteus, captures vividly the ambiguous and multifaceted nature of the sea gods. Glaucus, enamored of Scylla, tries to approach her, but she flees him, "not knowing if he was a monster or a god" (13: 912). Glaucus relates his transformation from a mortal to a sea-god, hoping to gain her sympathy, but frightened by his appearance, she flees from him.

Several points in these accounts are especially relevant to seventeenth-century drama; Proteus is, first of all, a trickster; he changes shape at will, and thus is an elusive figure. In Homer's account, ultimately he is himself a prey to trickery devised by Eidothea and Menelaus; he holds the key to Menelaus's return, but divulges information only under duress. In Ovid's account, he similarly aids Peleus. In all accounts he is also an ambiguous figure, both fearsome (perhaps even suggestive of evil) and helpful, dangerous and holding prophetic powers. A figure of the deep, he can even be associated with chthonic powers.

To varying degrees, all of these factors apply to protagonists in many Jacobean and Caroline plays. Iago in *Othello*. Bosola in *The Duchess of Malfi*, De Flores in *The Changeling*, Shakespeare's Macbeth, Malevole in *The Malcontent*, Maximus in Fletcher's *Vantentinian*, the Cardinal in Shirley's play by that name, and the Duke in *Women Beware Women* are only a few examples.

The image of Proteus is relevant also to the literary form of the masque, a form essentially about transformation and an important influence on Stuart drama. Two events are important in the development of the court masque as a form: the presentation of Jonson's masque *Proteus and the Adamantine Rock*, which ushered a change in the form, as critics have recognized,[2] and his invention of the antimasque in 1608, a feature which became very prominent in the masques of the Caroline period. *Proteus* introduced an idea that became central to all subsequent masques, that of transformation; of course, transformation always had been an important aspect of the masques, but the theme became more markedly central in the later masques. I am not suggesting that Jonson's masque and his interest in Proteus were responsible for this change; but I find it interesting that Jonson's composition stands at what has generally been recognized as a turning point in the development of the masque as a form and that it introduces an image that is primary in the masques and plays of the Stuart period.

The antimasque in particular influenced many Jacobean and Caroline plays. It must be remembered that the average man was excluded from the extravagant court performances and perceived them only from the outside through popular accounts and hearsay. But many plays of the period, either by incorporating masques or by invoking the masque in temper and mood, suggest some general opinions among the public about the form. People seem certainly to have been aware of its deficiencies, and plays such as *The Revenger's Tragedy* clearly express the falsity inherent in the form:

> The masque is treason's licence, that build upon
> 'Tis murder's best face when a vizard's on.
>
> (5.1. 181–82)

Strato, in *The Maid's Tragedy*, also describes the false flattery of masques:

> Yes; they must commend their king, and speak in praise
> Of the assembly, bless the bride and bridegroom

In person of some god; they're tied to rules
Of flattery.

(1.1. 11–14)

Strato's opinion about the masque is given in response to Lysippius's question, "Strato, thou hast some skill in poetry; / What think'st thou of a masque?" (5–6). Supposedly the opinion of the skilled poet, his attitude may be taken as similar to the dramatists' themselves.

Masques were often a part of celebrations; they thus shared traits with many popular festivals. The most important festival seasons in England were the Carnival and the twelve nights of Christmas, and masquing was a prominent aspect of these celebrations. In the present study, I have been interested not in the court masques themselves, but in their influence on the drama of the period, and the extent to which Stuart drama shares the transformative power of the masque. The masques in the drama are significantly different in temper from the Jacobean and Caroline court masques. On the popular stage, masques are multifaceted and eclectic, sharing aspects of the sophisticated royal masques and those of popular celebrations and communal customs such as the carnival, the charivari, and the dance of death that I discussed in the previous chapter. In form and temper, they incorporate subversion and the carnivalesque. By including masques within their plays, and by using these masques to comment on the central actions of their plays, Stuart dramatists invoke the transformative theme conventional in the masque and thus compel the audience or reader to extend that theme to the plays themselves.

Two other conventional figures from other traditions who shared some of Proteus's characteristics might also have contributed to the creation of Stuart protagonists: the trickster (who often was a variation of the medieval Vice figure) and the masque magician. The masque magician seems to have emerged in the later Jacobean masques; he was often the author of the antimasque (or antemasque as it was sometimes called), the spectacle that preceded the actual masque. Barbara Traister points out that "because of their involvement with the antimasque, the magicians themselves are grotesque characters, creators of chaos and disharmony" (1984, 158). These magicians of the stage are "both admirable and flawed, talented, but doomed to fail" (35). Iago, who directs the tragedy of *Othello*, Vindice, who directs *The Revenger's Tragedy*, and Lorenzo, who likewise stages *The Traitor*, are such figures, aware of the poetic and dramatic, yet agents of chaos and tragedy. Like conventional magicians, these figures change shape at will, are aware of most of the intrigues within the play, and mete out punishment to those they deem offenders; in the secular setting of the theater, dramatists have merely subsumed their conventional magical powers to emphasize instead their creative the artistic abilities.

The trickster was not a figure exclusive to drama; he was associated with many folk rituals and even with communal systems such as the marketplace and the fair. His influence on the drama provides an instance of the influence of plebian culture on the literary form. J.B. Russell argues that "the fundamental character of the trickster was the upsetting of order, but this can also release creative energies" (1977, 75), a characteristic that closely resembles Proteus's function in Ovid's account.

Ultimately all three figures, the protean malcontent, the trickster, and the masque magician, seem to have been mirror images of the dramatists themselves as they challenged convention and sought to effect a metamorphosis in society. In fact, critics have often regarded some of these figures as theatrical versions of the dramatists themselves; Dollimore notes that Vindice "is invested with a theatrical sense resembling the dramatist's own" (1984, 140). Muriel Bradbrook also emphasizes the relationship between dramatists and these stage-magicians:

> What is the magician but, as always in the old plays, a stage manager of shows, with his wand and his magic inscribed 'book'—what is this but a sublimated Master of Revels? (quoted in Traister 1984, 127)

We might even argue that Stuart dramatists themselves function within the theatrical role of the conventional trickster figure. Mircea Eliade's description of the trickster in mythology and religion as ambivalent and equivocal, responsible both for death and for transformation, may be applied to the dramatists (1969, 156). Like the trickster figure, dramatists succeed by dissimulation, through the theatrics of allusive representation. Usurping the conventional role of the trickster, dramatists mock the "sacred," and while their ridicule has a transforming effect, it ultimately turns against them in the closing of the theaters in 1642.

In this context, I would like to suggest that the dramatists, as they embody and effect this cultural transition, as they immerse themselves through their drama in "the transitional element of ritual passage," perform a function that Victor Turner ascribes to "liminaries" in the performance of ritual. Turner describes how these liminaries in many primitive cultures are frequently presented as masked, androgynous, and anonymous transvestites of the surrounding social structure (1986, 25–26). The protagonists in many Stuart plays, as they reflect and mirror the desires of the dramatists and the sociocultural system of which they are a part, also exhibit a similar complex and contradictory nature. Tourneur's Vindice, Beaumont's and Fletcher's Melantius, Fletcher's Maximus, and Shirley's Cardinal and Lorenzo, although villains themselves, also wreak vengeance on other villains. Figures such as Marston's Malevole function as agents of morality, but their language and actions nevertheless evoke ambivalent responses from the audience. Like the plays themselves, these figures exhibit dual and contradictory tendencies as they both affirm and negate the social structure of which they are a part.

The play that comes most to mind in this context, because of its frequent concern with masques, its depiction of the masque magician, and its interest in the theme of transformation by water (an invocation of the Proteus image), is probably Shakespeare's last play, *The Tempest*. Prospero constantly suggests the masque magician; but Ariel and Caliban, because they too know the magical world, share aspects of Prospero's character and seem in some senses to be extensions of his personality. These three figures manifest varying levels of a similar power: Ariel represents the spirit world and through his several transformations resembles Proteus; Prospero belongs to the human world, but like the masque magician, he has gained an awareness of the supernatural realm through study and practice; Caliban is also privy to some of these powers, but he is the trickster figure, seeking to regain power by wiles and cunning rather than by patient study.[3]

In fact, Shakespeare's *Tempest* contains many of the images that I have been discussing as central to Jacobean drama. The play even represents the dual bodies of the ruler—one divine and the other corruptible—in the characters of Prospero and Alonso. The work is about transformation wrought through the drama presented by Prospero, which includes a ritual cleansing by water and a masque. The play reasserts the patriarchal norm that had been undermined; at the end of the play, we can assume that Prospero has abandoned his earlier carelessness about his state, when he paid more attention to his books than to political affairs. It also invokes carnival and festival through image and action; the brutish Caliban is elevated to the status of a lord in the underplot, and the king's son is reduced to the level of a menial servant by Prospero. And, most important, Prospero invokes the presence of the poet-creator himself as a transformer of society; custom has regarded Prospero's farewell to his magic as also signifying Shakespeare's farewell to the stage. Thus, Shakespeare's play provides rich material for a simultaneous inquiry into many of the themes that I discussed in this study.

But the idea of the transformative power of drama is not exclusive to this play, or even to Shakespeare's work. It seems to have been inherent in the Renaissance concept of imitation and the theory of art as a mirror of life. Hamlet's famous thought on acting and playwriting may be remembered in this context. Critics have often suggested that *Hamlet* is about playwriting and that Hamlet's words on the subject may be treated as a reflection of what Shakespeare himself believed about the function of art and the artist, especially the dramatist. At any rate, Hamlet voices, if not Shakespeare's opinion, at least a theory of art that we may regard as common in his time. Describing the players (and by extension, plays themselves) as "the abstract and brief chronicles of the time," Hamlet requests that they be well received at court. At the end of the same scene, he articulates most fully what is expected of a good play:

> Hum, I have heard
> That guilty creatures sitting at a play
> Have by the very cunning of the scene
> Been struck so to the soul that presently
> They have proclaimed their malefactions.
>
> (2.2. 589–93)

In other words, the play does not simply reflect reality, *it prompts a response form the spectators and creates a new social situation.* Hamlet's concept of the play as provoking action is most fully apparent in what he expects from the staging of *The Murder of Gonzago.* Only in general outline does the play "mirror" the actions of Claudius; its plot, in fact, is "the image of a murder done in Vienna." In other words, its plot might mirror several such stories of deceit and murder. That is precisely why Hamlet spends so much time coaching the players in their art; only though accurate action can the play effectively "mirror" life. In a recent study of mirror imagery in the Renaissance, Herbert Grabes remarks on the particular fascination of early Stuart England with the image; the mirror appears with marked frequency in the century between 1550 and 1650, but decreases radically after the mid-century (1982, 12). He also points out various instances of the mirror as an agent of transformation (131–32). This central trope of the Renaissance theater perhaps indicates most emphatically the age's belief in the transformative power of art.

The transformative power of Hamlet's play, for example, emerges immediately at its staging. The play provokes immediate action from Claudius; it makes possible Gertrude's scene of repentance a little later; and it confirms Hamlet's own need to act promptly. Its success may be measured only by the degree of response it provoked; thus, Hamlet can claim that he may qualify for "a fellowship in a cry of players." The action of the play within the play parodies actions that had already occurred; if this inner play can be treatd as a stylized rendering of reality, Shakespeare's own tragedy of evil also demands that we regard it in those terms. Shakespeare provokes us into considering that his tragedy, another stylized version of reality, also has the power to trigger social changes.

This power of drama and language to create action is articulated throughout Shakespeare's works. In *Macbeth*, the drama staged by the witches prompts the rest of the action; in *The Tempest*, Prospero's drama results in a new social world to which the characters return at the end of the play; in *Othello*, Iago casually puts on a performance that has disastrous effects. Thus, New Historicist belief in the power of texts to transform sociopolitical situations is quite in keeping with Renaissance theories about the power of stage plays to "mirror" and thus transform life. Like Hamlet's version of *The Murder of Gonzago*, these Renaissance and Stuart plays were much more than passive reflectors of reality; vehicles of subversion and criticism, they determined the sociocultural transformations of the mid-century. Even as Hamlet's stylized tragedy on evil effected a change in Denmark, so Jacobean and Caroline depictions of evil had important effects on the sociocultural temper of seventeenth-century England.

Dramatic Legacies: Milton's Satan

These depictions of evil are not, of course, restricted to drama, although Stuart dramatists more than any other literary artists reveal a tenacious preoccupation with evil. As I have tried to suggest, the prose works of Dekker and Nashe also provide contexts through which seventeenth-century fascination with evil might be explored. Many poets of the period also evidence a similar concern with evil and dwell on the darker aspects of the human psyche. For example, in Phineas Fletcher's narrative poem *The Locusts, or Appolyonists* (1627), an important influence on Milton's representation of evil later in the century, Lucifer is described as a fall from self-hood:

> Thus fell this Prince of Darkness, once a bright
> And glorious star; he willful turned away
> His borrowed globe from that eternal light;
> Himself he sought, so lost himself: his ray
> Vanished to smoke, his morning sunk in night,
> And never more shall see the springing day.
>
> (1908, 171–76)

As in many dramatic versions of villainy, the essence of evil to Fletcher lies in Lucifer's lack of self.

In Milton's Satan, a vision of evil in which the age culminates, we have, in fact, an extended treatment of evil as lack of essence. Although he is not a figure on the stage, we can assume that Milton's Satan owes much to Stuart theatrical depictions of evil. Satan's transformation from angel to fiend becomes a central issue in the epic even as, for example, Vindice's transformation into a villain had been in *The Revenger's Tragedy*. In fact, our response to Satan during the epic is similar to our response to Vindice; we move gradually from involved sympathy to total condemnation. Satan's transformation is dramatically presented to us through the series of disguises that he takes, but most vividly in the scene in which Ithuriel exposes one of them, his disguise as a toad. Not recognizing Lucifer, Ithuriel questions him:

> Which of those rebel spirits adjudged to hell
> Comest thou, escaped thy prison, and transformed,
> Why sattest thou like an enemy in wait
> Here watching at the head of these that sleep?
>
> (4. 823–26)

Satan's pique at not being recognized by Ithuriel only emphasizes the discrepancy between his concept of self and the reality.

The most dramatic statement about Satan as lacking in substance is made early in *Paradise Lost*. In book 1, the poet describes Satan and his followers after their fall as

> godlike shapes and forms
> Excelling human, princely dignities,
> And powers that erst in heaven sat on thrones;
> Though of their names in heavenly records now
> Be no memorial blotted out and rased
> By their rebellion, from the books of life.
>
> (1. 358–63)

The erasure of the rebels' names metaphorically equates their fall into evil with the blotting of essence.

Stuart depictions of patriarchy and monarchy in decline may also be compared with Milton's treatment of the subject in *Paradise Lost*. Milton's quarrel, as Stevie Davies has recently argued, does not seem to be with patriarchy and monarchy themselves but with patriarchy and monarchy among men in its fallen state. (1983, 8). In his Satan, Milton combines many of the traits he saw in Charles I and provides us with two distinct visions of patriarchy: God's reign in heaven, marked by constancy and authority, and Satan's in hell, marked by changeability and corruption. Despite his affiliations with the Commonwealth, Milton's major poetic endeavor seems ultimately to support the patriarchal ideal, even as many Stuart plays did. But like them, he presents the system in its state of decline through the character (and influence) of Satan.

Milton also presents us with the carnivalesque verison of evil in *Paradise Lost*; Satan becomes a supreme example of the carnival-grotesque as he transforms from angel to tempter, and the poet repeatedly stresses his ambivalent and dual nature. In form he retains some of his earlier glory, and yet his expressions often give him away; even as a serpent during the temptation scene, he does not entirely mask his grotesque state between the human and animal bodies. Eve instantly remarks on this dual quality, although she remains oblivious of its danger and is drawn by it: "Redouble then this miracle, and say, / How camest thou speakable of mute" (9. 561–62). As in Stuart dramatic depictions, the grotesque body remains fascinating, although also dangerous and hideous. In the passage from Phineas Fletcher cited earlier, the poet depicts Lucifer's character as it changes from light to darkness but emphasizes the change after it has occurred. In Milton's Satan, however, we have a more intense representation of the carnival-grotesque; Milton dwells on Satan's protean nature, emphasizing his transformation even as it occurs from archangel to arch fiend. In *Paradise Lost*, therefore, we actually witness Satan's transformation as it occurs.

Again, Milton's repeated use of oxymorons to describe Satan's grotesque nature might be compared with Phineas Fletcher's description of Sin in *The Appolyonists*:

> The porter to the infernal gate is Sin,
> A shapeless shape, a foul deformed thing,
> Nor nothing, nor a substance, as those thin
> And empty forms which through the air fling

> Their wandering shapes, at length they're fastened in
> The crystal sight. It serves, yet reigns as king;
> It lives, yet's death; it please, full of pain;
> Monster. ah, who, who can thy being feign?
> Thou shapeless shape, live death, pain
> pleasing, servile reign.

(1908, 82–90)

In this passage and the one cited earlier, we have instances of the Bakhtinian grotesque; Fletcher presents Sin as an ambivalent and hideous combination of opposites. Milton extends the description of Sin to present us with several deformed bodies and with a vividly grotesque image of the endless assault on body by body. In Sin's description of her incestuous relationship with Death, the phallus and the womb are primary images; in book 2, Sin describes her rape by Death and the result of that rape:

> These yelling monsters that with ceaseless cry
> Surround me, as thou sawest, hourly conceived
> And hourly born, with sorrow infinite
> To me, for when they list into the womb
> That bred them they return, and howl and gnaw
> My bowels, their repast.

(2. 795–800)

The scene presents us with images explored on the stage in plays such as *The Revenger's Tragedy* and *The Maid's Tragedy* through their treatments of physical mutilation and decay. Feasting and bodily decay occur simultaneously. Milton's depiction of evil may thus owe a great deal to Stuart dramatic representations of the same. The grotesque in seventeenth-century literature derives, as Neil Rhodes argues, "from the unstable coalescence of contrary images of the flesh: indulged, abused, purged and damned" (1980, 4).

The carnivalesque-charivaric image of the woman-on-top also figures in *Paradise Lost*. In book 9, for example, Eve wishes to work separately from Adam primarily to prove her "firmness" as equal to his. The ambiguity that characterizes Milton's depiction of Eve is similar to dramatic depictions of women we have encountered earlier. Although not a carnival-grotesque in the mold of Lady Macbeth or Evadne, Eve's characterization emphasizes the ambiguity of the patriarchal system. Shakespeare's depiction of Kate in *The Taming of the Shrew* might be recalled at this point. Shakespeare's play emphasizes the patriarchal system, yet implies that that system is 'an exception rather than the norm. Similarly,

Milton champions the patriarchal system, yet his characterization of Eve insists on the discrepancy between ideal and actuality. This discrepancy is especially apparent in Eve's manipulation of Adam in book 9 in which Adam objects to their working separately:

> So spake the patriarch of mankind, but Eve
> Persisted, yet submissive, though last, replied.

(9. 376–77)

Milton's choice of words emphasizes the irony of the man-woman relationship. The "patriarch of mankind" speaks his mind, but Eve's "submissive" persistence nevertheless has the last word. Thus, the primal scene is itself fraught with such inconsistency; Milton seems to be implying that the discrepancy has always existed.

Thus, throughout the seventeenth century, both poets and dramatists seem to have been especially fascinated with the theme of evil. But this fascination does not indicate a general moral decadence as early critics of this literature often argued. Explorations of evil on the stage directly influenced the sociopolitical temper of the age and perhaps even precipitated the social drama of the mid-century. I have tried in this study to pinpoint some of these sociopolitical changes effected by Stuart drama.

Many of the ideas explored in this study apply also to Milton's Satan, the figure of evil with which the age culiminates. He is a carnival-grotesque, whose ever-changing protean nature links him with villains such as Vindice and the Cardinal. He is also the arch trickster who is ultimately a prey to his own trickery. Like Vindice and Iago, he is also the supreme artist, a magician, a fascinating creator of spectacular illusions. In Satan, Milton projects an intensely vivid variation on the protean trickster figures of the Stuart stage. It is perhaps no irony that Milton includes this supreme instance of evil, this creator of chaos and disharmony, in a work whose avowed purpose is to "justify the ways of God to men," to emphasize the good that would result from Man's fortunate fall to the power of evil. Stuart dramatic fascination with evil perhaps had a similar productive purpose.

Notes

Chapter 1. Dramatic Fascination with Evil

1. For traditional readings of the play as a comedy of mirth see Patricia Thompson, "The Old Way and the New Way in Dekker and Massinger," *MLR* 51 (1956): 168–78; H. E. Toliver, "*The Shoemaker's Holiday:* Theme and Image," *Boston University Studies in English* 5 (1961): 208–18; and Joel H. Kaplan, "Virtue's Holiday: Thomas Dekker and Simon Eyre," *Renaissance Drama* 2 (1969): 103–22.
    More recently, critics have recognized that the play is not so pure a comedy of mirth as it has traditionally been regarded. David Scott Kaston has argued that although the play resolves as a comedy and it idealizes work, "the idealization takes place in a commercial theatrical environment that itself exposes the fantasy" of the play's festive tone; the comedy, in other words, both creates a tone of ideal jollity and at the same time proclaims the illusion of its tone through self-conscious and extreme idealization (1987, 336). The darker elements have been recognized by other critics as well. I list the most interesting among these essays: Peter Mortenson, "The Economics of Joy in *The Shoemaker's Holiday*," *SEL* 16 (1976): 241–52; and Lawrence Venuti, "Transformation of City Comedy: A Symptomatic Reading," *Assays* 3 (1985): 99–134.
    2. Several essays in *The Anthropology of Evil*, ed. by David Parkin, explore the varying reasons for this disappearance.
    3. The following are a few examples: Anthony Harris, *Night's Black Agents*, Barbara Howard Traister, *Heavenly Necromancers: The Magician in English Renaissance Drama*, and David Woodman, *White Magic and the English Renaissance Drama*.
    4. See studies by Alan Macfarlane and Stuart Clark on the subject.
    5. Stuart Clark notes that "the witch craze in Scotland lasted till 1596, but . . . these were the last recorded personal contacts [for James] with witches in Scotland, and there is nothing comparable in his dealings with them in England" (1977, 161)
    6. This holds true even in plays which still use the supernatural; in a later revenge play such as *The Unnatural Combat*, for example, the ghosts of Malefort junior and his mother appear to Malefort senior, who had been responsible for their deaths. The dramatic scene certainly induces guilt in Malefort senior, but it occurs after his villainous actions have been completed and contributes little to the movement of the plot.
    7. Bataille remains unclear about the exact nature of this "intense communication." He seems to equate it simply with the evocation of a strong emotional response in the reader, as evoked by characters such as Heathcliff in *Wuthering Heights*. I am, of course, modifying Bataille's phrase and extending it to include more than an emotional response. The sociopolitical changes that take place in seventeenth-century England seem to me to be partly a result of the "intense communication" between literature and society in this period.

8. Thus, for example, in Christian explications of conflicts between God and Satan, the latter is always doomed to ultimate failure. Howver potent his power, Satan remains weak in comparison to God.

9. For an interesting application of Ricoeur's theory of evil to the seventeenth century, see John S. Tanner's essay on Milton in *PMLA* 103, no. 1 (January 1988): 45–56.

10. In this sense, as a deviation from desirable norms, Durkheim designates suicide an "evil" in the concluding chapter of his influential study of the subject. He thus provides an entirely secular definition of the term.

11. A recent issue of the *Critical Inquiry* (vol. 14, no. 3), for example, devoted to essays on the "sociology of literature," exemplifies this general trend during the past decade to emphasize sociocultural contexts. But, as the editors in their introduction to the volume point out, there is little agreement about what constitutes the "sociology of literature" even among its foremost practitioners.

12. The particular popularity of both psychoanalysis and deconstruction among critics of the nineteenth and twentieth centuries has been recognized by others (Selden 1985, 89). On the other hand, Renaissance (and eighteenth century) critics have for the most part been tentative about both theoretical schools. Stephen Greenblatt, for example, in a recent essay on psychoanalysis and Renaissance texts, notes their apparent incompatibility, a factor, he argues, that is apparent even in the writings of Sigmund Freud (1986, 210). Although his arguments are stunningly original, the essay itself is ultimately a reiteration of the old suspicion against psychoanalysis, because it is a post-Jacobean field of enquiry.

13. For example, see Greenblatt's "Improvisation and Power," pp. 57–99, and Girard's "'To Entrap the Wisest': A Reading of *The Merchant of Venice*," 100–19.

14. The shift in the last ten years in the criticism of sixteenth- and seventeenth-century drama has perhaps been sharper than that between the early half of this century and the 1970s, when the primary influence was that of T. S. Eliot and the New Critics. This becomes particularly apparent when one considers that even recent statements now seem almost dated. In 1977, Larry S. Champion was able to preface his book, *Tragic Patterns in Jacobean and Caroline Drama*, with the following statement: "Obviously, the plays are not allegories; with rare exceptions, they are not even suggestive of particular contemporary events, and there will be no attempt here to relate them to political and social contexts" (6). Thus, the New Critical stand, although qualified and modified by most critical schools, still echoes in works written even as recently as the last decade.

15. What I have said in favor of the New Historicism is not a plea for its sanction on account of its modishness; its importance as a critical methodology can hardly be underestimated, despite the voices of discontent that have already been raised against it. It has provided a powerful response to extremist positions that have dominated critical trends in recent years. It has not only destroyed belief in the self-sufficiency of texts but has also reawakened interest in historical contexts; it has opened the avenue for a truly interdisciplinary approach to literature; and, most importantly, it has relocated the power of the text in the ability of its words to *create* new environments. In other words, contrary to Champion's claim in 1977, Historicists have contended that playwrights and poets do indeed "represent the philosophical forefront of the age" (6); in fact, they helped create it.

16. My enthusiasm for the methodology is not simply a matter of personal bias; Peter L. Rudnytsky's description of the contemporary situation in a recent review essay is, I believe, an attitude shared by many; he suggests that the emergence of the New Historicism has made this "an exceptionally exciting period in Renaissance

literary studies" and that the new movement has "led to a fundamental rethinking of the interrelationships between literature and society" in which "the easy distinctioin between foreground and background, text and context" no longer holds (1987, 153)

17. This is true about most practitioners of the New Historicism, among them, Greenblatt, Dollimore, and Orgel.

18. For a thorough study of seventeenth-century antitheatrical attitudes, see Jonas Barish, *The Antitheatrical Prejudice* (Berkeley & Los Angeles: Univ. of California Press, 1981.)

19. My support of the New Historicism is not to imply that there are no differences among the critics whose writings fall under that category; as Peter Erickson points out, "though the New Historicism often conveys the effect of a united front, it has never been monolithic" (1987, 331). Critical of what he describes as the New Historicists's general apolitical temper, Erickson draws fine distinctions among Greenblatt's conservative conclusions, Goldberg's deconstructionist tendencies, and Montrose's feminist and cultural-materialist perspectives. While I disagree with Erickson's final analysis of the value of New Historicism, the distinctions he makes among the three groups and his description of the methodology of each is markedly accurate.

20. Bruce Robbins summarizes these voices of discontent that note the pitfalls of interdisciplinary work, particularly those that invoke "history":

> Scholars may know much in their own discipline remains controversial, but they tend to act as if this weren't true for other people's disciplines. A prime example is the appeal to "history" by literary critics, as if history were somehow less controversial than the texts it is brought in to resolve (1987, 83).

But, he concludes, "this systematic passing of the buck is the interdisciplinarity we now have," and a new methodology in which neither discipline is abused to suit immediate purposes awaits "the devising of a different interdisciplinarity" (96) While the about-turn by Robbins at the end of his essay seems almost a naive preservation of the state of things, there is a great deal of truth to his claim. Interdisciplinarity is a welcome alternative to viewing intellectual, artistic, and scientific endeavors as discrete areas of study, but it is unrealistic to demand that critics be fully aware of all the problems in every discipline, or that no partiality exists in interdisciplinary studies. As Rene Girard so eloquently argues,

> All around us, many walls and partitions have crashed to the ground. To pretend that we need a special license to do "interdisciplinary work" is to assume that these walls are still standing. ... The walls have crumbled because there never was a solid foundation underneath. ... The conditions are such that no research orientation can be presented as absolutely "authoritative." No research orientation, therefore, can be dismissed a priori. (1978, xvi)

21. Many historians regard the major turning point in public attitudes toward violence as occurring in the seventeenth century. Alan Macfarlane, for example, argues that the "eradicating of endemic violence and the personality changes associated with it" occurred after this period (1981, 1). For a detailed discussion of social histories that describe this period as a turning point, see Macfarlane's introduction in the same volume.

22. "Liminal" here is used (as it is by psychologists) to indicate the point of interchange between two equally powerful emotional stimuli; in many cases, this "threshold of discrimination" gradually ceases to be perceptible.

23. Greenblatt's argument centers on the theory that the modern concept of "self" is a post-Elizabethan phenomenon, a direct result of Elizabethan and Jacobean texts. The argument is not new; Dollimore in *Radical Tragedy* makes a similar claim when he notes that identity in the Jacobean drama is a fictional construct. Dollimore makes a distinction which, however, is collapsed in Greenblatt's essay to yield the startling conclusion he is then able to draw. While Dollimore indicates that the drama is self-consciously aware of the problem of identity, he nevertheless analyzes several plays as they depict the protagonists' search for the self. In other words, drama might ultimately posit the theory that the self is a construct, but the dramatic tension in most of these plays relies on the dialectic caused by *the need to believe in the self and the realization that the self is perhaps an artificial construct.*

Another major problem in Greenblatt's essay is that he assumes the Freudian model of the self as a non controversial and generally accepted belief among all psychologists. In the psychological theories of many others, notably Jung, the self, as in the drama of the Jacobean period, is a goal and a desire, not an inherent attribute in man. In fact, psychologists such as Jung are interested in precisely the phenomenon that Dollimore describes in the drama, man's *continuous* and therefore *always incomplete* search for the self.

I will argue in this study that the theories of psychoanalysis, especially non- and post-Freudian ones that have discarded the subjective model of the self, may indeed illumine the literature of this period (and any peiod, for that matter), and that psychological theories are hardly extraneous and post-Jacobean realizations.

In the final analysis, although I find Greenblatt's essays continually absorbing, I would have to agree with Peter Erickson's recent criticism that despite his original approach to texts, Greenblatt "does not finally change traditional readings of those works; rather, he confines and even justifies them from another angle" (1987, 333). To Erickson, "Greenblatt remains the key figure at the center of the new historicism because he epitomizes the bar against asking certain kinds of questions" (332). My own ultimate dissatisfaction with the New Historicism springs from its attempt (despite its theoretical claims to the contrary) to make certain fields of inquiry alien to the study of literature.'

I have elaborated on Greenblatt's arguments and dwelt on my own objections in detail, because the concept of the self in Stuart tragedy becomes crucial in my own arguments later in this study.

24. Interestingly, Bataille also finds Ford's play fascinating and cites it as one of only three works intensely and solely concerned with evil.

25. Although my argument emphasizes the importance of the audience, I do not mean to suggest that the revolutionaries who executed Charles I saw Stuart tragedies and were prompted to action by these plays. What I would like to suggest is that the remarkable degree of acquiescence from the nation as a whole in the matter of Charles's execution was made possible by Stuart dramatic depictions of corrupt or declining monarchical systems. Even silent acquiescence in the political events of the mid-century constituted political action. I will argue that such political action, this general social acquiescence, owes much to Stuart theatrical depictions of monarchy and patriarchy.

26. In a recent study of the relationship between carnival and theater, Michael D. Bristol seems to be making precisely the same claim. I would like to explore more fully the implications of some of the statements he makes in that study. Bristol's choice of "carnival" rather than ritual, I find particularly interesting, because carnival is a "festival without a patron," without "an owner," and in this

definition, "there is a strong distributive, democratic, and naturally compensatory content" (Matta 1984, 225). Treated as a whole, Jacobean and Caroline drama may be seen as exhibiting features of the carnival; it expresses collective festivity.

27. Hayward discusses the relationship between the madmen's scene in Webster's *The Duchess of Malfi* and the charivari, an essentially disruptive form of folk culture. He concludes his essay with a provocative suggestion about the relationship between Elizabethan drama in general and the charivari, a relationship I will explore most fully in chapter 4.

28. My use of the term *ritual* to describe Stuart drama is, of course, an over simplification, and I am aware that I lay myself open to the charge of generalization. But by invoking ritual, I do not mean to imply that ritual and drama are identical. I hope merely to stress the ritual origins of the drama in this age; much may be gained by discussing some of the attributes that ritual and dramatic performance share, especially as the forms seem to be closely allied in these periods.

Several recent studies have discussed the close alliance between these forms, especially in earlier or "primitive" cultures. The following are a few examples: Victor Turner, *From Ritual to Theatre*; John J. MacAloon, ed. *Rite, Drama, Festival, Spectacle*; Michael D. Bristol, *Carnival and Theater*. For an interesting discussion of the manner in which literature both imitates and differs from ritual, I refer the reader to opening pages of a recent essay by Sophia S. Morgan on Borges's fiction.

29. This is true especially of earlier critics. See, for example, Paul V. Krieder's and Hardin Craig's studies.

30. For a detailed study of the mirror as more than a reflector of attitudes, see Herbert Grabes's *The Mutable Glass*. He make the interesting point that although the mirror is used frequently during the century between 1550 and 1650, there is a marked decrease in its use in the latter half of the seventeenth century (12). The period of its greatest frequency seems to parallel the emergence of drama as a major artistic form.

31. See, for example, Rene Girard's most recent works on the subject of imitation, especially *"To double business bound."*

32. Evidence for this "intertextuality" can be found in several aspects of the play but most vividly in important Biblical analogies that focus on the issue of the Christian versus the Jew. Interestingly, Shakespeare avoids any mention of two associations, Cain and Barrabas, that had been characteristic of previous depictions of Jews, including Marlowe's. However, he retains certain characteristics relevant to both Barrabas and Cain through other Biblical analogies.

The most important of these references, the reference to Jacob, occurs in a key speech by Shylock in Act 1, Scene 3. Though justification of usury forms the focus of Shylock's speech, his reference to Jacob carries more important resonances. First, he uses Jacob as a common forbear of both Jews and Christians. But he also makes a passing reference to Jacob's other famous instance of cheating, namely, his cheating his brother of his birthright, an act devised by his mother and condoned by God; the speech may thus be a veiled reference to the displacement of the Jews by the Christians as the favored children of God. The substitution of Jacob for Cain in order to represent paternal favoritism necessarily complicates the Christian versus Jew issue. The moral outcome of the Cain and Abel encounter remains unquestionable; Cain is a jealous murderer and undoubtedly in the wrong. Esau, on the other hand, is deceived, and though one might accept God's preference of Jacob as an inexplicable divine preference, Esau evokes some sympathy through his unwarranted loss.

Shylock later suggests yet another parallel between the Christian-Jew issue and a Biblical tale about brothers. In Act 2, Scene 1, the line "But yet I'll go in hate, to feed upon / The prodigal Christian," may simply be a reference to the fact that Antonio lends money gratis, but the context of its occurence suggests that it may actually be a veiled reference to the new Testament story of the prodigal son. Shylock, like the older brother in the Biblical story, had earlier refused to dine with the Christians, but has now been persuaded to participate in their "feast." The reference once again makes the relationship between the Christians and the Jews similar to the relationship between two brothers, the younger of whom, despite his spendthrift ways, receives special treatment from his father. Again, Shylock sees himself as the older brother displaced perhaps unfairly by the younger, and thus made an outsider within his own family.

A similar use is made of another Biblical story about a rejected brother, Ishmael. The incident of Abraham's rejection of Ishmael after the birth of Isaac, creates an emotional response similar to that created by the stories of Jacob and the prodigal son, for it arouses our sympathy for the unfortunate Ishmael. But the reference to Ishmael in *The Merchant*—"What says that fool of Hagar's offspring?" (2.5. 43)—is interesting for more than that reason. It follows immediately after Launcelot's little song which raises the Christian versus the Jew issue, and may thus be intended as a gloss on it from the Jewish perspective. At any rate, Shylock sees his daughter, Jessica, and by extension, himself and all Jews, as Hagar's offsprings cast out unfairly by a patriarch who favors his younger son.

Shakespeare seems to be using these Biblical references to dramatize two themes: the theme of conflict between brothers, and the theme of inexplicable paternal preference. Had he wished simply to make the issue between Christianity and Jewishness a clear-cut moral issue between brothers, the story of Cain and Abel would have served him well. Again, had he wished simply to make the point about favoritism through an ironic parody, he could have used the story of Barrabas. But both Cain and Barrabas were murderers; this may account for Shakespeare's analogical substitutions.

G. K. Hunter argues in a discussion of the theology of Marlowe's *The Jew of Malta* that the frequent references to Job in that play function as counter references to Barabbas's character and that Barabbas acts as an anti-Job whose "career can be seen as a parody of Job's" (1964, 219). The numerous Biblical images in Shakespeare's play may point to the intertextuality between his play and Marlowe's. Shakespeare's work deliberately rejects Marlowe's characterization of the Jew as a Barabbas figure, and the references in *The Merchant of Venice* serve as recognizable parallels (rather than anti-patterns) to issues raised in the play. In every instance, they complicate rather than explicate the play's central conflicts; they also suggest the dialogic relationship of this play to earlier depictions of the same issue.

33. In essence, therefore, mimesis is not unlike the express-repress desires that Freud characterizes as basic to the act of artistic creation itself, or the desecration and appropriation of the talents of the father-figure that Harold Bloom describes as basic to the act of literary creation in the Romantic age.

34. For discussions of the "Cult of Elizabeth," see Roy Strong, *The Cult of Elizabeth* (London: Thames and Hudson, 1977); Frances Yates, *Astrae* (London: Routledge, 1975); and more recently, the opening chapter in R. Malcolm Smuts's *Court Culture and the Origins of the Royalist Tradition in Early Stuart England* (Philadelphia: University of Pennsylvania Press, 1987).

35. This distancing of the populace from the court had begun even during James's reign, but as historians such as Robert Ashton and Christopher Hill have

argued, Charles's court continued to increase the distance and thus to alienate the public.

36. Many critics tend to minimize these intertextual links. N. W. Bawcutt, for example, in his edition of *The Changeling*, insists that, except for a superficial similarity between De Flores and Iago, the play has little in common with any of Shakespeare's tragedies (1958, xxxv).

37. This reworking of original patterns has been recognized more recently, and many later plays have been studied as variations of Elizabethan plays, especially Shakespeare's. Ford's *"Tis Pity She's a Whore*, for example, has been compared frequently with Shakespeare's *Romeo and Juliet*; in a recent volume, E. A. J. Honigmann *Shakespeare and His Contemporaries*, brings together a number of such comparative essays on Elizabethan and Stuart drama.

38. See, for example, discussion of the subject in the collection, *Patronage and the Renaissance*, edited by Lytle and Orgel.

Chapter 2. Evil as Nonbeing

1. Of course, the importance of madness in this literature has always been recognized, and my study will differ from previous studies only in my emphasis on how depictions of madness signify more than mere fascination with its theatricality. As Penelope Doob has argued in her study of madness in medieval literature, "Finding Nebuchadnezzar's children is easy," but "knowing what they signify is much harder" (1974, ix). My study will concern itself with the *significance* of Jacobean and Caroline theatrical depictions of madness, especially as the theme relates to aspects of the society's culture and politics.

2. Elizabethan and Jacobean plays abound with references to this notion of the dual bodies of the king; Hoffman's proud claim, "I am half monarch and half fiend," for example, in Chettle's gory tragedy, *Hoffman*, is probably an allusion to the two halves of the monarch.

3. In retrospect it would seem as if Elizabeth, James, and Charles, much more than the earlier monarchs, felt their positions to be particularly precarious and therefore made much of the theory to retain their hold over a more questioning populace. Ironically, James and Charles also consciously fashioned their court in the elaborate Roman manner and probably found sanction for the theory of the monarch as god in the style of the Roman emperors.

4. As I hope to show in chapter 3, the christological terminology in which kingship was expounded can be linked directly with the activation of the scapegoat psychology in the mid-century.

5. In many Elizabethan plays, the theme of the dual bodies had found a natural correlative in depictions of familial disruption caused by enmity between brothers, the Cain and Abel pattern. Duke Senior and Duke Frederick and Oliver and Orlando in *As You Like It*, and Prospero and Alonso in *The Tempest*, for example, maintain such a relationship.

In many Stuart plays, however, brothers are often accomplices in crimes; the difference between them becomes not a difference between good and evil, as in the earlier plays, but between extreme and lesser villainy. Vindice and Hippolito in *The Revenger's Tragedy*, the Cardinal and Ferdinand in *The Duchess of Malfi*,

Melantius and Diphilus in *The Maid's Tragedy*, and Sciarrha and Florio in Shirley's *The Traitor* are only a few examples where one brother draws the other into villainy. the Cain and Abel archetype itself thus undergoes some variation in the Stuart era; many plays present us with two Cains.

6. See, for example, Francis Barker's *The Tremulous Private Body*, the essay by Houston Diehl in *Renaissance Drama*, and more recently, John Hunt's essay on *Hamlet* in *Shakespeare Quarterly*, and Frank Whigham's on Renaissance drama in *ELH*.

7. The theme of the grotesque body had existed also in *Hamlet* in the hero's choice of an "antic disposition." The term *antic*, as Arthur McGhee points out, derived from the Latin "antico," from its application to the fantastic carvings found in the ruins of ancient Rome (1987, 76). These ruins were the source also for Bakhtin's term, *grotesque*. "Antic" seems to have been used by Hamlet to mean *fantastic*, *grotesque*, or *ludicrous*, and the term points to the conjunctive presence of the comic and the horrible in his personality.

Chapter 3. Evil as Corruption and Decline

1. My description summarizes Girard's theories expounded in *Violence and the Scared, The Scapegoat*, and *Violent Origins*.

2. It may be interesting that in his last play, *The Tempest*, also concerned with a potential parricide and regicide, Shakespeare returns to this theme to emphasize and reinstate patriarchal authority. The play begins appropriately with the conscious regaining of patriarchal power by Prospero after his sufferings, the consequence of his earlier neglect of patriarchal power.

3. Interestingly, in a later reworking of *Hippolytus*, however, in Racine's *Phaedra* (1677), this open structure is substituted by a closed and more satisfying one. In Racine's play, Theremanes conveys the news of Hippolytus's death to Theseus together with his dying wish that Theseus take care of Aricia, a request to which Theseus answers in the affirmative. At the close of the play, Theseus, although dejected and distracted, has some understanding of the events, because Phaedra has confessed her plot against Hippolytus.

4. The following are a few essays that discuss the issue: Karl Holzknecht, "The Dramatic Structure of *The Changeling*," in *Shakespeare's Contemporaries*, ed. Max Bluestone and Norman Rabkin (Englewood Cliffs; Prentice Hall, 1961), 261–72; Henry E. Jacobs, "The Constancy of Change: Character and Perspective in *The Changeling*," *Texas Studies in Language and Literature* 16 (1975): 651–74; Paula Johnson, "Dissimulation Anatomized: *The Changeling*," Philological Quarterly 56 (1977): 329–38; Peter F. Morrison, "A Cangoun in Zombieland: Middleton's Teratological Changeling," in *"Accompaninge the players": Essays Celebrating Thomas Middleton 1580–1980*, ed. Kenneth Friedenrich (New York: AMS Press, 1983).

5. The controversy over natural versus created nobility dramatized in this play was very popular on the Stuart stage. In a recent essay on the subject, James Day, without adequately exploring its dramatic relevance, discusses how both ideas of nobility were equally current in the period (1987, 69). The Stuart monarchs' extravagance in the creation of knights probably added to the potency of the debate. *A King and No King* refrains, however, from resolving the issue that it raises, and

may be regarded as continuing the discourse on seventeenth-century ideas about nobility.

6. The tendency to dismiss later Stuart plays as decadent was, of course, typical of earlier critics of this literature. T. M. Parrott, for example, in his discussion of *Revenge for Honour*, debates the issue of authorship through several pages, and after settling on Henry Glapthorne, concludes with the assertion that the question of Glapthorne's contributions "does not greatly matter. If we have freed Chapman from the charge of having written so theatrical and insincere a piece of work as this, and established a connexion between it and an obsure playwright of the last days of the decadence of drama, our task is done" (Chapman 1910, 720).

7. Of course, such a claim necessarily causes some problems. After all, what do we mean by the term *society*? Society consists of several factors, political, cultural, economic, etc. But my point is simply that we need to break down barriers between these factors. Especially in the seventeenth century, these areas of human activity form an integrated and often indistinguishable entity. It is to this total body that I give the term *ritual*.

Chapter 4. Evil as Deviations from the Norm

1. An increasing interest in plebian culture within seventeenth-century contexts has resulted in a number of books and articles. The following are only a few among them: Jean-Christophe Agnew in *Worlds Apart: The Market and the Theater in Anglo-American Thought* traces the influence of the market on theater; Michael D. Bristol, in the wake of Bakhtin's influential study of Rabelais, has studied the carnivalesque in seventeenth-century drama in *Carnival and Theater*; Frank Wadsworth in " 'Rough Music' in *The Duchess of Malfi*" explores the charivaric tradition in Webster's *The Duchess of Malfi*; and Jan Kott has recently studied the carnivalesque in Marlowe and Shakespeare in *The Bottom Translation*.

2. The term *festival* was used in the seventeenth century to denote communal events, both tragic and celebrative. Thus, at the close of *Revenge for Honour*, a sad and bewildered Tarifa characterizes the events of the tragedy as "black sorrow's festivals" (5.2. 336).

3. The spirit of carnival is not exclusive to the masques on the stage, however. In the late masques of the Caroline period, we encounter a similar tendency toward the carnivalesque. In the unusual masque, *Brittania Triumphans* (1637), William D'Avenant transforms the benevolent magician, Merlin, into an antimasque magician (Traister 1984, 160). As Barbara Traister argues, D'Avenant ignores history and tradition in this masque, and "Merlin, the usual upholder of monarchy and traditions, is transformed" almost beyond recognition (160). The masque still indulges in extravagant praise of the monarch, Charles, but it seems to me that this praise is deliberately undercut by so drastic a transformation in the character of its principal figure. Moreover, the praise of the monarch has been wrested from Merlin (from whom when it issued in the past, it had the merit of prophetic accuracy) and placed in the mouths of the sea nymphs, whose association with water aligns praise with suggestions of transitoriness. In masques such as this one, we encounter the carnivalesque spirit (that seems to have been prominent during the Caroline period) when traditional associations are negated or inverted.

4. See Ronald Huebert's recent study of Ford.

5. It may be worth noting that the "related meaning" that Bakhtin talks about is little different from the "doctrine of correspondences" that critics regard as operative in most Renaissance drama.

6. See James Craigie's introduction to the *Declaration of Sports* in *Minor Prose Works*, pp. 217–30.

7. I exclude Alonso de Piracquo only because he does not figure in the action of exchanging places; even though his early murder is central, he emerges as a passive figure who is easily eliminated in the early stages of the game. Because we know very little about the actual manner in which the game was played, the relevance of the metaphor to the play's actions remains unclear, and we can only speculate on the issue. It is very likely, of course, that there were variations of the game with more or fewer players than six.

8. Perhaps my characterization of suicide as a valiant act requires some explanation. Our conception of suicide as an act of weakness, "the feminization of suicide," evolved after the seventeenth century, as Margaret Higgonet points out (1986, 70). We are, of course, often expected to see female suicide even in the seventeenth century (Ophelia's, for example) as weak, but male suicide is almost always an act of valor, an attitude which probably drew from the Roman tradition.

9. See, for example, Ronald Huebert's recent study.

10. Kurtz points out that there was also a painting of the dance at Whitehall, although it was destroyed in 1697 (1939, 139). The motif was certainly familiar to the English, and the greatest artist of the dance of death, Holbein, spent some time in England in the court of Henry VIII (190).

11. In fact, some critics even regard Vesalius's work as related to the dance of death:

> Quite out of the ordinary is the physician Vesalius's treatise *De Humani Corporis Fabrica*, showing strangely animated corpses peeled down to their bones in most graceful fashion (Eichenberg 1983, 3)

Chapter 5. Evil and Sociocultural Transformation

1. Chapman's famous translations of Homer were published in installments; his translation of book 4 of the *Odyssey* was published in 1613. At any rate, we can safely assume that most writers were familiar with the general outlines of the story of Proteus. Yet another classical source for the figure of Proteus is Vergil's *Georgics* 4. 386–528.

2. Enid Welsford, for example, marks the presentation of this masque as a turning point in the history of the form (1962, 162).

3. In a recent essay, Orgel argues that Caliban's interest in Miranda, far from being the result of brutish desire, is calculated to strengthen his rights to the island by peopling it with his progeny (1986, 64). Orgel's discussion insists on our viewing Caliban as more than a brutish idiot; my own description of him as trickster emphasizes precisely this aspect of Caliban's nature.

Works Cited

Adelman, Janet. 1987. "'Born of Woman': Fantasies of Maternal Power in *Macbeth*." In *Cannibals, Witches, and Divorce*, edited by Marjorie Garber, 90–121. Baltimore: Johns Hopkins University Press.

Agnew, Jean-Christophe. 1986. *Worlds Apart: The Market and the Theater in Anglo-American Thought, 1550–1750*. Cambridge: Cambridge University Press.

Anderson, Donald K. 1986. *"Concord in Discord": The Plays of John Ford, 1586–1986*. New York: AMS Press.

Anglo, Sidney. 1977. *The Damned Art: Essays in the Literature of Witchcraft*. London: Routledge & Kegan Paul.

Artaud, Antonin. 1970. *The Theatre and its Double*. Translated by Victor Corti. London: Calder and Boyars.

Ashley, Maurice. 1987. *Charles I and Oliver Cromwell: A Study in Contrasts*. London: Methuen.

Ashton, Robert, ed. 1969. *James I by His Contemporaries*. London: Hutchinson and Company.

———. 1979. *The City and the Court: 1603–1643*. London: Cambridge University Press.

Babb, Lawrence. 1951. *The Elizabethan Malady: A Study of Melancholia in English Literature from 1580–1642*. East Lansing: Michigan State College Press.

Bacon, Francis. 1876. "On Revenge." In *Bacon's Essays*, edited by Edwin A. Albott. 2 vols. London: Longmans.

———. 1954. *The Advancement of Learning*. In *The Renaissance in England*, edited by Hyder E. Rollins and Herschel Baker, 907–13. Lexington, Mass.: D. C. Health and Co.

Bakhtin, Mikhail. 1968. *Rabelais and His World*. Translated by Helene Iswolsky. Cambridge M.I.T. Press.

———. and P. N. Medvedev. 1978. *The Formal Method in Literary Scholarship: A Critical Introduction to Sociological Poetics*. Baltimore: Johns Hopkins University Press.

Barber, C. L. 1959. *Shakespeare's Festive Comedies: A Study of Dramatic Form and its Relation to Social Custom*. Princeton: Princeton University Press.

Barkan, Leonard. 1975. *Nature's Work of Art: The Human Body as Image of the World*. New Haven: Yale University Press.

Barish, Jonas. 1981. *The Antitheatrical Prejudice*. Berkeley and Los Angeles: University of California Press.

Barker, Francis. 1984. *The Tremulous Private Body: Essays on Subjection*. London: Methuen.

Barry, Jonathan. 1985. "Popular Culture in Seventeenth-Century Bristol." In

Popular Culture in Seventeenth Century England, ed. Barry Reay, 59–90. London: Croom Helm.

Bataille, Georges. 1973. *Literature and Evil*. Translated by Alastair Hamilton. New York: Urizen Books.

Beaumont. Francis and John Fletcher. 1933. *The Maid's Tragedy*. In *Elizabethan Plays*, edited by Hazelton Spencer, 839–80. Lexington, Mass. D. C. Heath and Co.

———. 1963. *A King and No King*. Ed. Robert K. Turner. Lincoln: University of Nebraska Press.

———. N.d. *Valentinian*. In *Plays of Beaumont and Fletcher*, edited by J. St. Loe Strachey, 411–520. New York: Charles Scribner's Sons.

Belsey, Catherine. 1985. *The Subject of Tragedy: Identity and Difference in Renaissance Drama*. London: Methuen.

Bernstein, Michael Andre. 1983. "When the Carnival Turns Bitter: Preliminary Reflections on the Abject Hero." *Critical Inquiry* 10 (December): 283–305.

Bowers, Fredson. 1940. *Elizabethan Revenge Tragedy: 1587–1642*. Princeton: Princeton University Press.

Bright, Timothy. 1940. *A Treatise on Melancholy* (1586). New York: Columbia University Press.

Bristol, Michael D. 1985. *Carnival and Theater*. New York: Methuen.

Brooke, Nicholas. 1979. *Horrid Laughter in Jacobean Tragedy*. London: Open Books Publishing.

Burke, Kenneth. 1973. *The Philosophy of Literary Form*. Berkeley: University of California Press.

Burke, Peter. 1978. *Popular Culture in Early Modern Europe*. New York: New York University Press.

Burkert, Walter, Rene Girard, and Jonathan Z. Smith. 1987. *Violent Origins*. Stanford, Calif.: Stanford University Press.

Burt, Richard. 1987. "'Licensed by Authority': Ben Jonson and the Politics of Early Stuart Theater," *ELH* 54, no. 3 (Fall): 529–60.

Burton, Robert. 1927. *The Anatomy of Melancholy* (1621). Edited by Floyd Dell and Paul Jordan-Smith. New York: Tudor Publishing.

Butler, Martin. 1984. *Theatre and Crisis 1632–42*. Cambridge: Cambridge University Press.

Carey, Lady Elizabeth. 1914. *The Tragedy of Mariam*. Malone Society Reprints. London: Oxford University Press.

Castle, Terry. 1986. *Masquerade and Civilization: The Carnivalesque in Eighteenth Century English Culture and Religion*. Standford, Calif.: Stanford University Press.

Cervantes, Miguel de. 1930. *Don Quixote*. New York: Modern Library.

Champion, Larry S. 1977. *Tragic Patterns in Jacobean and Caroline Drama*. Knoxville: University of Tennessee Press.

Chapman, George. 1910–14. *Revenge for Honour*. In *The Plays and Poems of George Chapman*, edited by Thomas M. Parrott. 2 vol. London: Routledge.

Charles I. 1966. *Eikon Basilike*. Edited by Philip A. Knachel. Ithaca: Cornell University Press.

Christian, Roy. 1966. *The Country Life Book of Old English Customs*. London: Country Life.

Clark, James M. 1950. *The Dance of Death in the Middle Ages and the Renaissance*. Glasgow: Jackson, Son & Co.

Clark, Stuart. 1978. "King Jame's *Daemonologie*: Witchcraft and Kingship." In *The Damned Art: Essays in the Literature of Withcraft*, edited by Sidney Anglo, 156–81. London: Routledge and Kegan Paul.

Dahl, Mary Karen. 1987. *Political Violence in Drama: Classical Models, Contemporary Variations*. Ann Arbor, Mich.: U. M. I. Research Press.

Davies, Stevie. 1983. *Images of Kingship in Paradise Lost*. Columbia: University of Missouri Press.

Davis, Natalie Zemon. 1975. *Society and Culture In Early Modern France*. Stanford, Calif.: Stanford University Press.

Day, James F. 1987. "Trafficking in Honor: Social Climbing and the Purchase of Gentility in the English Renaissance." *Renaissance Papers*: 61–70.

Dekker, Thomas. 1925. "The Wonderfull Yeare." In *Dekker's Plague Pamphlets*, edited by F. P. Wilson, 1–62. Oxford: Clarendon Press.

———. 1979. *The Shoemaker's Holiday*. Edited by R. L. Smallwood and Stanley Wells. Baltimore: Johns Hopkins University Press.

Deleuze, Gilles and Felix Guattari. 1972. *Anti-Oedipus*. Translated by Robert Hurley, Mark Seem, and Helen R. Lane. New York: Viking Press.

Denham, John. 1928. "The Prologue To His Majesty." In *The Poetical Works of John Denham*, edited by Theodore Howard Banks, Jr. New Haven: Yale University Press.

Derrida, Jacques. 1978. *Writing and Difference*. Chicago: University of Chicago Press.

Diehl, Huston. "The Iconography of Violence in English Renaissance Tragedy." *Renaissance Drama* 11: 27–44.

Dollimore, Jonathan. 1984. *Radical Tragedy*. Chicago. University of Chicago Press.

Doob, Penelope B. R. 1974. *Nebuchadnezzar's Children: Conventions of Madness in Middle English Literature*. New Haven: Yale University Press.

Douglas, Mary. 1970. *Natural Symbols*. London: Barrie and Rockcliffe.

Eco, Umberto. 1984. "The Frames of Comic 'Freedom.'" In *Carnival*, edited by Thomas A. Sebock, 1–10. New York: Mouton Publishers.

Eichenberg, Fritz. 1983. *Dance of Death: A Graphic Commentary on the Dance Macabre Through the Centuries*. New York: Abbeville Press.

Eliade, Mircea. 1969. *The Quest: History and Meaning in Religion*. Chicago: University of Chicago Press.

Erickson, Peter. 1987. "Rewriting the Renaissancce, Rewriting Ourselves." *Shakespeare Quarterly* 38, no. 3 (Autumn): 327–37.

Ferguson, Priscilla Parkhurst, Phillipe Desan, and Wendy Griswold. 1988. *Critical Inquiry*. Vol. 14, no 3 (Spring).

Fletcher, Anthony and John Stevenson, eds. 1985. *Order and Disorder in Early Modern England*. London: Cambridge University Press.

Fletcher, John. 1966. *The Woman's Prize or the Tamer Tamed*. Edited by George B. Ferguson. London: Mouton and Co.

Fletcher, Phineas. 1908. *The Locusts or Appolonyists*. In *The Poetical Works of Giles Fletcher and Phineas Fletcher*, 2 vols., edited by F. S. Boas, I: 125–86. Cambridge: Cambridge University Press.

Folkenflik, Robert. 1987. "Recent Studies in the Restoration and Eighteenth Century," *SEL* 27, no. 3 (Summer): 503–53.

Ford, John. 1966. *'Tis Pity She's a Whore*. Edited by N. W. Bawcutt. Lincoln: University of Nebraska Press.

Foster, Vera. 1988. "*'Tis Pity She's a Whore* as City Tragedy." In *John Ford: Critical Revisions*, edited by Michael Neill, 181–200. Cambridge: Cambridge University Press.

Foucault, Michel. 1965. *Madness and Civilization*. New York: Random House.

———. 1980. *Power/Knowledge: Selected Interviews and Other Writings*. Edited by Colin Gordon. New York: Pantheon.

Friedenrich, K, edited by 1983. *"Accompanying the Players"*: *Essays Celebrating Thomas Middleton*. New York: AMS.

Fromm, Erich. 1962. *beyond the chains of illusion*. New York: Simon and Schuster.

Garber, Majorie. 1987. *Cannibals, Witches, and Divorce: Estranging the Renaissance*. Baltimore: Johns Hopkins University Press.

Geertz, Clifford. 1978. *The Interpretation of Cultures*. New York: Basic Books, Inc.

———. 1986a. "Hamlet's Dull Revenge." In *Literary Theory/Renaissance Texts*, edited by Patricia Parker and David Quint, 281–302. Baltimore: Johns Hopkins University Press.

———. 1978. *"To double business bound": Essays on Literature, Mimesis, and Anthropology*. Baltimore: Johns Hopkins University Press.

Girard, Rene. 1972. *Violence and the Scared*. Baltimore: Johns Hopkins University Press.

———. *The Scapegoat*. 1986b. Baltimore: Johns Hopkins University Press.

Goffman, Irving. 1955. "Performances." In *Ritual, Play and Performance*, edited by Richard Schechner and Mady Schuman, 89–96. New York: Seabury Press.

———. 1959. *The Presentation of Self in Everyday life*. New York: Overlook Press.

Goldberg, Jonathan. 1983. *James I and the Politics of Literature*. Baltimore: Johns Hopkins University Press.

Grabes, Herbert. 1982. *The Mutable Glass: Mirror Imagery in Titles and Texts of the Middle Ages and the Renaissance*. New York: Cambridge University Press.

———. 1980. *Renaissance Self-Fashioning: From More to Shakespeare*. Chicago: Chicago University Press.

———. 1981. "Invisible Bullets: Renaissance Authority and its Subversion." *Glyph* 8: 40–61.

———. ed. 1982. *The Forms of Power and the Power of Forms in the English Renaissance*. Norman, University of Oklahoma Press.

———. 1986. "Psychoanalysis and Renaissance Culture." In *Literary Theory/ Renaissance Texts*, edited by Patricia Parker and David Quint, 210–24. Baltimore: Johns Hopkins University Press.

———. 1988. *Shakespearean Negotiations: The Circulation of Social Energy in Renaissance England*. Berkeley: University of California Press, 1988.

Hallett, Charles A. and Elaine S. Hallett. 1980. *The Revenger's Madness: A Study of Revenge Tragedy Motifs*. Lincoln: University of Nebraska Press.

Halverson, John. 1970. "Dynamics of Exorcism: The Sinhalese Saniyakunaa," *History of Religions* 10: 330–44.

Harris, Anthony. 1980. *Night's Black Agents: Witchcraft and Magic in Seventeenth Century English Drama* Manchester: Manchester University Press.

Heinemann, Margot. 1980. *Puritanism and Theatre: Thomas Middleton and Opposition Drama Under the Early Stuarts*. Cambridge: University of Cambridge Press.

Higgonnet, Margaret. 1986. "Speaking Silences: Women's Suicide." In *The Female Body in Western Culture*, edited by Susan Rubin Suleiman, 68–83. Cambridge: Harvard University Press.

Hill, Christopher. 1972. *The World Turned Upside Down: Radical Ideas During the English Revolution*. London: Temple Smith.

———. 1984. *The Experience of Defeat: Milton and Some Contemporaries*. New York: Viking.

———. 1986. "The Word 'Revolution' in Seventeenth-Century England." In *For Veronica Wedgewood: These Studies in Seventeenth Century History*, edited by Richard Ollard and Pamela Tudor-Craig. London: William Collins Sons and Co.

Hobbes, Thomas. 1968. *Leviathan*. Middlessex: Penguin.

Hodges, Devon L. 1985. *Renaissance Fictions of Anatomy*. Amherst: University of Massachusetts Press.

Holzknecht, Karl. 1961. "The Dramatic Structure of *The Changeling*." In *Shakespeare's Contemporaries*, edited by Max Bluestone and Norman Rabkin, 261–72. Englewood Cliffs, N. J.: Prentice-Hall.

Homer. 1946. *The Odyssey*. Translated by E. V. Rieu. Baltimore: Penguin.

Honigmann, E. A. J. 1986. *Shakespeare and his Contemporaries*. Manchester: Manchester University Press.

Hooker, Richard. 1954. *Of The Lawes of Ecclesiastical Polity*. In *The Renaissance in England: Non-Dramatic Prose and Verse of the Sixteenth Century*, edited by Hyder E. Rollins and Herschel Baker. Lexington, Mass. D. C. Heath and Co.

Huebert, Ronald. 1977. *John Ford: Baroque English Dramatist*. Montreal: McGill Queen's University Press.

Hunt, John. 1988. "A Thing of Nothing: The Catastrophic Body in *Hamlet*." *Shakespeare Quarterly* 39, no. 2 (Spring): 27–44.

Hunt, Maurice. 1988. "Compelling Art in *Titus Andronicus*." *SEL* 28, no. 2 (Spring): 197–218.

Hunter, G. K. "The Theology of Marlowe's *The Jew of Malta*." *Journal of the Warburg and Courtlaud Institutes* 27: 211–40.

Ingram, Martin. 1985. "Ridings, Rough Music and Mocking Rhymes in Early Modern England." In *Popular Culture in Seventeenth Century England*, edited by Barry Reay, 166–97. London: Croom Helm.

Ivanov, V. V. 1984. "The Semiotic Theory of Carnival as the Inversion of Bipolar Opposites." In *Carnival*, edited by Thomas A. Sebock, 11–36. New York: Mouton Publishers.

Jacobs, Henry E. 1975. "The Constancy of Change: Character and Perspective in *The Changeling*." *Texas Studies in Language and Literature* 16: 651–74.

James VI. 1918a. *Basilikon Doron*. In *The Political Works of Jame I*, edited by Charles Howard McIlwain, 3–52. Cambridge: Harvard University Press.

———. 1918b. "Speech of 1603–04." In *The Political Works*, edited by Charles Howard McIlwain, 269–80. Cambridge: Harvard University Press.

———. 1918. "A Declaration of Sports." In *Minor Prose Works*, edited by James Craigie, 103–9. Edinburgh: Scottish Text Society.

———. 1981. "The True Lawe of Free Monarchies." In *Minor Prose Works of*

James VI and I, edited by James Craigie, Edinburgh: Scottish Text Society.

Johnson, Paula. 1977. "Dissimulation Anatomized: *The Changeling.*" *Philological Quarterly* 56: 329–38.

Jonson, Ben. 1966. *Sejanus His Fall.* Edited by W. F. Bolton. London: Ernest Benn Limited.

Jung, C. G. 1933. *Modern Man in Search of a Soul.* New York: Harcourt Brace.
———. *Portable Jung.* 1971. Edited by Joseph Campbell, translated by R. F. C. Hull. New York: Viking.

———. *Essential Jung.* 1983. Edited by Anthony Storr. Princeton: Princeton University Press.

Kantorowicz, Ernst H. 1957. *The King's Two Bodies: A Study in Medieval Political Theology.* Princeton: Princeton University Press.

Kaplan, Joel H. 1969. "Virtue's Holiday: Thomas Dekker and Simon Eyre." *Renaissance Drama* 2: 103–22.

Kaston, David Scott. 1987. "Workshop and/as Playhouse: Comedy and Commerce in *The Shoemaker's Holiday.*" *Studies in Philology* 84, no 3 (Summer): 324–37.

Kerenyi, C. and C. G. Jung. 1949. *Essays on the Science of Mythology.* Princeton: Princeton University Press.

Kinsman, Robert S. 1974. *The Darker Vision of the Renaissance.* Los Angeles: University of California Press.

Kott, Jan. 1987. *The Bottom Translation: Marlowe and Shakespeare and the Carnival Tradition.* Evanston, Ill.: Northwestern University Press.

Kristeva, Julia. 1983. *The Power of Horrors.* New York: Columbia Press.

Kurtz, Leonard P. 1939. *The Dance of Death and the Macabre Spirit in European Literature.* New York: Gordon Press.

Kyd, Thomas. 1951. *The Spanish Tragedy.* Edited by Charles T. Prouty. New York: Appleton-Century-Crofts.

Levi-Strauss, Claude. 1975. *The Raw and the Cooked.* New York: Harper.

Limon, Jerzy. 1986. *Dangerous Matter.* Cambridge: Cambridge University Press.

Locke, John. 1969. *An Essay Concerning Humane Understanding.* In *Eighteenth Century English Literature*, edited by Geoffrey Tillotson, et al, 188–201. New York: Harcourt Brace Jovanovich.

Lyons, Bridget Gellert. 1970. "The Iconography of Melancholy in the Graveyard Scene in *Hamlet.*" *Studies in Philology* 67: 25–58.
———. 1971. *Voices of Melancholy: Studies in Literary Treatments of Melancholy in Renaissance England.* London: Routledge and Kegan Paul.

Lucian. 1913. *The Dialogues of the Dead.* In *Lucian*, vol. 7, translated by M. D. Macleod, 1–175. Cambridge: Harvard University Press.

Lytle, Guy Fitch and Stephen Orgel. 1981. *Patronage in the English Renaissance.* Princeton: Princeton University Press.

MacAloon, John J., ed. 1984. *Rite, Drama, Festival, Spectacle: Rehearsals Toward a Theory of Cultural Performance.* Philadelphia: institute for the Study of Human Sciences.

Macfarlane, Alan. 1970. *Witchcraft in Tudor and Stuart England.* London: Routledge and Kegan Paul.

———. 1981. *The Justice and the Mare's Ale: Law and Disorder in seventeenth-century England.* New York: Cambridge University Press.

Marcus, Leah. 1986. *The Politics of Mirth: Jonson, Herrick, Milton, Marvel, and the Defense of Old Holiday Pastimes*. Chicago: University of Chicago Press.

Marvell, Andrew. 1972. "The Last Instructions to a Painter." In *Andrew Marvell: The Complete Poems*, edited by Elizabeth Story Donno, 157–83. London: Penguin.

Massinger, Philip. 1976. *The Unnatural Combat*. In *The Plays and Poems of Philip Massinger*, edited by Philip Edwards, 195–271. Oxford: Clarendon Press.

Matta, Roberto Da. 1984. "Carnival in Multiple Planes." In *Rite, Drama, Festival, Spectacle*, edited by John MacAloon, 208–40. Philadelphia: Institute for the Study of Human Issues.

Maturin, Charles. 1977. *Melmoth the Wanderer*. London: Penguin Books.

McGhee, Arthur. 1987. *The Elizabethan Hamlet*. New Haven: Yale University Press.

McIllwain, Charles Howard. 1910. *The High Court of Parliament and its Supremacy*. New Haven: Yale University Press.

McMillan, Scott. 1984. "Acting and Violence: *The Revenger's Tragedy* and its Departures from *Hamlet*." *SEL* 24: 274–91.

Melinkoff, Ruth. 1973. "Riding Backwards." *Viator* 4: 153–76.

Middleton, Thomas. *A Game at Chesse*. 1929. Edited by R. C. Bald. Cambridge: Cambridge University Press.

———. 1958. *The Changeling* (1622). Edited by N. W. Bawcutt. London: Methuen.

———. *Women Beware Women*. 1975. Edited by J. R. Mulryne. Manchester: Manchester University Press.

———. 1958. *The Changeling* (1622). Edited by N. W. Bawcutt. London: Methuen.

Milton, John. 1941. *Paradise Lost*. In *The Complete Poetical Works of John Milton*, edited by Harris Francis Fletcher, 138–387. Cambridge, Mass. Riverside Press.

———. 1953. *Complete Prose Works of John Milton*. Edited by Don M. Wolfe. Vol. 3 of 8. New Haven: Yale University Press.

Mora, George. 1984. "Reification of Evil: Witchcraft, Heresy, and the Scapegoat." In *Evil: Self and Culture*, edited by Marie Coleman Nelson and Michael Eigen, 36–60. New York: Human Sciences Press.

More, Sir Thomas. 1931. *The Four Last Things*. In *The English Works of Sir Thomas More*, edited by W. E. Campbell and A. W. Reed, et al. 2 vols. London: Eyre and Spottiswoode.

Moretti, Franco. 1983. *Signs Taken for Wonders: Essays in the Sociology of Literary Forms*. London: Verso Editions and NLB.

Morgan, Sophia S. 1984. "Borges's 'Immortal': Metaritual, Metaliterature, Metaperformance." In *Rite, Drama, Festival, Spectacle*, edited by John J. MacAloon, 79–101. Philadelphia: Institute for the Study of Human Issues.

Mortenson, Peter. 1976. "The Economics of Joy in *The Shoemaker's Holiday*." *SEL* 16: 241–52.

Murray, Peter B. 1984. *A Study of Cyril Tourneur*. Philadelphia: University of Pennsylvania Press.

Myerhoff, Barbara. 1964. "A Death in Due Time: Construction of Self and Culture in Ritual Drama." In *Rite, Drama, Festival, Spectacle*, edited by John J. MacAloon, 149–78. Philadelphia: Institute for the Study of Human Issues.

Myers, Jeffrey Rayner. 1987. "*Ut Picturae Poemata.*" In *Renaissance Papers*, edited by Dale B. J. Randall and Joseph A. Porter. 71–94. Durham, N. C.: South Eastern Renaissance Conference.

Nashe, Thomas. 1954. *The Unfortunate Traveller.* In *The Renaissance in England*, edited by Hyder R. Rollins and Herschel Baker, 788–99. Lexington, Massachusetts; D. C. Heath and Company.

Neill, Michael, ed. 1988 *John Ford: Critical Re-visions.* London: Cambridge University Press.

Nelson, Marie Coleman and Michael Eigen, eds. 1984. *Evil: Self and Culture.* New York: Human Sciences Press.

Neumann, Eric. 1972. "The Scapegoat Psychology." In *The Scapegoat: Ritual and Literature*, edited by John B. Vickery and J'nan Sellery. Boston: Houghton Mifflin.

Nietzsche, Friedrich. N. d. *The Birth of Tragedy.* In *The Philosophy of Nietzsche*, 164–340. New York: The Modern Library.

Opie, Peter and Iona. Opie. 1969. *Children's Games in Street and Playground.* Oxford: Clarendon Press.

Orgel, Stephen. 1986. "Prospero's Wife." In *Rewriting the Renaissance: The Discourses of Sexual Difference in Early Modern Europe*, edited by Margaret Ferguson, Maureen Quilligan, and Nancy J. Vickers, 50–64. Chicago: University of Chicago Press.

Ornstein, Robert. 1954. "The Ethical Design of *The Revenger's Tragedy.*" *ELH* 21 (June): 81–93.

———. 1960. *The Moral Vision of Jacobean Tragedy.* Madison: University of Wisconsin Press.

Ovid. 1916. *Metamorphoses.* Translated by Frank Justus Miller. 2 vols. Cambridge: Harvard University Press.

Parkin, David, ed. 1985. *The Anthropology of Evil.* New York: Basil Blackwell.

Parry, Graham. 1981. *The Golden Age Restored.* New York: St. Martin's Press.

Pechter, Edward. 1987. "The New Historicism and its Discontents: Politicizing Renaissance Drama." *PMLA* 102, no. 3 (May): 292–303.

Prosser, Eleanor. 1967. *Hamlet and Revenge.* Stanford, Calif.: Stanford University Press.

Rackin, Phyllis. 1987. "Androgyny, Mimesis, and the Marriage of the Boy Heroine on the English Renaissance Stage." *PMLA* 102, no. 1 (January): 29–41.

Reay, Barry, ed. 1985. *Popular Culture in Seventeenth Century England.* London: Croom Helm.

Rector, Monica. 1984. "The Code and Message of Carnival: Escolas-de-Samba." In *Carnival*, edited by Thomas A. Sebock, 37–165. New York: Mouton Publishers.

Reed, Robert R. 1952. *Bedlam on the Jacobean Stage.* London: Oxford University Press.

Rhodes, Neil. 1980. *Elizabethan Grotesque.* London: Routledge and Kegan Paul.

Ricks, Christopher, ed. 1971. *English Drama to 1710.* London: Sphere Books.

Ricoeur, Paul. 1967. *The Symbolism of Evil.* Boston: Beacon Press.

Robbins, Bruce. 1987. "Poaching off the Disciplines." *Raritan* no: 4 (Spring): 81–96.

Rudnytsky, Peter L. 1987. Review of David Norbrook's *Poetry and Politics in the English Renaissance*. In *Renaissance Quarterly* 40, no. 1 (Spring): 153–54.

Russell, Jeffrey Burton. 1977. *The Devil: Perceptions of Evil from Antiquity to Primitive Christianity*. Ithaca: Cornell University Press.

Said, Edward, ed. 1980. *Literature and Society*. Baltimore: Johns Hopkins University press.

Salingar, Leo. 1986. "*The Revenger's Tragedy* and the Morality Tradition." In *Dramatic Form in Shakespeare and the Jacobeans*, 206–21. London: Cambridge University Press.

Schechner, Richard and Mady Schuman, eds. 1976. *Ritual, Play, and Performance*. New York: Seabury Press.

Schoenbaum, Samuel. 1954. "*The Revenger's Tragedy*; Jacobean Dance of Death." *MLQ* 15: 201–7.

———. 1955. *Middleton's Tragedies: A Critical Study*. New York: Columbia University Press.

———. ed. 1962. The Bloody Banquet. Malone Society Reprints. Oxford: Oxford University Press.

Selden, Raman. 1985. *A Reader's Guide to Contemporary Theory*. Lexington: University Press of Kentucky.

Shakespeare, William. 1980. *The Complete Works of Shakespeare*. Edited by David Bevington, 191–226. London: Scott, Foresman.

Sharpe, Kevin and Steven N. Zwicker. 1987. *Politics of Discourse: The Literature and History of Seventeenth-Century England*. Berkeley: University of California Press.

Shirley, James. 1965. *The Traitor*. Edited by John Stewart Carter. Lincoln: University of Nebraska Press.

———. 1966. *The Maid's Revenge*. In *The Dramatic Works and Poems of James Shirley*. Edited by William Gifford, 99–185. New York: Russell and Russell.

———. 1986. *The Cardinal*. Edited by E. M. Yearling. Manchester: Manchester University Press.

Simmons, J. L. 1977. "The Tongue and its Office in *The Revenger's Tragedy*." *PMLA* 92: 56–68.

———. 1980. "Diabolical Realism in Middleton and Rowley's *The Changeling*." *Renaissance Drama* 11: 135–70.

Slack, Paul. 1985. *The Impact of the Plague in Tudor and Stuart England*. London: Routledge and Kegan Paul.

Smuts, R. Malcolm. 1987. *Court Culture and Origins of a Royalist Tradition in Early Stuart England*. Philadelphia: University of Pennsylvania Press.

Somerset, J. A. B. 1975. "'Fair is foul and foul is fair': Vice-Comedy's Development and Theatrical Effects." In *The Elizabethan Theater* V. Edited by G. R. Hibbard, 54–75. Hamden, Conn.: Shoe String Press.

Spinrad, Phoebe S. 1987. *The Summons of Death on the Medieval and Renaissance English Stage*. Columbus: Ohio University Press.

Stowe, John. 1945. *A Survey of London*. London: J. M. Dent.

Strong, Roy. 1977. *The Cult of Elizabeth*. London: Thames and Hudson.

Suckling, Sir John. 1971. *Fragmenta Aurea*. In *The Works of Sir John Suckling*, ed. Thomas Clayton, 9–13. Oxford: Clarendon Press.

Suleiman, Susan Rubin. 1985. *The Female Body in Western Culture*. Cambridge: Harvard University Press.

Sutherland, Sarah P. 1983. *Masques in Jacobean Tragedy*. New York: AMS Press.

Tanner, John S. 1988. "'Say First What Cause': Ricoeur and the Etiology of Evil in *Paradise Lost*." *PMLA* 103, no. 1 (January): 45–56.

Tayler, Edward W. 1979. *Milton's Poetry: Its Development in Time*. Pittsburgh: Duquesne University Press.

Tennenhouse, Leonard. 1986. *Power on Display: The Politics of Shakespeare's Genres*. New York: Methuen.

Thomas, Keith. 1971. *Religion and the Decline of Magic*. London: Weidenfeld and Nicholson.

Thompson, Patricia. 1956. "The Old Way and the New Way in Dekker and Massinger." *MLR* 51: 168–78.

Todorov, Tzvetan. 1984. *Mikhail Bakhtin: The Dialogical Principle*. Minneapolis: University of Minnesota Press.

Toliver, H. E. 1961. "*The Shoemaker's Holiday*: Theme and Image." *Boston University Studies in English* 5: 208–18.

Tourneur, Cyril. 1966. *The Revenger's Tragedy*. Edited by Lawrence J. Ross. Lincoln: University of Nebraska Press.

Traister, Barbara Howard. 1984. *Heavenly Necromancers: The Magician in English Renaissance Drama*. Columbia: University of Missouri Press.

Turner, Victor. 1976. "Social Dramas and Ritual Metaphors." In *Ritual, Play, Performance: Readings in the Social Sciences/Theatre*, edited by Richard Schechner and Mady Schuman. New York: The Seabury Press.

———. 1982. *From Ritual to Theater*. New York: Performing Arts Journal Publications.

———. 1986. *The Anthropology of Performance*. New York: Performing Arts Journal Publications.

Underdown, David. 1985. *Revel, Riot, and Rebellion: Popular Politics and Culture in England, 1603–1660*. Oxford: Clarendon Press.

Venuti, Lawrence. 1985. "Transformation of City Comedy: A Symptomatic Reading." *Assays* 3: 99–134.

Wadsworth, Frank. 1984. "'Rough Music' in *The Duchess of Malfi*: Webster's Dance of Madmen and the Charivari Tradition." In *Rite, Drama, Festival, Spectacle: Rehearsals Toward a Theory of Cultural Performance*, edited by John J. MacAloon, 58–78. Philadelphia: Institute for the Study of Human issues.

Warthin, Aldred Scott. 1931. *The Physician of the Dance of Death: A Historical Study of the Evolution of the Dance of Death Mythus in Art*. New York: Paul B. Hoebber.

Webster, John. 1959. *The Duchess of Malfi*. Edited by F. L. Lucas. New York: Macmillan.

———. 1960. *The White Devil* (1612). Edited by John Russell Brown. Cambridge: Harvard University Press.

Welsford, Enid. 1962. *The Court Masque*. New York: Russell and Russell.

Whigham, Frank. 1988. "Reading Social Conflict in the Alimentary Tract: More on the Body in Renaissance Drama." *HLH* 55, no. 2 (Summer): 333–50.

White, Lynne, Jr. 1974. "Death and the Devil." In *The Darker Vision of the Renaissance*, edited by Robert Kinsman, 25–46. Berkeley: University of California Press.

Williams (Bishop). 1969. "James I and King Solomon: Bishop Williams Funeral Oration on James, 1625." In *James I by His Contemporaries*, edited by Robert Ashton, 19–21. London: Hutchinson and Company, Ltd.

Williams, Raymond. 1973. *The Country and The City*. New York: Oxford University Press.

———. 1977. *Marxism and Literature*. Oxford: Oxford University Press.

Wilshire, Bruce. 1982. *Role Playing and Identity*. Bloomington: Indiana University Press.

Woodman David. 1973. *White Magic and the English Renaissance Drama*. Rutherford, N. J.: Fairleigh Dickinson University Press.

Wymer, Rowland. 1986. *Suicide and Despair in Jacobean Drama*. Sussex: The Harvester Press.

Yates, Frances. 1971. *Astrea: The Imperial Theme in the Sixteenth Century*. London: Routledge.

Index

190